Science Fiction and Indian Women Writers

I0585647

Science fiction, as a literature of fantasy, goes beyond the mundane to ask the question: what if the world were different from the way it is? It often challenges the real, builds on imagination, places no limits on human capacities, and encourages readers to think outside their social and cultural conditioning.

This book presents a systematic study of Indian women's science fiction. It offers a critical analysis of the works of four female Indian writers of science fiction: Rokeya Sakhawat Hossain, Manjula Padmanabhan, Priya Sarukkai Chabria and Vandana Singh. The author considers not only the evolution of science fiction writing in India, but also discusses the use of innovations and unique themes including science fiction in different Indian languages; the literary, political, and educational activism of the women writers; and eco-feminism and the idea of cloning in writing, to argue that this genre could be viewed as a vibrant representation of freedom of expression and radical literature.

This ground-breaking volume will be useful for scholars and researchers of English literature. It will also prove a very useful source for further studies into Indian literature, science and technology studies, women's and gender studies, comparative literature and cultural studies.

Urvashi Kuhad is Assistant Professor in the Department of English at Ram Lal Anand College, University of Delhi, India. She was awarded a Fulbright Foreign Language Teaching Assistant Fellowship (2010–11) to visit the University of Texas at Austin, USA, where she served as a young ambassador to the host country. She was also invited for a graduate teaching assistantship to the University of Western Ontario, Canada in 2011–12. Dr Kuhad's work has been published in several national and international publications on the intersections of identity and imagination. Her research taps into the latest developments in Indian science fiction to investigate its radical potential.

Science Fiction and Indian Women Writers
Exploring Radical Potentials

Urvashi Kuhad

Routledge
Taylor & Francis Group

LONDON AND NEW YORK

First published 2022
by Routledge
2 Park Square, Milton Park, Abingdon, Oxon OX14 4RN

and by Routledge
605 Third Avenue, New York, NY 10158

*Routledge is an imprint of the Taylor & Francis Group, an
informa business*

© 2022 Urvashi Kuhad

British Library Cataloguing-in-Publication Data
A catalogue record for this book is available from the British
Library

Library of Congress Cataloging-in-Publication Data
A catalog record has been requested for this book

ISBN: 978-0-367-51106-7 (hbk)
ISBN: 978-0-367-52776-1 (pbk)
ISBN: 978-1-003-05832-8 (ebk)

Typeset in Sabon
by SPi Technologies India Pvt Ltd (Straive)

Contents

Foreword

Science Fiction and Indian Women Writers adopts a new perspective to investigate the much-discussed field of science fiction. Using the concept of Radical Potential – an attempt to change which is new and unconventional – Dr Kuhad offers a fresh viewpoint on the subject of Indian women's science fiction. With its detailed analysis of this new wave of female writers, namely Vandana Singh, Rokeya Sakhawat Hossain, Manjula Padmanabhan, and Priya Sarukkai Chabria, the book highlights the manifold contribution made by the Indian women SF writers. It makes a significant contribution to the critical stock of writing on the new genre of female science fiction. The aim of the work is to enlighten both students and teachers in higher education institutions about the increasing importance of this genre. It is clear that *Sciece Fiction and Indian Women Writers: Exploring Radical Potentials* will prove a valuable precious acquisition for both personal and public libraries.

Professor Bhim S. Dahiya
Formerly Vice-Chancellor, Kurukshetra University, India

Acknowledgments

I would like to express the deepest appreciation to each and every individual who helped me in some way or the other and contributed towards the compilation of this book.

This book would not have been possible without the support of many people. First of all, I want to thank my advisor, Prof. Bhim Singh Dahiya, former vice chancellor at Kurukshetra University, Kurukshetra, for constant encouragement around the research and the systematic organization of my work. I am equally grateful to Prof. P. C. Pattanaik, of the Department of Modern Indian Languages and Literary Studies, University of Delhi, for his complete support and guidance over the course of this project. Heartfelt thanks are also due to Dr. Anand Prakash, reader (retd) from University of Delhi. Without his moral support and advice, this work would have proved much more onerous. I would also like to extend my heartiest gratitude to Dr. Rakesh Gupta, Principal, Ram Lal Anand College, University of Delhi, for his encouragement of my work and to all the teachers in the university's Department of English for their kindness and cooperation.

I am deeply indebted to my father, Prof. R. C. Kuhad, vice chancellor, Central University of Haryana, Mahendragarh, my mother, Mrs. Saroj Kuhad, and my brother, Harsh Kuhad, for their repeated efforts to motivate me. I am deeply grateful to them for their unconditional love and support without which I would not have been able to complete this project. I could walk this path because of the support and help of my dear husband. He is the only person who kept me going, despite the challenges around. Thanks to you, Vivek.

Urvashi Kuhad

1 Introduction

Science fiction as a genre

Needless to emphasize that the SF is an established literary genre which has its origin in the West and has received tremendous response from writers belonging to different countries in the world. The popularity of SF has become manifold. Perhaps it is for this reason the SF has emerged as a separate field of investigation in the literary analysis. Considering its growth in the present literary scenario of the world, attempt has been made here to focus on the origin and growth of SF in the West.

The origin of science fiction in the world can be traced back to the 17th century writers who were producing speculative fictions about new technologies and discoveries. A genre conducive to science fiction was that of utopian fantasy, which included an imaginary voyage to a far off land. The rich tradition of science fiction traveler's tales was started by Francis Bacon which was considered as one of the first and foremost champions of the scientific style of writing. His work *New Atlantis* (written in 1617; published in 1627) is an example of this style. Most such works of the period, the utopian fantasies, did give importance to scientific and technological advancement, yet relegated to them a minor role in the face of matters of social, political and religious reform, which assumed the centre stage. The writers who laid emphasis on matters of scientific progress were not always enthusiastic about it.

The narrative form of the imaginary voyage also came to be used by many writers in a satirical format. Such writers were: Margaret Cavendish's *The Blazing World* (1666) and the third book of Jonathan Swift's *Gulliver's Travels* (1726). Their works gave rise to a tradition of 'anti-science fiction' or dystopias. The narratives of fantastical voyages appeared alongside the standard format of religious fantasy, the dream story. The seventeenth and eighteenth century science fiction literatures began to use the dream as a plausible means of allowing themselves to access the future. This tradition was common until the late nineteenth century. An early example of this can be seen in *Somnium* (A Dream, 1634) by Johannes Kepler. The work is an attempt to understand/imagine how life on the moon might have adapted to the long cycle of day and night. Johannes Kepler was the first to take the Copernican theory of the solar system and put it into the form of a dream vision to articulate his queries.

Mary Shelley's *Frankenstein* (1818) gave science fiction a form that became established in the last decade of the nineteenth century as the principal narrative form. The "formula of an unruly and unfortunate artifact bringing about the downfall of its creator became established in the last decade of the nineteenth century as the principal narrative form."[1]

Most science fiction criticisms place the origin of science fiction in the nineteenth century, taking a few select texts from earlier (epochs) centuries as precursors. For instance, the science fiction critic Peter Nicholls is of the view that science fiction requires a scientific outlook and the "'the scientific way of looking at the world did not emerge until the 17th century, and did not percolate into the society at large until...the 19th'"[2]. He asserts that before the 19th century, science fiction could not be considered as a genre. Similarly, Brian Aldiss, SF author and critic, considers Mary Shelley's nineteenth century novel, *Frankenstein* as the first SF text.

It is common enough to find critical histories of science fiction that begin, after a brief mention of a few earlier texts, with the works of H.G. Wells and Jules Verne. Both the writers are called as 'The Father of Science Fiction.' They greatly influenced the development of SF in the 20th century. On the other hand, there are critics who refer to earlier texts to mark the origin of SF. Lucian's second century A.D. text, *True History* is treated as an example of proto science fiction. In this particular work, the narrator's ship while sailing is caught by a hurricane and gets tossed into the sky. The ship then sails to the Moon. In another work by Lucian, the *Icaromenippus*, the protagonist flies to the Moon by using the wings of a vulture and an eagle. Some critics even go onto mention texts as early as The *Epic of Gilgamesh* and the Bible, because they have brought together passages that can be considered as both 'realist' as well as fantastic, carrying the impossible and imaginary.

A text like *Gilgamesh*, one of the oldest pieces of literature we have, becomes interesting in the sense that while it tells us the story of a hero who encounters supernatural happenings and monsters, it enables us an encounter with differences. The monsters that the reader comes across can be called as nova. Another work of proto science fiction is Thomas More's *Utopia*, often cited as a starting point for SF. Written in 1516 in Latin, *Utopia* was translated into English in 1551. The work as the title suggests is a utopia, an ideal society in which everybody coexists harmoniously. The setting is a fictional island. *Utopia* creates an alternative world, which gives it the status of being a science-fiction. In showing the island as a place where all the 'goodness' are available, the rest of the world is considered as a place for the evils and full of problems. As such, the text is not concerned with an encounter with the 'other'.

Another critic namely, Robert Adams considers SF to be 'post-Romantic,' the literature which came after the revaluation of culture and metaphysics linked with the Romantic period, from around 1780-1830.[3] He adds that SF shares certain characteristics with the sub-genre of 'Gothic fiction,'[4] evolved from the Gothic style. Brian Aldiss says that the Gothic stressed on the remote and unearthly. "But the Gothic was only a symptom of the larger literary and cultural phenomenon known as 'Romanticism', and in particular it is the notions of the Imagination and the Sublime associated with Romantic writing that sets the agenda for the development of SF."[5] These two, Imagination and the Sublime contribute to what is also referred to as 'Sense of Wonder SF'[6], which provided the artistic structure for all SF writers of today to work in.

Robert Adams does not locate the origins of SF in Mary Shelley's *Frankenstein* even though the text may play a significant role in the development of SF. But in the *Paradise Lost* (1674), Milton allows his imagination to move about freely through the whole of the solar system: to think of things such as whether the Moon is inhabited by a race of aliens.

if land be there,
Fields and inhabitants: her spots thou seest
As clouds, and clouds may rain, and rain produce
....
....
With their attendant moons thou wilt descry[7]

Adams interprets the text as one that represents Otherness (Satan) with the aim to demonise him.

The crucial thing is that this is a text about the most alien of aliens its authors could imagine: an alien who is so radically Other than God that he cannot be contained within the universe God has created. Milton's Satan is the original bug eyed monster.[8]

Reading this way, one can say that Milton's poem becomes science fiction. Besides, the epigraph of *Frankenstein* has been taken from Milton's poem, ('Did I request thee, maker, from clay to mould me man?') and one can say that the novel could be a retelling of *Paradise Lost*. Frankenstein's monster too is in many ways like Satan and the first book he learns to read is Milton's *Paradise Lost*. The alienated monster is Shelley's *novum*. The novel, according to Darko Suvin, set in motion a common theme of SF, that progress is inseparable from disaster. According to him, *novum* is the main formal device of SF. This term was coined by him and it is the Latin term for 'new' or 'new thing' (the plural being *nova*). *Novum* in science fiction refers to the 'point of difference' that distinguishes the world rendered in SF from the world which we inhabit. This *novum* crucially distinguishes between SF and other forms of imaginative or fantastic literature.

Adams clarifies that although Shelley's novel played a significant role in the development of SF, yet it is with the works of Verne and Wells, at the end of the 19th century that the genre grew as a meaningful category, since this period saw a range of SF works were written, rather than an isolated single novel. And it is more through Wells' involvement, rather than Verne's which led to the growth of fiction concerned with the experience with difference.

John Clute, another SF critic, defines the experience of reading Verne as "a sense of coming very close to but never toppling over the edge of the known."[9] Similarly, Patrick Parinder describes Wells as a pivotal figure, who facilitated the movement of scientific romance into modern SF. Wells is credited with mastering a range of themes, such as time travel, biological mutation, alien invasion, anti-utopia etc. In his novels, he beautifully articulates the familiar and the strange and its relationship, which is also the cognitive estrangement. Wells also uses his novels to explore the concerns of the age and to comment upon them. He brings the reader's attention towards alarming and pressing issues of the period, urging them to develop a better and clearer understanding of things. In *The War of the Worlds*, Wells symbolically explores a deeper set of concerns through the story of Woking, in Surrey, England, where a cylinder drops on Earth from Mars. Martians emerge from it and make war upon humanity. As a result, London is deserted due to the Martian threat. This is symbolic of the ongoing project of Imperialism. He articulates concerns about the Empire, the violence caused by Empire-building, the fears and anxieties of otherness and the experience of being the 'other' that the Empire forces upon the Imperial population. According to Aldiss, Wells' novel "showed the Imperialist European powers of the day how it felt to be on the receiving end of an invasion armed with superior technology."[10]

While mainstream fiction cannot directly comment upon the larger project of Imperialism, SF can reflect on its darker reality through the use of different themes and ideas. There is no doubt that British SF flourished at the time of Wells, H. Rider Haggard (1865–1925), Bram Stoker (1847–1912) and Olaf Stapleton (1886–1950). Similarly, when the USA emerges as a world power after the Second World War began a period called the 'Golden Age' of SF. American SF prospered through the 1950s and 1960s. American SF texts during this period did not deal solely with issues such as Imperial anxiety, but also explored new frontiers, moving the subject of colonization of the American continent onto the whole galaxy.

The beginning of SF as a serious genre is also marked by the popular market in America, the growth of so-called pulp fiction.[11] These were in the cheap magazine format, popularly known as 'Pulp.' The popular topics for such writings were romantic love stories and detective fiction. *Amazing Stories* was the first magazine with any commercial value, published in 1926. It was founded by Hugo Gernsback, who worked hard to shape the development of the genre. He insisted and laid emphasis on SF, "that was grounded thoroughly in science, that was 'educational' almost to the point of being openly didactic".[12] Another editor of a rival publication, *Astounding Science Fiction*, in 1937 concurred with Gernsback's view. Campbell professed that SF should both educate and entertain.

Despite the efforts of editors like Gernsback and Campbell, the 'Pulps' did not carry a very sound reputation. These tales were clumsily written, poorly conceptualized, and morally crude. According to Edward James, "'the American Pulps may have bequeathed a largely unfortunate heritage to SF in the second half of the twentieth century'".[13] Two authors, in fact, irrespective of being 'Pulp' writers proved long-lasting. They were able to produce something that consistently attracted the interest of a large number of readers, both being prolific and inventive. They are Rice Burroughs (1875–1950), best remembered for inventing Tarzan, Lord of the Jungle and E. E. 'Doc' Smith (1890–1965). He is responsible for inventing the subgenre, 'Space Opera.'[14]

Although America was producing a great deal of bad SF before World War II, it was also beginning to develop a framework to deal with the representation of the radical others. As the American society flourished, American SF also received some of the luster and grew with it. This led to 'the Golden Age' in SF, which is usually referred to occur between the late 1930s and early 1940s or sometimes more specifically in the period 1938–1946, when American 'Pulp' was being published. This period, though short, saw a wealth and diversity of talented writers: Isaac Asimov, L. Sprague De Camp, Clifford Simak, Theodore Sturgeon, A E Van Vogt, Robert Heinlein.

Just as the brilliance of America of the 1940s is reflected in its SF, similarly, the increasing unease of 1950s is mirrored in SF of that period. During the 1950s, American society was carrying out a campaign against communism, being led by Senator Joe McCarthy. Under this campaign, those people who did not embrace 'American values' were accused of being agents of the old Soviet Union. The SF of the period portrayed the secret 'evil' communists as Alien and the American citizens as 'good'. The Cold War led to paranoia of all kinds.

John Huntington, a critic, remarks that it was only by the 1960s, the period of the 'New Wave SF' that the genre achieved the status of a popular phenomenon. Huntington says,

> The growth of new wave SF in the sixties can be seen as a rendering of attitudes implicit in the SF of the middle and late fifties. It is not accidental that the flourishing of new wave in SF coincides with a decade of political activism and of skepticism about technological solutions to social and environmental problems.[15]

Also, during the 1950s and 1960s, the number of novels published increased and there was a decline in the publication of magazines. The growth of the genre is also signaled by the rise in the number of authors of colour; the rise of women authors writing SF, to such an extent that two of the greatest writers of the field are Ursula Le Guin and Octavia Butler, who made significant contributions. The popularity of the genre grew not only through the novels published but what also attracted a large number of people to SF are TV and cinema. The first TV serial is *Star Trek*, which also became the most successful science fiction TV serial in America. This further ignited the interest of audiences for reading and watching SF.

Fantasy as a genre incorporates into itself a range of works of fiction which employ magic, the supernatural, or seemingly supernatural in their plot, central idea or setting. Most of these works are set in an imaginary world where fantastical events take place. Fantasy makes a departure from the genre of SF and horror, in that it does not offer a scientific explanation for the strange phenomena or make use of macabre themes. Although, there tends to be overlapping between the genres of fantasy, SF and horror since they are subgenres of speculative fiction.

Fantasy as a genre in the twentieth century took to rendering dream worlds, such as Lewis Carroll's *Through the Looking Glass* or portraying unconvincing or impossible domains and happenings like Kafka's *The Metamorphosis*. However, not all works which contain elements of the supernatural or the other-worldly can be called fantastic. A particular work can be described as a fantasy when its world and myths are logically structured. What make these worlds more believable and inclusive are references to daily, commonplace activities in them. The amalgamation of elements from everyday life and the supernatural signal to a world that contains more opportunities for a better life and conveys a sense of completeness, than everyday life can offer. Even if in a work of fantasy, the 'real' world is distinctly represented from that of fantasy, the transition of the characters from one sphere to another is smooth, such that the character is always present in either of the spheres. The reader goes through an extraordinary and incredible experience, and is full of admiration as against feeling puzzled.

One significant feature of fantasy is that the text ensures the reader does not know completely how to explicate and react to the series of events in the text. Some critics believe that a clear demarcation between the possible events in a text (due to the laws of nature) and the impossible or supernatural is necessary for a fantastic work to prevail. Others believe that the fantastic entails the intrusion of possible events into the impossible or mysterious. This shocking experience, however, is not the only thing that makes the reader awe-struck. There are other reasons why the reader experiences the bewilderment associated with fantasy. Poe's stories can be an example where the author tries hard to sustain the suspense in the events for as much time and increase the experience of mystery and horror. Very often, the language contributes to increasing the reader's feeling of awe and amazement.

> The style is lucid, even crystalline, but poor in undertones, repetitive in its creation of atmosphere. The lucidity often resides in an over general statement of the narrator's or protagonist's impressions: Poe's reference to 'the thrilling and enthralling eloquence' of Ligeia's 'low musical language' (*Ligeia* 1838) leaves the reader unsure what kind of speech and auditory sensations to imagine, more aware of the intensity of the narrator's response than its quality.[16]

The lucidity and intensity present reflect an amount of insanity. The confusion thus generated tends to draw attention to the personality of the main character. The leading actors are consciously presented as unsociable. "Family life, a steady career, friendship, even common everyday activities are either meaningless to them or highly problematical."[17] In fantasy, there is a tendency to create a stable world where worries can be forgotten, and repressed. By showing that one could stretch their limits, the reader is encouraged to fantasize such a world and hence discouraged to condemn a seeming ambiguity.

According to modern criticism, there is a connection between texts of fantasy and the circumstances in which they were written and which they depict. Critics identify the supernatural terrors found in a fantastical text as a reference to the social terrors present in the society of the time. Fantasy allows an outlet for the doubts that spring up in society, but which are not considered in mainstream literature.

Based upon the observations of various SF works, whether Western or Eastern, certain characteristics have been identified. It is because of these characteristics that they can be classified as SF, irrespective of their cultural or linguistic differences. They are:

1   Relationship with Science: All SF stories discuss facts and details regarding the science and technology of the future. Scientific facts and principles are interwoven into the plot of the story or novel. These scientific principles or theories are also partially true and partially fictitious. It is ensured by the writers that the scientific content is not entirely unbelievable, because in that case the particular work ventures into the domain of fantasy. SF is accordingly the right blend of scientific theories (often dealing with space and technology) and fiction. Science is an extremely crucial factor in the writing of a work of SF, hence maintaining the accuracy of the scientific facts is vital.

2   Setting: SF works are often set in the future, depicting an alternative timeline, a different world or universe. Very rarely are SF works set in the present.

3   Impact of Science: SF stories tend to explore the impact of new scientific or technological developments on people in the future, such as the effect of faster than light travel or cloning. While SF speculates on the effects of new discoveries and happenings on people, they ask the question to the readers: "What if?" This speculative question is also the starting point for SF literature. H.G. Wells' *The Time Machine* investigates the results of creating a time machine that would transport the person that inhabits it.

4   Scientific Discoveries: Inventions are key in SF. Many SF works have predicted or introduced scientific or technological innovations which later led to future discoveries. It has been rightly said that today's SF will be the science of tomorrow. Arthur C. Clarke predicted geostationary satellites and Jules Verne wrote about a journey to the moon and both became a reality.

5   Aliens: Aliens are considered to be a major feature of science fiction. They are often present in SF novels, short stories, motion pictures and so on. Encounters with aliens could happen in different ways; the alien

may land on Earth, or the humans may come in contact with aliens on their expedition to space, to mention a few ways. Aliens can be both friendly as well as serve as enemies. It is the work of the writer's imagination and the requirement of the plot that determines the nature of the alien.

6   Space Travel: Many SF works have attained glory due to the element of space travel in them, such as *Star Wars* and *Star Trek*.[18] It is a truly fascinating feature for the readers and viewers. It fuels fire to the reader's curiosity about life in space, and about aliens, if they do exist. However, not all SF works space travel involve an encounter with aliens.

7   Time Travel: Time travel is a well-known feature of the genre of SF. Not possible in real life, the concept of time machine has been explored by many writers. The fantasy for the future or the ability to alter events of the past are dealt with in this feature of SF.

8   Enquiry into Sensitive Issues: Its central ideas allow the author and also the readers to reflect upon the pressing issues of society that need most immediate attention. Common issues explored include destruction caused by wars, pollution of various kinds, population explosion, and so on.

It is the beauty of SF that it offers the reader science in an easily understandable manner, while being educative at the same time. SF delights the reader and also offers a platform through which science and scientific developments can be communicated. It also encourages the cultivation of a scientific awareness in the reader. In addition, SF alerts the readers of future changes so that the society can prepare and reduce damages in the future with such valuable advice and insight. SF is also an examination of the society and human nature. Examples of writers from India who have shown proficiency in research in their writings, thereby enriching the genre, are Rahul Sankrityayan, Sampoornanand, and Satyajit Ray. Amongst recent writers, Jayant Narlikar's SF rests on explicit scientific principles. There are, of course, many more authors whose works can be clearly labelled SF. Nonetheless, not all works which call themselves as SF are science fiction. A work qualifies to be called SF, only if science or technology is an important component of it and does not appear by chance. Facts that are offered in a work of SF must be explained in a logical fashion. The author is not authorized to alter the laws of science. The author must not tamper with the existing scientific laws and should also have a proficiency in the subject. In case any liberty is taken, the author has to offer a valid reason. It is up to the imagination and creativity of the author how he/she uses both to create fascinating plots, even though with slight modifications in scientific content. The SF which depends upon genuine scientific facts and knowledge is known as 'hard' SF, which is the most appreciated and relished by scientists. Such hard SF also relies heavily upon scientific facts and knowledge to develop its storyline. A new idea is acceptable in SF as long as it is presented logically. In the case, where no reasoning is given for a certain scientific fact, innovation or invention, that work would be called as fantasy. For instance, if a work talks about the falling of an asteroid and does not explain its impact on Earth - such as the resultant change in atmosphere - its effect on the gravitational force, and how a common man's life can be disturbed by it, then it should be seen as a work of fantasy rather than SF. For it to be SF, it is necessary for the reader to have an understanding of what an asteroid is. However, a mere explanation of scientific laws is insufficient to make a popular work of SF. For it to be engaging, it must also be interesting. For this reason, certain attenuations in science are permitted, but without any falsification. Science is the significant bind that unites all the constituents of SF.

C.M. Nautiyal,[19] in his essay, "The Dividing Lines between Science Fiction, Science Fantasy and Fantasy: A Perspective from Films," mentions the essential components of science fiction. According to Damon Knight, the initiator of the Science Fiction Writers of America and also a writer, editor and critic, these elements are "science, technology and invention, the future and the remote past, including all time travel stories, extrapolation, scientific method, other places- planets, dimensions etc., including visitors from the above, catastrophes (natural or manmade)."[20] Nautiyal informs us that (as conjectured by Knight) a story deserves to be called SF if it contains at least three of the above-mentioned elements; if it contains two elements, then the story is on the margins of being both an SF and science fantasy; stories employing one or none of the elements cannot be called SF.

Nautiyal points out that very often what is passed off as SF to the readers is simply either science fantasy or a work of pure fantasy. There is no clear segregation of these categories; they may, in fact, be some overlap. The demarcation can be influenced by the environment in which the reader or critic is present. Although the range of SF is quite vast, it is felt that what is marketed as SF is, in reality, science fantasy. The Indian motion picture, *Koi Mil Gaya*, comes nearest to being called an SF amongst Indian films, yet it is not wholeheartedly one. But this does not mean that if a work is not SF, then it is bad literature. There is a need for writers and movie makers to put in concentrated efforts to produce better works, considering the educational potential of SF.

Various attempts have been made by scholars and critics to define SF, but there is no single universally accepted definition. Furthermore, there is a relation between three terms: science fiction, science fantasy, and fantasy. The term 'fantasy' is too wide in its scope and highly imaginative literature, with no specified bounds. But SF and science fantasy can overlap, with no clear boundary. It also depends on the reader, how they choose to interpret it, and the context in which they are placed. Nautiyal gives the example of Indian mythology, which is seen as SF by some, although many reject the claim. Yet as a general rule one can maintain that SF must not transgress the established laws of science, disregarding only for a reasonable cause, with a logical explanation.

SF in the West matured from pulp magazines, which then gradually found its place in movies, dramas, video games, television serials, apart from novels and short stories. The beginning of SF has been traced back to a number of sources, of which the most agreed upon is the imaginary voyages of *Gulliver's Travels* (1726) by Jonathan Swift. Also, both H.G. Wells and Jules Verne are regarded have been labelled the fathers of science fiction. The origin of SF has also been located in Sir Thomas More's *Utopia* (1516), which is concerned about creating a better society in the present. A similar work is by Francis Bacon, who in *The New Atlantis* (1627) presents a better place to live in and the novel is set on a fictional island, Bensalem. Such works were followed by works of dystopia, where life was imagined to be as bad as it could be.

Another noteworthy novel belonging to the genre of SF, whose central ideas were science and technology, is Mary Shelley's *Frankenstein* (1818). The novel is filled with mystery and horror and explores the various potentials of science. Between the years 1890 to 1914 emerged a subgenre of SF which was called future war fiction. Under this category, novels and short stories preoccupied themselves with narratives of the forgotten cultures, places which remained unexplored, whose occupants held with them surpassing secrets of science and technology. Elaborate accounts were also given of the weapons involved. A popular writer of this subgenre is Sir Arthur Conan Doyle. The first leading SF writer from Britain was H.G. Wells. He gave the name scientific romance to the genre of SF. Aldous Huxley and George Orwell also contributed significantly to the field of SF. SF was also produced in languages other than English, between 1890 and 1930.

The SF production was meager in the interim period between World War I and World War II. However, the genre grew significantly from the late 1940s and 1950s, taking American SF to a dominating position. At the turn of the 20th century, SF magazines emerged, such as Hugo Gernsback's *Amazing Stories* (1926). Gernsback also founded the magazine *Wonder Stories* in 1929. The period from 1926 to 1962 is characterized as the time in which SF magazines flourished. Most SF written was then published in these magazines in a serialized form. The next crucial milestone in the development of American SF is the 'Golden Age' of SF which occurred between 1939 and 1949. A popular magazine of this period is *Astounding Stories* (1937), edited by John Wood Campbell.

SF writing also suffered the impact of World War II and largely fluctuated during the period. However, post-World War II, more SF magazines evolved, such as *Fantasy and Science Fiction* (1949) and *Galaxy Science Fiction* (1950). This period of SF is often called the Silver Age of science fiction. Feminism emerged as a prominent theme in SF in the 1970s while the genre of cyberpunk evolved in the 1980s. The genre of 'hard' SF was revived in the 1990s. Such fiction explores and offers solutions to challenges making use of only science and technology. The subgenre of space opera (stories set in outer space) and alternative history fiction also developed. These subgenres have been discussed in detail at the end of this chapter. Science fiction in the West did not remain confined to fiction but also spread to the radio, TV shows, movies and other means of mass media.

The origin of science fiction in India can be traced back to the mid-nineteenth century, with Pandit Ambika Dutt Vyas as the first identified writer. His "Ascharya Vrittant" (1884) was published in a magazine, namely *Piyush Pravaha*. *Chandrakanta*, a very well-renowned work of science fiction in Hindi, was produced by Devki Nanadan Khatri. He wrote two novels, *Chandrakanta* and *Chandra Kanta Santati*, which were turned into TV serials in the twentieth century. Another novel, *Chandra Lok Ki Yatra* by Babu Keshav Prasad, was published in a famous magazine, *Saraswati*, in 1900. This was followed by Acharya Chatur Sen Shastri's three novels: *Khagraas* (1959), and *Neelmani* and *Adbhut Manav* (1960).

A key writer of the 20th century was Guru Dutt, who achieved immense popularity with his novel *Sangharsh* (*The Struggle*). He was succeeded by Rahul Sankrityayan, who wrote *Baeesvi Sadi* (*The Twenty Second Century*) in 1924. The 1970s was a very fertile period, as far as science fiction novels are concerned. The major writers were Ramesh Verma, Malaprasad Tripathi, Kailash Shah and Devendra Marwari. It becomes necessary to say that the wave of science fiction in Hindi which ensued from 1995 onwards is continuing to the present day and the major writers that have contributed to the field are Kalpana Kulshrestha, Manoj Potrairiya, Harish Goel, Sukhdev Prasad, Amit Kumar, Yugal Kumar and Zeashan Zaidi. Science fiction is also abundant in other Indian languages as Marathi, Oriya, Bengali, Telugu.

There are a number of overarching themes to be found in Western SF, such as the study of how the universe was created, how it evolved and its eventual fate; stories dealing with alternate histories; predictions for the future with the help of science; omega point; space warfare, with the use of specialized weapons; gender, sex and sexuality; alien invasions; and many more. Out of this tremendous storehouse of themes and issues, Indian SF writers have picked out themes and also come up with new themes in accordance with the Indian environment, as not all may be applicable in an Indian context. The Indian writers tried to understand SF issues in the West and respond to them in accordance with their experience in an Indian context. Many SFs are also used as knowledge-based books, to present scientific content in simple language and style. Issues popular in Indian SF are to do with the environment, such as different kinds of pollution which cause a threat to the environment, ecology and wildlife. These issues can differ in relevance from Western SF to Indian SF. For instance, the issue of population explosion surfaces in many works in Indian SF, such as Manjula Padmanabhan's play *Harvest*, but it is not a significant part of Western SF. Other issues can include the psychological problems resulting from joblessness followed by suicide. These can often be encountered in a developing country such as India. Hence, Indian writers assessing the needs of the society choose to respond to ideas such as population, female foeticide etc. to make the readers aware of the need to act accordingly, so that they may attempt to repair the situation. Similarly, there is a difference in the presentation, form and content in Indian SF from Western SF. The setting also tends to differ. The language used is also very often a vernacular language, as opposed to

English. The language has to suit the people of the nation because the ideas or scientific knowledge will not reach them unless it is communicated in a language understood by them. Otherwise, it will be difficult for people to understand what the writer is trying to convey. The social circumstances cannot be ignored.

In contrast to the West, SF has not found a prominent place in the school or university curriculum in India. There is a great degree of skepticism associated with studying the genre as a discipline and for M Phil and PhD research purposes. However, this response is in contrast to the way Indian SF is being accepted by the readers. There are a large number of writers who are providing to the readers SF not just in English, but also in a range of different vernacular languages, such as Bengali, Odia, Gujarati, and so on. Detailed accounts of SF in these languages are discussed in the next chapter. In fact, SF literature has been written for children and there is also an attempt to produce more SF for children. The National Book Trust (India) also publishes books on SF, and on the various advances in science and technologies for the benefit of children. In addition, the National Book Trust organized an online story-writing contest for children in 2013, using the theme of science fiction. There is also an increase in the number of SF films made in India in the recent past. They are also being accepted and appreciated by the audience, especially children. These films include *Koi Mil Gaya* (2003), and its sequels *Krrish* (2006) and *Krrish* (2013). Another notable SF film is *Ra.One* (2011). Sequels to these films are being planned.

Ashok Banker, a popular Indian writer who has been writing SF since he was 15 years old, claims that Indians have, for many centuries, been endowed with immense knowledge of technology and it is due to some unknown reasons that the same knowledge became dissipated and could not be further utilized. In an email interview he remarked:

> Anyone familiar with our ancient Indian epics knows that we have more exciting ideas, technology and fantastical scenarios than any dozen sci-fi novels. I think the Indian mind associates these tropes and devices with the ancient past, as part of reality then.[21]

He also adds that while the genre of SF likes to believe that our generation is not adequately advanced with respect to science and technology and that is why we need to look into the future, where SF writers invent newer mechanisms. But, according to Banker, India has already experienced all this in the past and that may be the reason why the Indian mind is not easily receptive towards the genre.

Furthermore, Jayant Narlikar, an astrophysicist, the mathematician Padma Vibhushan and an SF writer (English and Marathi) during a lecture series in Goa said that well-known writers of fiction must attempt to write in the genre of SF. He expressed the need for more skilled SF writers in India. Narlikar asserted: "I know I am not a good writer. I am only an amateur. Well-known writers of short stories and novels in India should take up science fiction."[22] Narlikar stressed that there are too few writers of SF in India and the genre requires accomplished writers.

Vandana Singh, in her interview with Anil Menon, states that SF in India has a long history, but since there are so many languages, in addition to English, it is not so easy to keep track of all Indian SFs. The lack of translations makes this task tougher and she adds that translations into English from non-English languages are only a recent development. Singh tell us that there is a heritage of SF in Bengali, Marathi, Tamil, but she knows little of it as she can only read and write in Hindi and English. However, she shows her awareness of modern Hindi SF and the regular workshops and conferences organized by Indian Association for Science Fiction Studies (IASFS). Singh mentions the names of a few writers of Indian SF in English, such as herself, Anil Menon, Payal Dhar, Kalpana Swaminathan, Manjula Padmanabhan, Priya Sarukkai Chabria, and so on. Singh tells us that she appreciates Menon's writings for the way he uses language and the way in which emotions are conveyed in his SF, which is not to be seen commonly, especially in the work of male SF writers.

Menon remarks that on his recent visit to India, he was glad to find a new set of SF writers emerging, including Samit Basu and Priya Sarukkai Chhabria, and that he was greatly impressed by their work. Menon also applauds the writings of Suchitra Mathur, a member of faculty at IIT, Kanpur. He feels that she is contributing in a great way to the development of SF. According to Menon, Indian SF is thriving in English, Bengali and Marathi. According to him, there is also some SF in Assamese and Tamil, but none in Malayalam. Menon mentions that our ancient texts of Hindu mythology did include things such as *Pushpak Viman*, *Sudarshan Chakra*, yet no scientific explanation was offered for their presence.

> Hindu mythology does not talk about stuff like flying vehicles, world-nets and mantra guided missiles. But I don't think we really had a science fiction tradition till the British arrived. However, we seem to have had a speculative-fiction tradition that's remarkably postmodern in temperament.[23]

To this, Vandana Singh adds that the mythological stories did surely encourage her to write SF but she too does not consider them to be SF.

Various attempts have been made to define SF by both scholars and critics. Some of the most important contributions are discussed below:

1.1 Darko Suvin

The genre of science fiction operates in reality as well as imaginations through the imaginary worlds it creates. In this context, a definition of science fiction that takes into account the correlation between reality and fiction proposed by Darko Suvin in 1979[24] needs to be discussed. According to him, science fiction is "a literary genre whose necessary and sufficient conditions are the presence and interaction of estrangement and cognition, and whose main formal device is an imaginative framework alternative to the author's empirical environment."[25] The above lines generate interest to focus the investigation on two important terms: "estrangement", and "cognition". The "estrangement" to which Suvin refers to is "the new idea that shocks us into perception."[26] This idea of Suvin was supported by Carl D. Malgren, who explains that "estrangement" forces the reader to look at things from a different perspective. To him, the reader is made to inhabit this perspective and take it back to their everyday world. Similarly, the term "cognition" from the definition argues that the aspects of SF that prompt us to try and understand, to comprehend the alien landscape of a given SF book, film or story. Further, Elise Edwards, in her book *Race, Aliens and the U.S. Government in African American Science Fiction*, supports this by saying that it is only by the balance of the two, "cognition" and "estrangement", that the SF texts can be made relevant to our world, and that they will be in a position to challenge the ordinary and taken for granted. In addition, the "imaginary framework" or the "alternative world" of which Suvin speaks of "need to be conceivable in regard to the field of science".[27] Thus, any "alternative" world should be based on "certain logical principles" that do not contradict each another.[28]

When talking of the 'science' aspect of 'science fiction' Suvin implies that for him the discipline is based on certain logical principles that refrain from self-contradiction, that science is rational, not emotional or based on instincts. Science is most accurately described as a discipline which works by building a hypothesis and it is tested by experiment. Adam Roberts is of the opinion that it is not the use of 'science' in SF that gives the text an access to the truth but SF itself which gives science the access to truth. It is not about the 'truth' of science in SF, but the entry into "a particular, material and often rational discourse."[29]

According to the critic Gwyneth Jones:

> 'Science' in Science Fiction has always had a tacit meaning other than commonly accepted. It had nothing in particular to say about the subject matter, which may be just about anything so long as the formal conventions of future dress are observed. It means only, finally, that whatever phenomenon or speculation is treated in the fiction, there is a claim that it is going to be studied to some extent scientifically -that is objectively, rigorously; in a controlled environment. The business of the writer is to set up the equipment in a laboratory of the mind such that the 'what if' in question is at once isolated and provided with the exact nutrients it needs.[30]

Hence it is not the 'truth' of science used in a SF text, but it is the scientific method, the logical progression of a certain idea. Suvin remarks, "SF is distinguished by the narrative dominance or hegemony of a fictional 'novum'... validated by cognitive logic".[31] The *novum* is most important and dominates a SF text.

1.2 Robert Scholes

While Suvin may place a lot of emphasis on the science part of SF, another highly influential critic, Robert Scholes, chose to focus on the literary aspects of SF texts. In his book *Structural Fabulation*, Scholes emphasizes the metaphorical element of SF. According to him, 'fabulation' is any "fiction that offers us a world clearly and radically discontinuous from the one we know, yet returns to confront that known world in some cognitive way."[32] He clarifies that although SF is interested in things which are different or unlike the world in which we live, this does not mean that SF is an escapist kind of literature. According to Scholes, the world in SF is simultaneously both different and the same as reality. While this world can be called as 'discontinuous' from the ordinary world, it also confronts that world in a certain logical manner. Scholes' term 'fabulation' as a category encompasses all imaginative or fantastic literature, and even non-SF works. He adds the term 'structural' to his 'fabulation' definition in such a way that both 'science fiction' and 'structural fabulation' become synonymous: "Structural fabulation is neither scientific in its methods, nor a substitute for actual science. It is a fictional exploration of human situations made perceptible by the implications of recent science."[33]

Damien Broderick has given Scholes the status of being one of the first American scholars to established a place for SF in the academy. Scholes regards the genre of SF highly because of the possibilities it opens up as a scientific mode of literature of the 20th century, being distinctive from other kinds of literature. He is more inquisitive about the fictionalizing aspect of SF and the 'science' is only a starting point.

1.3 Damien Broderick

The Australian SF author and critic, Damien Broderick, defines SF as:

> SF is that species of storytelling native to a culture undergoing the epistemic changes implicated in the rise and supercession of technical-industrial modes of production, distribution, consumption and disposal. It is marked by (i) metaphoric strategies and metonymic tactics, (ii) the foregrounding of icons and interpretative schemata from a collectively constituted generic 'mega-text' and the concomitant de-emphasis of 'fine writing' and characterization, and (iii)certain priorities more often found in scientific and postmodern texts than in literary models: specifically, attention to the objects in preference to the subject.[34]

'Metaphoric strategies and metonymic tactics' refer to the idea that while SF represents the world metaphorically, in such a manner that the alternative world of SF refers to a part of the real world, the elements of the novel will not be metaphorical but metonymic. These elements are derived from a body of accepted and existing 'nova,' such as starships, time machines, robots and so on. They connect with a certain 'estranged' form of our reality.

For Broderick, SF that effectively reflects periods of technological and cultural change, and the present age can offer a good illustration. Broderick not only develops and extend Suvin's sense of 'cognitive estrangement' and Scholes' idea of 'structural fabulation'; he also extends it to bring into the picture some aspects not thought of by other critics. Broderick takes into account the fact that SF is considered as a popular genre, that it is populist, catering even to the "lowest common denominator" seen to be an adolescent mode/style of writing, not 'serious' or 'high art.' This opinion of Broderick originates from the larger critical unease associated with SF as a genre. Many are of the opinion that it is lacks in many respects and that hence it should not be considered serious literature. These are given as, firstly, beautiful or experimental writing styles; secondly, detailed and subtle analyses of character; and thirdly, psychological analyses. But an SF focuses on concept, subject and narrative, rather than style. Preference is given to the concrete instead of the abstract.

Jones, like many others, comes to the defense of SF and argues:

> A typical science fiction novel has little space for deep and studied characterization, not because writers lack the skill (although they may) but because in the final analysis the characters are not people, they are pieces of equipment...the same reductive effect is at work on the plot, where naked, artless, urscenarios of quest, death and desire are openly displayed.[35]

Broderick suggests that SF's emphasis is on 'object' and not the subject.

1.4 Samuel Delany

Ascribed as one of the genre's most distinguished practitioners, Samuel Delany defines SF as a symbolist genre, which attempts to replicate the world instead of reconstructing it. Suvin also agrees and sees SF as a 'symbolist system,' which tries to represent the world instead of replicating it. Symbolism provides richness to the probable interpretation. While the symbols or 'nova' used in SF may be limited; however, they are not to be shunned as a narrow and exhausted set of clichés. They should rather be seen as flexible and "wide referencing body of material *symbols*." Various symbols, such as the catlike mrem, though used widely, are more than anything a potent symbol of alienness in SF.

Science fiction can be divided into two major categories as 'hard' science fiction and 'soft' and social science fiction. The various subgenres fall under these broad categories. Hard science fiction or "hard SF"[36] refers to those works which pay careful and exhaustive attention to details in the natural sciences, such as chemistry, physics, astrophysics, or which depict future worlds in precise ways that could be possible due to advanced technology. It is believed that the hard science fiction subgenre has made some predictions which have been realized in the future. The idea of genetic engineering and

DNA, for example, were predicted in Aldous Huxley's *Brave New World* and were later introduced into the scientific world. Some hard SF authors, such as Jayant Narlikar and Vandana Singh, have professional careers as scientists, and other notable hard science fiction authors from the West include Isaac Asimov, Arthur Clarke, and Stephen Baxter. Some hard SF authors are also mathematicians.

"Soft"[37] science fiction include those works of science fiction which utilize social sciences such as political science, sociology, psychology, economics, and anthropology. Such stories tend to focus primarily on emotion and character. Noteworthy writers in this genre include Ursula K. Le Guin, Philip K. Dick, Manjula Padmanabhan, and Rokeya Sakhawat Hossain. One of the most skilled practitioners of this art was Ray Bradbury. Some writers do not observe the boundary between hard and soft science fiction and consequently tend to blur them. Both utopian and dystopian stories are related to soft and social SF.

1.5 Subgenres

It is difficult to categorize science fiction into different subgenres because these categories are not watertight. One work may be classified under more than one subgenre, whereas there are some works which may not be classified under any single category.

The genre of Cyberpunk evolved in the 1980s, with the term having been coined by Bruce Bethke who gave the title to his 1980 short story *Cyberpunk*. The term combines cybernetics and punk. "Cybernetics is a transdisciplinary approach for exploring regulatory systems, their structures, constraints, and possibilities. Cybernetics is relevant to the study of systems, such as mechanical, physics, biological, cognitive and social systems."[38] In 1948, Norbert Weiner defined cybernetics as "the scientific study of control and communication in the animal and the machine."[39]

American critics first used the term 'punk' in the early 1970s, in relation to rock music, to refer to garage bands and their followers. In 1977, punk rock became a widespread cultural phenomenon in the U.K. Punk itself became associated with the rejection of the mainstream. A simultaneous punk culture also developed, which expressed youth rebellion. This rebellion expressed itself through a distinct style of dressing and a range of anti-authoritarian ideologies.

Cyberpunk stories mostly take place in the near future, in a dystopian setting.

> Common themes in cyberpunk include advances in information technology and especially the Internet, visually abstracted as cyberspace, artificial intelligence, and prosthetics and post-democratic societal control where corporations have more influence than governments. Nihilism, post-modernism and film noir techniques are common elements, and the protagonists may be disaffected or reluctant anti-heroes.[40]

Time travel stories date back to the 18th and 19th centuries. The most famous time travel novel, for example, is H.G. Wells' *The Time Machine* (1985). In such stories, a vehicle permits an operator to travel "purposefully and selectively." The term "time machine"[41] was coined by H.G. Wells and is now used universally to refer to such an invention. Time travel remains a popular topic in modern science fiction, whether in movies, on television, and in print.

Alternate (alternative) history stories are based on the idea that certain events in history may turn out to be disparate. Such stories use time travel either to change the past, or simply to set the story in a time frame with a different history from our own. The author, Turtledove, is called the "master of alternate history" and one of the most remarkable authors of this subgenre. Rokeya Sakhawat Hossain's "Sultana's Dream" is also set in an alternate world called Ladyland where the men are kept strictly in the *mardana* (a male version of the *zenana*) and the women are in charge of the affairs of the state.

Military SF shows a conflict between national, interplanetary, or interstellar armed forces. The main characters in this type of fiction are soldiers. These stories give detailed discussion of topics such as the technology used in military, procedures followed to implement it, the various rituals, and their history. Military stories may also tend to base themselves upon certain conflicts within history. Among the most prominent military SF authors are John Ringo, David Weber, John Car, and Don Hawthorne.

Superhuman stories revolve around the evolution of human with extraordinary abilities, beyond the norm. These abilities could result from natural causes or due to scientific developments. Superhuman stories tend to focus on the psychological angle of the characters, which is the experience of alienation of such individuals and how society reacts to them. These stories have also contributed to discussions of human enhancement in real life.

Apocalyptic fiction depicts the end of civilization, either due to war, an astronomic or pandemic impact, environmental disasters, or other man-made or natural disasters, or depicts the state of a world or civilization after any of the above mentioned disasters. Apocalyptic fiction concerns itself mostly with the disaster and its direct effects, whereas post-apocalyptic fiction concerns itself with events leading after the disaster to a long period of time, even several centuries into the future. In video game, apocalyptic science fiction is a popular genre.

Space opera is the name given to adventurous science fiction, with its setting in outer space or on faraway planets. The focus here is on heroic conflicts that take place on a large scale. The term 'space opera' is used sometimes in a deprecatory manner, to refer to stories involving unconvincing plots, ludicrous science, and unreal characters. However, the term is also used to recall a glorious time, the 'golden age' of science fiction and its accompanying sense of wonder. Edward E. (Doc) Smith is considered to be the primary figure of the subgenre. George Lucas's *Star Wars* is one of the most popular cinematic space operas, with its story revolving around the battles between good and evil across the entire galaxy.

Space Western is set against a backdrop of "futuristic space frontiers."[42] These stories show colonies that have recently been settled and help to comment on the idea of lawlessness and economic expansion. These ideas were the over-riding ideas in the American West. An example is Sean Connery's film, *Outland*.

Apart from these subgenres, there are also a few more.

The subgenre of anthropological science fiction is understood as literature in relation to anthropology. It analyses anthropology and the investigation of the human mind. According to Jo Walton, a writer of SF and fantasy, the main idea that describes anthropological science fiction is

> one lone traveler, from a spaceship culture that is recognizably connected to our future, as an outsider exploring the culture of a planet populated with low-tech and culturally fascinating people. There may be other people from the spaceship culture around, but the lone traveler is central.[43]

Jo considers Ursula Le Guin's *The Left Hand of Darkness* (1968) as an example of such fiction. The feature which stands out in most books belonging to this subgenre is the culture that seems either unfamiliar or extra-terrestrial. The protagonist is the stranger who finds him/herself in a culture that is difficult to understand, yet is placed in that culture and struggles to understand it in the process along with the reader.

Comic science fiction is a subgenre that uses the genre's norms to bring about a comic reaction. As a trait, comic science fiction tends to make fun of or satirize conventional SF elements such as space travel, invasion by aliens or futuristic scientific innovations. Not only is the subgenre popular in novels and short stories, but it also has a sizeable presence in television, films, video games, radio as well as theatre. A popular work of comic SF is the *Pete Manx* serials produced by Henry Kuttner and his associate, Arthur K Barnes. *The Sirens of Titan* by Kurt Vonnegut is another example of this genre. Comic science fiction includes stories for children, adolescents, and even adults. These comics make use of illustrations and different displaying methods like Photoshop, Paintshop and Corel Paint to make the reading of the fiction more catchy and interesting.

> Biopunk science fiction is a subgenre of cyberpunk fiction that focuses on the near-future unintended consequences of the biotechnology revolution following the discovery of recombinant DNA. Biopunk stories explore the struggles of individuals or groups, often the product of human experimentation, against a backdrop of totalitarian governments and mega corporations which misuse biotechnologies as means of social control and profiteering.[44]

Popular works of biopunk include *Ribofunk* (1996) by Paul di Filippo and *White Devils* (2004) by Paul J. McAuley.

The subgenre of feminist science fiction explores social issues and asks difficult and interesting questions such as: what are the consequences of female foeticide on a society? The genre explores and questions how and why the society has subordinated women and placed the men on a higher pedestal. The issue of gender inequality is primary most and is articulated through using both utopias and dystopias.

Utopia has been defined as "an ideal commonwealth whose inhabitants exist under seemingly perfect conditions. Hence, utopian and utopianism are words used to denote visionary reform that tends to be impossibly idealistic."[45] The word *utopia* was first used by Sir Thomas More in his book, *Utopia*, published in Latin in 1516. He derived the word *utopia* from the Greek word '*ou-topos*' which means 'no place' or 'nowhere.' He intended this to be a pun - another identical Greek word is *eu-topos* which means 'a good place.' More wanted to place a significant question through this word, that does an ideal/perfect place really exist? In the book, More gives the name *utopia* to the imaginary island where the social, political and legal system is an ideal one. The underlying idea is that "no place" can be flawless. Over the years, the term *utopia* refers to a model society where there is a system of political and social eminence prevails. More made an ironic comparison between the island, *utopia*, and 16th-century British society - recognition by him that an ideal society cannot exist.

A work of *utopia* postulates that the significant modifications in social and political establishments can result in an objective society for the readers to sustain an exemplary life and hence encourage specific political beliefs. Thomas More's *Utopia* depicts fictionally a society organized in the most rational manner, and the tale is narrated by Raphael Hythlodaeus, an explorer. The imaginary island is a republic where the property is common and hence belongs to no one in particular. There are no lawyers, no crime or violence and they hire mercenaries from the neighbouring islands in times of war to fight on their behalf. Since More's *Utopia*, the title is used as a common term to refer to both fictional works where the author prescribes theories and dramatizes how the society can be organized in a better manner; and actual societies which are brought into being by implementing such theories in practice.

The *utopia* can be one where idealism dominates or that which is pragmatic, but over the years the term has also come to connote optimism, idealism and perfection that is impossible to achieve. The *utopia* can be contrasted with a *dystopia* or anti-utopia and the satirical utopia. Utopia can be of different types, a few of them being economic socialist and communist *utopias*, political and historical *utopia*, religious *utopia*, and scientific and technological *utopia*.

Economic socialist and communist *utopias* emphasize the equitable distribution of goods, normally through the total abolition of money, and citizens being given the freedom to do the work which they find enjoyable, providing them with sufficient time to indulge in their interests of arts and sciences and subsequent enrichment of the same. A religious *utopia* emphasizes the ideas of heaven as found in Christianity and Islam, leading to speculations about a life that is free from sin, poverty or sorrow that is far away from the control of death. A religious *utopia* may also be one which stresses on the Buddhist idea of *Nirvana*. A religious *utopia* is often described in broad terms as a delightful garden, where one can exist without worries, in a blissful state rejoicing almost god-like power. These reasons encourage the readers towards a greater understanding and the importance of being dedicated to a religion which can also serve as a stimulus to include new members in the religion. Scientific and technological *utopias* are those which are set in the future, where, with the help of advanced science and technology, high or utopian standards of living are made possible. These could be conditions such as deprivation of suffering, disease and so on.

A *dystopia* can be described as a society which is unpleasant and unacceptable, and there could be many reasons for this. The term *dystopia* was invented by John Stuart Mill, to denote just the opposite of *utopia* and to refer to an imaginary place which is nightmarish, and where things are as bad as they can be. Most works of *utopia* and *dystopia* are observed as the subgenres of SF. It is the author's point of view which determines whether a fictional work is a *utopia* or a *dystopia*. *Dystopias* often serve the purpose of conveying a warning or work as satires, presenting to the audience a current issue/scenario taken to its nightmarish extremes. This marks a *dystopia* as being significantly different from a *utopia*, since a *utopia* shows an ideal society that is completely unlike the present society, being set in a different time and space.

A *dystopia* works in close association with the concerns of the contemporary society. A large number of Cyberpunk SFs make use of a dystopian setting, where the world is dominated by a highly sophisticated world defined by technologies that reduces the importance of and gradually replaces national governments. The genre of post-apocalyptic SF commonly includes dystopias. Works of *dystopia* ask from the readers for social and political action. Dystopian fiction apprises the readers of the outcome of the ongoing social and political movements.

Dystopian works depict a world in which the tyrannical control maintained by the society and the mirage of an ideal society could be sustained through different types of command. These could include control by the corporate, where one or more than one corporations assume control over the society through means of media, advertising, and so on. Another form of command exercised in a *dystopia* is by the bureaucracy. Here the dysfunctional bureaucracy attempts to handle the society through never-ending regulations and amateurish government administrators. Another form of control exercised in *dystopia* is the control of society through technology. This is achieved through use of robots, computers, and other technically advanced gadgets. Philosophical or religious control is also a significant means of controlling society where a philosophical or religious teaching is executed forcefully in an autocratic manner.

Often, the protagonist in a *dystopia* feels suffocated in the prevailing circumstances and scrambles to escape from the same. He/she disputes the social and political arrangements or the workings of their contemporary society. The protagonist is perturbed at the state of affairs in the society and feels that things are becoming worse. This is the author's way of making the audience acknowledge the negative features of the dystopian world through his or her outlook.

In a *dystopia*, a political cause or point of view is disseminated in the society in order to control its citizens. There is a restriction on the citizens' freedom, individualistic thinking is discouraged and people do not have access to the desired information. Fear of the outside world is also manifested in the citizens. In addition, the citizens lead an automated life, where individuality is curbed and they are not allowed to advance alternative arguments. The citizens are compelled to lead a static life. Additionally, a *dystopia* tries to give the illusion of a perfect utopian society.

Notes

1 James, Edward and Farah Mendlesohn, eds., *The Cambridge Companion to Science Fiction*. 2003, p.19
2 Roberts, Adam. *Science Fiction*. 2000, p. 48
3 Roberts, Adam. *Science Fiction*. 2000, p. 54
4 Gothic fiction: Gothic fiction as a genre is believed to combine the elements of horror, fiction and Romanticism. The term was first used in 1763 in Horace Walpole's novel *The castle of Otranto (A Gothic Story)*. Melodrama and parody are two other characteristics of gothic fiction. A good example of this genre is the works of Edgar Allan Poe. The term Gothic makes a reference to the medieval buildings in which many of these stories are set
5 Roberts, Adam. *Science Fiction*. 2000, p. 54
6 Ibid., p. 54
7 Milton, John. *Paradise Lost*. 1993, p.184
8 Roberts, Adam. *Science Fiction*. 2000, p.56
9 Clute, John and Peter Nicholls, eds., *The Encyclopedia of Science Fiction*. 1993, p. 1276
10 Aldiss, Brian. *Billion Year Spree: the History of Science Fiction*. 1973, p. 71
11 Pulp fiction: The expression "pulp fiction" was first used to refer to a paper magazines printed on low-quality paper, made from wood pulp in the 19th century, hence the name 'pulp.' These magazines published the works of many inventive writers such as Arthur Conan Doyle, H.G. Wells, Edgar Rice Burroughs. The pulp fiction proved as a launch pad for many prolific writers and is also responsible for increasing the popularity of SF and building an audience.
12 Roberts, Adam. *Science Fiction*. 2000, p. 68
13 James, Edward. *Science Fiction in the 20th Century*. 2000, p. 48
14 Space Opera: This is a subgenre of science fiction and the term space opera was coined Wilson Tucker in 1941. Its vital features include interstellar space travel at a superfast pace, daring exploits by impulsive heroes, and disastrous weapons. It is a far future SF and *Star Wars* is a suitable example of a space opera.
15 Huntington, John *Rationalising Genius: Ideological Strategies in the Classic American Science Fiction Short Story*. 1989, p. 2
16 The Routledge Dictionary of Literary Terms

17 Ibid

18 *Star Wars* is both a popular American Television serial and a number of Hollywood films are titled on it. *Star Trek* is similarly a well-known American TV serials and a Hollywood film is also made on it. Both fall under the category of Science Fiction.

19 C M Nautiyal is a Scientist-in-Charge, Radiocarbon Lab, Lucknow.

20 Nautiyal, C M. "The Dividing Lines between Science Fiction, Science Fantasy and Fantasy: A Perspective from Films". Science Fiction in India: Past, Present and Future. 2011, p. 57

21 Banker, Ashok K. "Ashok Banker talks about his sci-fi book". *Woodpie blog.* September19,2013.Web.May15,2014.http://blog.woodpie.com/ashok-banker-talks-sci-fi-book/

22 Narlikar, Jayant. "Jayant Narlikar talks about Writers Need to Take Up science Fiction". *News Yaps.* 12 November 2012. Web. January 11, 2013. http://www.newsyaps.com/writers-need-to-take-up-sci-fi-genre-jayant-narlikar/93260/.

23 Vandermeer, Jeff. *The Southern Reach.* October 7, 2007. Web. May 15, 2014. http://www.jeffvandermeer.com/2008/10/07/in-search-of-indian-science-fiction-a-conversation-with-anil-menon/.

24 Suvin, Darko. *Positions and Presuppositions in Science Fiction.* 1986, p. 66

25 Ibid., p. 66

26 Edwards, Elise. *Race, Aliens and the US Government in African American Science Fiction.* 2011, p. 8

27 Roberts, Adam. *Science Fiction.* 2000, p. 8

28 Ibid., p. 8

29 Ibid., p. 9

30 Jones, Gwyneth. *Deconstructing the Starships: Science, Fiction and Reality.* 1999, p. 4

31 Suvin, Darko. *Positions and Presuppositions in Science Fiction.* 1986, p. 63

32 Scholes, Robert. *Structural Fabulation: An Essay on Fiction of the Future.*1975, p. 2

33 Roberts, Adam. *Science Fiction.* 2000, p. 11

34 Broderick, Damien. *Reading by Starlight: Postmodern Science Fiction.* 1995, p. 155

35 Jones, Gwyneth. *Deconstructing the Starships: Science, Fiction and Reality.* 1999, p. 5

36 Clute, John, David Langford. "SFE: The Encyclopaedia of Science Fiction". *SFE Content.* 28 February, 2013. Web. June 13, 2014. http://www.sf-encyclopedia.com/archives/hard_sf/124546.

37 Ibid.

38 Leh, Leeahna. "Cybernetics Lecture". *Academia Edu.* 19 September, 2013. Web. 15 May, 2014. https://www.academia.edu/36189720/Cybernetics_Lecture.

39 Ibid.

40 Ibid.

41 Chandler, Otis. "GoodReads:. *GoodReads.* n.d., 19 October, 2013. Web. 15 April, 2014. https://www.goodreads.com/book/show/2493.The_Time_Machine.

42 Best science Fiction Books. 2015. *BestScienceBooks.com.* September 19, 2015. Web. 15 November, 2015. https://bestsciencefictionbooks.com/space-western-science-fiction.php.

43 Walton, Jo. August 23, 2012. Web. June 16, 2014. http://www.tor.com/blogs/2012/08/some-thoughts-on-anthropological-science-fiction-as-a-sub-genre.

44 *World Heritage Encyclopaedia*, "Biopunk". World Heritage Encyclopaedia, ed. By World Library Edition, Project Gutenberg Self-Publishing Press, 10 October 2014. http://www.self.gutenberg.org/articles/eng/Biopunk.

45 Britannica. "Utopia". *Encyclopaedia Britannica*, July 22, 2014. Web. August, 2014. http://www.britannica.com/EBchecked/topic/620755/utopia.

2 Indian science fiction

2.1 Science fiction in India

2.1.1 The beginning of science fiction in India

The origins of SF in India have been traced back to two adventure stories written in Hindi between 1884 and 1888: "Aascharya Vrittant" (A Strange Tale) by Pandit Ambika Dutt Vyas and "Chandra Lok Ki Yatra" (Journey to the Moon) by Keshav Prasad Singh. These two have been compared with Jules Verne's *Voyages Extraordinaires*. *Voyages Extraordinaires* are Verne's fifty-four novels, which were published sequentially between 1863 and 1905. Written in an unconventional style, both "Aascharya Vrittant" and "Chandra Lok Ki Yatra" are filled with wonder, mystery and suspense.

During the said period, the country also produced a number of works which can be called as proto SF. These works carry certain features of SF, such as the element of wonder and the use of extraordinary gadgets, but they do not offer any scientific explanation for the fantastical events that occur. The scientific themes are also absent. Under this category comes the 'Tilism'[1] literature of Devki Nandan Khatri, who wrote two renowned novels of proto SF: *Chandrakanta* (1888) and *Chandrakanta Santati* (1896). In fact, Khatri is also credited as being the first writer to popularize reading in the Hindi language. Many people took to learning Hindi in order to read his novels. Such was the experience of mystery and wonder to be found in Khatri's works.

Among mainstream SF writers are two authors: Swami Satyadev Parivrajak and Rahul Sankrityayan. Parivrajak's work, "Aascharya Janak Ghanti," was published in 1908 in the magazine *Saraswati* and Sankrityayan wrote his novel, *Baisvee Sadi*, in 1924. This novel is a utopia set in the 22nd century, where the author introduces us to a society of the future that has embraced the political and social refinements of the 24th century due to advancement in technology. This novel has some resemblances to Louis Sebastian Mercier's *Memoirs of the Year Two Thousand Five Hundred* (1772). It is also a work of utopia set in the 25th century and the society presented here is one obsessed with science. It is considered to be a crucial milestone in the development of Indian SF. This was the first utopia to be set in the future and also indicated that the future is directly linked to progress.

A large number of magazines made a significant contribution and have provided platforms to aspiring SF writers. The earliest SF magazines in India were *Vigyan Jagat*, published by Indian Press in Allahabad, and *Vigyan Lok*, published by Mehra Newspapers. These magazines both evolved during the 1960s. Writers such as Dr. Nawal Bihari published their scientific stories in these magazines. Two of the most prominent of these stories, "Prithvi Se Saptarishi Mandal" and "Khagras," co-authored by Dr. Sampoornanand and Aacharya Chatursen Shastri, were published in 1953 and 1960, respectively.

The first major leap in Indian SF came in 1970 with Hindi writers such as Maya Prasad Tripathi, Rajeshwar Gangavar, Kailash Sah, Devendra Mewari and Sukhdev Prasad, all of whom became consistent producers of SF. Two anthologies of SF by Devendra Mawadi gained immense popularity among a Hindi-reading audience. The two anthologies are *Bhavishya* (1994) and *Kokh* (1998). In the 1980s a concerted effort was made to give SF its recognition and this was made successful through the establishment of the Indian Science Fiction Writers' Association (ISFWA) in 1995. This association further supports the growth of SF by issuing a quarterly magazine, *Vigyan Katha*, in which SF stories and critical articles on SF are published under the Chief Editorship of Dr. R.R. Upadhyay.

2.1.2 The history of science fiction in India

The second major milestone for Hindi SF came with the appearance of Dr. Arvind Mishra's story, "Ek aur Kraunch Vadh" (1989) in a well-known magazine *Dharmayug*. The story focuses on harmful experiments made on animals and the adverse effects of pesticides on the animal kingdom. With these developments, many more writers joined the band of already existing SF writers which bestowed on the genre of Indian SF a variety, thus enriching it. We now have an abundance of SF writers in India, including Zeashan Haider Zaidi, Kalpana Kulshreshtha, Manoj Patririya, Sukhdeo Prasad, Swapnil Bhartiya, Harish Goyal, and Yugal Kumar. Kalpana Kulshreshtha has been accorded the status of being an outstanding SF writer with her anthology, *Baisevee Sadi Ki Baat* (2005), which received remarkable reviews. She in fact chooses to label her SF as soci-fi as it focuses more on sociological issues.

Contemporary Indian SF writers make use of innovations and unique themes in their works, including the blend of myth and modern technology. One example of this is Ashok K. Banker's writings. He has written an eight-part adaptation of the *Ramayana* series. Using the plot of the Hindu epic, *The Ramayana*, he rechristened it within the framework of fantasy and science fiction. Banker does not exactly portray the tale as done by Valmiki, however. Banker utilizes the Hindu traditions of Vedic mathematics, astronomy and science, and depicts them in an imaginary style. He offers a modern interpretation of *The Ramayana* in the 21st century. In Banker's tales ancient

Indian traditions such as *yoga* help the warriors to master the movements of their bodies. One can say that *yoga* serves as a magic ritual. *Ravana* is portrayed in a unique light as a fixed arch-villain instead of being just one among many characters in an epic. Through his rendering, Banker is said to have reinvented the epic, *The Ramayana* in much the same way as *The Chronicles of Narnia* by C.S. Lewis was a reimagining of *The New Testament*.

The use of settings drawn out of the Indian subcontinent and epics is quite common in Indian SF, but it is interesting to note that some SF writers in the West, such as Alan Dean Foster and Bruce Sterling, have also set some of their tales in India. There has also been a moderate shift in contemporary Indian SF in terms of the themes it addresses. In earlier fiction, the focus was more on fantasy and magic; gradually, however, the emphasis has shifted to scientific areas such as nanotechnology, robotics, genetic engineering, and biotechnology, etc. There is also an increasing preoccupation with depicting the effects on science and technology on our lives. *Tokyo Cancelled* by Rana Dasgupta is an effective example that examines the force and effects of globalization in the world. The main issues present in the novel are artificial intelligence, cloning and memory loss. The novel is set in many parts of the world such as the US, England, Japan, India, Nigeria to name a few, and hence the novel cuts across geographic and cultural boundaries. The story is about thirteen passengers from different parts of the world, left stranded on the airport. In order to pass time, they narrate tales to one another. Each chapter contributes a different story by a traveler. One of the stories, "The Billionaire's Sleep," is set in Delhi and this concerns the adventures of an extremely wealthy man, Mr. Malhotra, who marries a Bollywood heroine. The pair enlist the help of a scientist for giving birth to a child, but something goes wrong and three God-like children are born. One of them, a girl, carries the gift of fertility to the world.

Any study of Indian SF is also incomplete without a reference to SF films and television shows. Bollywood films such as *Koi Mil Gaya* (2003) and *Krrish* (2006) are worthy of mention in this respect, since they have given a new dimension to the SF genre. *Koi Mil Gaya* features communication with aliens in space, and the subsequent arrival of a friendly alien on Earth, Jaadu, who transfers his superpowers to the protagonist, Rohit. *Krrish* is a sequel to this movie. Other films that classify as SF or carry its elements are *Kaadu* (1952), which translates into English as *Jungle*. *Kaadu* is a co-production between Tamil and American cinema. It focuses on the peculiar behaviours of animals. *Patalghar* (2003) is a Bengali SF film and an adaptation of Shirshendu Mukhopadhyay's story by the same name. This movie also has visitations by aliens.

In addition to SF movies, there have been SF shows on Indian television such as *Karma: Koi Aa Raha Hai Waqt Badalne*. It appeared on Star Plus Channel from 2004 to 2005, as a one-hour weekly episode. It was launched keeping in mind the success of the film, *Koi Mil Gaya*. Another popular serial that aired on DD1 in 2004 was *Parle Bongo*. It used 2-D and 3-D animation to portray cartoon characters interacting with human characters.

Another show, which appeared on Star Plus in 2006, was *Antariksha: Ek Amar Katha*. It was set 10,000 years into the future and was inspired by *The Ramayana*. Furthermore, Mani Ratnam has directed a film categorized as SF, *Rudraksh* (2004). The rising potential of animation and content development has made a large contribution largely to the increase in SF films and TV shows, where we find a mix of mythology, science and fiction.

Indian SF was not always labeled as such. In the beginning, it was usually regarded as just one aspect of 'mainstream' fiction. The earliest works of Hindi SF were considered to be part of 'mainstream' or 'commercial' literature. Pandit Ambika Datt Vyas' SF story "Aascharya Vrittant" first appeared in a popular literature magazine, *Piyush Pravaha* from 1883 to 1884 in a serialized form. This story familiarized the reader with a new kind of literature, not commonly published in a popular magazine. This story proved as a trend-setter, as it encouraged other SF writers to contribute their works to such established magazines. For instance, Keshav Prasad Singh's SF story, "Chandra Lok Ki Yatra," was published in *Saraswati*, a well-known magazine of the period. Following this, many other stories were published in *Saraswati*, including Parivrajak's "Aascharyajanak Ghantee." A significant achievement for Indian SF came with the publication of Rahul Sankrityayan's *Baisvee Sadi* in 1924. Two of the other prominent SF writers of this period whose work was disguised as mainstream literature are Aacharya Chatursen Shastri and Sampooranand.

Hence, one can clearly admit that the early SF writings in Hindi were being popularized and circulated as mainstream fiction, and no reference was made to them being SF. However, we cannot blame anyone for not reading SF as SF because the term 'science fiction' did not come into use until the 1930s, even in the West. Even the most renowned writers in the West also marketed their SF as simply fiction for a long time. They realized only by the 1940s that they could possibly sell their works as SF. Even Aldous Huxley's SF novel, *Brave New World* (1932), was initially aimed at a conventional audience and no genre category in specific. It is speculated that the genre of SF was in existence when Hugo Gernsback founded the magazine *Amazing Stories* in 1926, but the genre was not particularly popular or talked about. *Amazing Stories* was the first American science fiction magazine and also the first one solely devoted to that genre. The genre of SF gained popularity and prominence after 1937, after John W. Campbell Jr. became the editor of the science fiction magazine, *Astounding Fiction*. Since this development, SF became established as a recognized genre. Before this, the term 'scientific romance' had been used to refer to the works of authors such as H.G. Wells and Jules Verne.

The successful transition for seeing SF literature produced in India as serious and no longer as solely commercial came with the writings of Naval Bihari Mishra and Yamunadatt Vaishnav Ashok, from the 1930s. Both of these writers were quite vocal about the need for their fiction to be described as SF/Fantasy. Vaishnav deserves special mention for introducing 'Indianness' in his writings, as against some writers who merely aped the western tradition of SF. This 'Indianness' could be seen in the setting, a localized plot and characters with which the Indian audience could identify. At the same time, however, he included the latest scientific themes and elements in his stories. It was Vaishnav's efficiency and skill as a writer which allowed him to sustain both the 'Indianness' and the element of scientific romance in his writings. Dr. Arvind Mishra, a well-known Hindi SF writer, emphasizes that the genre of SF developed and received recognition in India as a result of the efforts of the two above-mentioned writers. From the 1980s onwards, there has been a clear divide between mainstream SF fiction that refuses to be categorized as SF and makes its occasional appearance every now and then and the genre of SF which makes a regular appearance in Hindi science magazines. Examples of such magazines include *Vigyan, Vigyan Pragati, Vigyan Ganga, Vaigyanik, Garima Sindhu* and *Awishkar*. *Awishkar*, however, no longer publishes works of SF, for some unknown reasons. Among the most renowned Hindi magazines which have published mainstream SF include *Dharmyug, Sarika, Saaptaahik Hindustan*, and *Navneet*. In the recent past, all other magazines, with the exception of *Navneet*, have discontinued publishing. This has unfortunately affected the opportunities for mainstream SF in Hindi of late. But Dr. Mishra, the secretary of the ISFWA, sees this as a good sign as SF will be accepted and acknowledged as a separate branch of literature, even if it is restricted to a select Hindi audience. He appreciates the magazine *Vigyan Pragati*, an initiative of CSIR for publishing SF as a consistent feature that continues to the present day, and this was put into action by Bal Phondke, the editor of the magazine, in the 1990s.

Dr. Mishra argues that the genre of Hindi SF has a considerable way to go before it can gain complete academic acceptance from Indian intelligentsia, more so in the field of Hindi literature. There is an evident bias against it and this is due to the dismissive attitude of the literati, the critics and so on.

> It's the self-appointed conservator of literary taste, in literary criticism, who remains deliberately most critical in their attitude towards sf in general and genre sf in particular. Science fiction is still struggling to attract the attention of mainstream literati. It is still looked down with contempt and ridicule by a group of self-appointed and so called great connoisseurs of Hindi literature.[2]

Scholars such as Anwesha Maity suggest that there is a striking similarity in approach towards SFs of the two countries, India and Japan. Indian SF has been greatly influenced by Japanese SF. There is a clear resemblance between the history of Japan and Bengal, in the sense that both experienced the influence of Western literature and style since the early 19th century. A similarity can be seen in the political and social arena. The period of Bengal Renaissance finds parallel in the progress made in Japan in the Meiji Restoration era between 1868 and 1912. The likeness is also found in the inclination of the intellectuals to gain knowledge from and emulate Western culture. In addition, India and Japan have both had recent historical experiences of being colonies. India was under British rule between 1757 and 1945 and Japan was a colony of the US for a short period after World War II (1945 to 1952).

In the literary context, the evolution of SF involved the adoption of Western literary forms such as the novel and short story, in both Bengal and Japan. This was also met with resistance in both places. The acceptance of these dominant forms was crucial for expressing and dealing with the 'new age' themes of science and technology. To convey a new genre of literature, a new medium was mandatory. It is believed that the earliest SF in Bengali was written in the late 19th century, a period during which the region was experiencing the effects of increased Industrialization. Early SF in Bengali can also be seen as an articulation of awe and veneration for SF produced in the West. During its colonization, Indian writers saw science as a 'Western' phenomenon.

As mentioned before, the earliest SF writings in Japan were produced during the Meiji era. The literature composed also reflected crucial happenings, such as Imperial Restoration and the successive modernization that came. The Japanese were also influenced by the West and looked to Western literature as a model for including revolutionary ideas. The Japanese also translated Jules Verne's adventure tales. In both Japan and Bengal, a number of educational and scientific institutions emerged, which encouraged research. This took place at the end of the 19th century. The result was the growth of a scientific temperament amongst the educated class. Alongside this, the general public learnt a great deal about the basic scientific concepts and theories due to their newly formed education in Japan. The early SF writers in Bengal had to work slightly more to proliferate a scientific outlook in the general public. This was necessary to generate interest and respect for the genre.

In Bengali SF, Hemlal Dutta's story "Rahasya" (1882), which was published in *Vigyan Darpan*, a pictorial magazine, in two parts, can be considered to be the first SF written in Bengali. In Japan, the first SF written is a story named "Ukeshiro Monogatari" by Yano Ruykei. It is an adventure story and hence categorized as an SF, written around 1884–1886. There tends to be a close likeness between the development of SF in the two languages and also the thematic ideas and trends explored in both.

If we compare SF literature from Japan and Bengal, with respect to the first phase, which is believed to have occurred between the late 19th century and the early 20th century, there are differences in what each of the literatures chose to focus upon. In Bengal, the writers centralized on presenting to the readers a simplified scene, and in fact a worldview that was both fantastic and scientific at the same time. The Japanese counterparts instead concentrated upon more serious issues like those of death, war, and destruction. These had to do with the regime of armed forces and Japan's aim to be on the same level as the Western powers. Unforgettable works of this are Harada Masaemon's "The Bitter Future Ten-Year War between Japan and Russia" (Ikon Junen Nichiro Miraisen) and Oshikawa Shunro's "Warships on the Bottom of Sea" (Kaitei Gunkan). In Bengal, it was Jagadishchandra Bose's short story "Palatak Tufan" (The Runaway Storm) and Jagananda Roy's "Shukra Bhraman" (Travels to Jupiter).

The period during which Japanese SF really took off is identified as the Taisho era (1912–1926). This period also saw the advent of a number of magazines that published SF, the most popular ones being *Shinseinen* (*New Youth*) and *Kagaku Gaho* (*Science Pictorial*). It was from the Showa period (1926–1989) that imaginative writing gained popularity and became familiar. The period between 1926 and 1930 was especially productive as many SF stories were published in magazines such as *Ryoki*, *Daisho Bungei* and *Modan Nihon*. The element of mystery dominated in these stories, although they also contained certain scientific elements. From the 1930s onwards, scientific themes became more ascendant and the element of mystery faded into the background. In the period around World War II, SF in Japan was virtually forbidden. However, stories which engaged in defaming the Soviet or the 'Western' world, or those which venerated the Japanese empire, were both encouraged and supported. It was acceptable to write about adventure stories and scientific developments and one had to be careful about condemnations of social and political policies of Japan.

As against the productive phase in Japanese SF and abundant production, Bengali SF only produced two great works: "Heshoram Hushiyarer Diary" by Sukumar Ray and "Sultana's Dream" by Rokeya Sakhawat Hossain. While there is a difference in the volume of production, Japanese and Bengali SF addressed similar issues. Both gave attention towards including scientific or semi-scientific components as central to the stories. The element of satire was also present in both, as a means of critiquing the wrongdoings in society in general, and, more specifically, the evil desires of man.

It has been widely agreed that the Golden Age of SF came in Japan in the 1960s. A number of reasons have been cited for this. The post-war situation was conducive to increase in SF writing as there was an improvement in living conditions. Since the war had now ended, the Japanese could think of things other than mere survival. In addition, when Yuri Gagarin went into space, it encouraged a period of scientific innovations and adventure. Yuri Gagarin was a pilot and cosmonaut from Soviet Russia. A popular magazine of SF, namely *SF Magajin* (1968), had been started by the Hayakawa Shobe Publishing Company. This development triggered interest in foreign undertakings and contributed outstandingly towards the progress of Japanese SF. Many publishing houses came forward in 1970s that continue to publish SF to the present day, including Kobunsha, Shinchosha, Kodansha and Kadokawa. Hayakawa published the *Compendium of World SF* (*Sekai SF Zenshu*) and it devoted six volumes (out of a total of thirty five) to Japanese authors. Noteworthy writers included in the collection are Arai Motoko, Yumemakura Baku, Hoshi Shin'chi, Sakyo Komatsu, and Abe Kobo. Bengal did not experience a similar 'golden age' in SF; but one of the prominent writers of Bengali SF was Premendra Mitra (1904–1988), who is famous for the innovative scientific stories he wrote, such as "Piprey Puran"

(The Story of the Ants) and "Mangalbairi" (The Martian Enemies). But connoisseurs of Bengali SF think of Mitra as the maker of the fictional character, Ghanada. The first adventure story in which he appeared is "Mosha" (Mosquito) in 1945. The persona, Ghanada, is a tall, middle-aged man and is the storehouse of many stories. The others often coax him to narrate stories on a wide variety of topics from adventure stories, historical stories to science fiction. Through these stories, Mitra had once stated that he wanted to educate readers, especially children about various unknown and unexplored facts in subjects such as science, geography and history.

Satyajit Ray's *Professor Shanku* series also became well known for its Bengali SF stories. The first story in this series was "Byomjatrir Diary" (The Spaceman's Diary). This was published in 1961 in *Sandesh*, a popular children's magazine in Bengali. These stories are filled with new inventions, adventures and travels.

Upon careful observation, one can say that there are many similarities between the Japanese and Bengali SF stories that were written after World War II. The similarities can be seen in terms of the issues dealt with in both. These issues are war, the ability of the individual to win over any obstacles, the tussle between the 'good' and 'bad' for mankind. Similarities are also seen in the way the hero or protagonist strives to achieve the 'good' or at least to attain a balance between the two. Both fictions base their works in a past or present setting, rather than the sorts of future settings that are usually found in Anglo-American SF. In addition, in both Bengali and Japanese SF texts, the protagonist belongs to the same social strata as the author and tends to be at the centre of the narrative throughout. The idea that machines, however more skilled and efficient, can never rise above their creator is also significantly recurrent in both.

2.1.3 Science fiction in different languages

Other parts of the country have shown special liking towards SFs in the 20th century and, as a result, a number of SFs are found in other Indian languages, such as Bengali, Marathi, Kannada, Telugu and Tamil. It is true that both Indian writers and the readers have responded positively and thus, SF in India has been established as an important genre of Indian literature.

2.1.3.1 Science fiction in Bengali

Science fiction in Bengali is referred to as "Kalpabigyan."[3] The earliest work of SF in Bengali is considered to be "Shukra Bhraman" (Travels to Venus) that came out in 1879. It has most of the characteristics of SF, including the presence of aliens, space travel, and the use of scientific contents. Hence, it was not purely a fantasy. The story also contained a discussion of Darwin's theory of evolution. The readers also find in the story the description of aliens on Mars, which was taken much later by H.G. Wells in his novel, *The War of the Worlds* (1898). Another writer who deserves mention as one of the first few who wrote SF in Bengali is Hemlal Datta for his story, "Rahasya" (The Mystery) in 1882. A remarkable tale of this period is "Nirussesher Kahini" (1896) by Jagadish Chandra Sen. He has also been given the status of being the 'father' of Bengali SF. Later the story came to be called "Palatak Tufan" (Runaway Cyclone).

One writer who made a large contribution to the field of Bengali SF is Rokeya Sakahwat Hossain, the author of "Sultana's Dream." It is a work of feminist science fiction and one of the first few works in the genre of any language. The first SF novel was written by Premendra Mitra, *Kuhoker Deshe* (In the Land of Mystery). *Meghduter Morte Agomon* by Hemendra Kumar Ray also deserves mention in this regard.

Bengali SF produced in the time of British Raj, that is the 19th and the early 20th century, showed signs of being affected by the Industrial Revolution. In fact, the effects were as visible as they might have been in the US and Europe. The genre achieved great heights through the writings of Sukumar Ray (1887–1923), who produced stories full of adventure. Ray's writing seems to be influenced by Sir Arthur Conan Doyle and more so by H.G. Wells when he wrote *The Diary of Heshoram Hushiar*. He is often referred to as the pioneer of science fiction. His son, Satyajit Ray (1921–1992), was also quite experimental in the language he uses in the *Professor Shonku* series (1961). These stories are abundant in terms of their use of unique gadgets and devices.

2.1.3.2 Science fiction in Marathi

SF is a firmly established genre in Marathi. All of the key elements of SF are present in Marathi SF, such as effective characterization, the presence of a central issue, a significant progression of events and scientific laws. The scientific laws and facts are present as they exist and are usually not tampered with. In addition, one can note the presence of imagination. All of these elements contribute to the development of an interesting and tantalizing plot. Most of the Marathi SFs can be seen to belong to the category of 'hard' SF. A scientific theory or concept is used to predict new developments, which have not yet been discovered. Through the story, the SF conveys what the effects of science and technology will be on the human society. However, many SFs in Marathi are predominantly concerned with the exploration of social issues, at the same time they sustain a close association with science. Some works also fall under the category of soft science fiction.

The earliest inspiration for writing SF in Marathi came from translations of western SF, in this case the works of Jules Verne. *Keral Kokil*, a well-known magazine, mentions a translation of *Journey to the Moon* in an article written in 1912. Another of Verne's novel's translation was published in *Granth Mala*. S. B. Ranade's short story "Tareche hasya" (1911) is given the credit for being the first SF story in Marathi. It is believed to be the first original SF, although a few critics argue that Nath Mahadev's novel *Srinivasa Rao* (1908) is the first original work of SF. The argument surfaces because Srinivasa Rao does not fulfill all the traits of the genre, as we have today.

W. M. Joshi is considered to be the next champion of SF in Marathi as he gained renown from two of his stories published in 1914. They are "Aprakash kiranancha divya prakash" and "Wamalochana." The years of freedom struggle only received occasional SF works. There was little consistency, but after the Independence during the 1950s, there was a renewed interest in the genre. This was also due to better access to translations of SF writers of the West. B R Bhagwat, a renowned scholar, translated a number of works of Jules Verne and H. G. Wells and made them available as useful resources. He did not merely translate but he offered adaptations of them, adding a local flavour, concepts, etc. Bhagwat also wrote children's literature.

SF, which had started with a bang in the 1960s, had declined in importance by the end of the decade. This was because SF increasingly began to be regarded as children's literature or plain adventure stories. This affected the enthusiasm of many writers who produced original works. The one figure who prevented SF from totally disappearing from the scene was Anant Antarkar, the editor of the monthly magazine, *Naval*. He encouraged that SF be printed consistently in the magazine. The genre had picked up by the 1970s as circumstances improved. Schools emphasized on science in curricula and stress was also laid upon mathematics. Hence, studying science became compulsory up to the 10th standard. So, it was a period for the revival of SF. The Annual Science Fiction Writing Competition under the guidance of the Marathi Vigyan Parishad also encouraged the genre. Additionally, Jayant Narlikar, a well-known astrophysicist, also began to write SF. His works were published in the *Maharashtra Times Annual* and *Kirloskar*, two reputable periodicals. Jayant Narlikar's writings took the genre to a higher level and since then there has been no looking back. Other notable writers, apart from Jayant Narlikar, include Bal Phondke, Niranjan Ghate, Laxman Londhe, Subodh Jawdekar, G. K. Joshi etc.

2.1.3.3 *Science fiction in Gujarati*

It was the short stories of science fiction published by Kailash Jadav in the 1950s in *Kumar* that attracted critical notice towards SF in Gujarati. Following this, Nagin Mody published a few short stories with their foundation in science, in the magazine *Chandrani*. Apart from this, no major works of Gujarati SF have been produced to date. However, one cannot say there has been no activity in the field of SF either through writing or translating. Sukanya Zaveri, for example, translated the *Professor Shanku* series by Satyajit Ray, which was published in 1981. Another collection of short stories of SF was translated by Bharat Pathak in 1987; these were *Troyno ghodo* by Jayant Narlikar. Both of these collections were well appreciated by the Gujarati readership. The last decade of the 20th century saw the publication more stories which used science as the foundation. These were

"Sahasna grahman," "Chandrana patalman," and "Sat samandar par" by Yashwant Mehta and "Ret Manav" by Kishore Pandya.

Nagin Mody has also authored two collections of SF stories for children, *Virat dadani vigyan vartao* (1990) and *Kautuk* (1991), in which he both explains and illustrates basic scientific principles and theories. Two other short story collections were produced by Yashwant Mehta and Bipin Mehta, *Virenkakani vigyan vartao* (1986) and *Bal vigyan Kathao* (1988), respectively. In addition, an SF novel, *Apurva Apeksha* (1976), was written by Damodar Balar. The novel was analyzed in detail by Ramlal Joshi and a comprehensive work of SF, *Narasur*, was written by Ramlal Soni.

One can conjecture that more science stories or novels were published than purely SF. The emphasis of much literature was more on educating the readers, especially children, about different fields in science such as biology, chemistry etc., with the help of illustrations. These writings could be seen as prospective SF, but not SF itself.

2.1.3.4 *Science fiction in Kannada*

Before 1965, hardly any SF had been written in Kannada. Initially, stories, novellas, and novels came out which were based on scientific principles or concepts. Such writings came into being with Rajashekar Bhoosnurmath (Rabhoo), whose writings were published in popular magazines of the period, such as *Sudha* and *Mayura*. The works received widespread response. Rabhoo referred to his short stories as *Vaignanika Kathegalu* and called his novels *Vaignanika Kadambarigalu*. It was from here that SF in Kannada was given the name, *Vaignanika Katha Sahitya*. SF was accepted and printed in many magazines of the period, which contributed to its popularity and spread.

The very beginning of SF in Kannada was inspired by translations of Jules Verne by Gopalakrishna Adiga, a renowned poet. A story that used rational science was rare and did not appear on the scene until the first half of the 20th century. A deviation from this was Sadanand Nayak's short story in the 1930s. He wrote a love story in which he used the idea of heart transplant, leaving a fateful message.

Apart from Rabhoo, who is given the status of being the pioneer of SF in Kannada, there are many writers who have attempted to write SF. H. S. Bhaimanatti wrote regularly. Among women writers there is only Sarita Jnanananda. Among the prolific writers are Sanjay Havanur, Manu and M. S. K. Prabhu. Some writers have even attempted writing full-length novels, but they did not succeed at it. The scientific facts or ideas used by them are displeasing and do not qualify to be called SF.

The maximum contribution to Kannada SF is by Rabhoo, before and even today. Special issues have been brought especially devoted to his works in the periodicals, *Taranga* and *Maurya*. We could attribute the credit to the well-constructed plot and innovative style of Rabhoo that has elevated the level of SF in Kannada and also attracted a large readership. His works range from fantasy to space exploration to a disturbing vision of a future scenario. Rabhoo is also the master of science fiction for children. His most popular work is *Nalina makkala kathegalu*. The total published books of SF in Kannada are above sixty and half of them have been written by Rabhoo. Hence, one can say that SF is an entrenched genre in Kannada language. Some terms invented by Kannada writers have been accepted in the vocabulary of SF, such as 'Psychorama' and 'Touchyrama.'

2.1.3.5 Science fiction in Telugu

The genre of SF in Telugu is a relatively recent development. While Telugu poetry was greatly influenced by literary movements in the West, the impact on science fiction in Telugu was nearly missing. H. G. Wells and Jules Verne were lesser known than Tolstoy and Gustave Flaubert. The influence of Wells and the likes reached Telugu literature towards the beginning of the 20th century. The earliest works of Telugu SF were produced by a founder of social research, Tekumalla Rajagopala Rao. In his novel, *Vihanga yanam* (Bird's Flight), he draws on Jules Verne when the protagonist journeys in a submarine. Another credible work is *Haa haa hoo hoo* by Viswanatha Satyanarayana. The novel reports the event of a Gandharva that lands in Trafalgar Square, London.

Ravuri Bhardwaj also wrote a short story after the invention of spaceships, "Chandra mandala yatra." While writers wrote in abundance, the response of the publishers was not very supportive. A work of SF that surfaced after a considerable gap was *Grahantara jatrikulu* (Transplanetary travelers) by Bollimunta Nageswara Rao. This was also followed by a short gap when no works were written, until Kommuri Venugopala Rao wrote his novel *Okeraktam oke manushulu*. Other remarkable works include Paruchuri Raja Ram's *Mabbu vidichina vennela* (1983) and *Japmala*. A recent development in the field of Telugu SF is the increase in number of periodicals that promote the writing of SF.

2.1.3.6 Science fiction in Odia

Even though the tradition of SF in Odia goes back to a time before Independence, it is still not considered seriously even today, irrespective of its popularity among the literate class. Stories with elements of SF in Odia could be seen as early as pre-Independence in the novel, *Nirvasita* by Godavarish Mishra (1886–1956). The writer given the credit of spearheading the movement of SF in Odia is Gokulnanda Mahapatra (1922–2013). His first work, *Prutibhi Bahare Manisha* (Man outside the Earth), was published in 1954. This work has been accorded a unique status by many critics. In his books, he explores the effects of science on human society and how human life is impacted due to scientific and technological discoveries, innovations and inventions. Mahapatra's fiction contributed to developing a scientific bent of mind in the people of his time. He combined scientific realism with fantasy in his novels. He has written a number of science novels, including *Krutrima Upagraha* (Artificial Satellite, 1958), *Udanta Thalia* (The Flying Saucer, 1963), and so on. Mahapatra is accorded the status of being the H.G. Wells of Odia fiction.

Other well-known SF writers in Odia include Amulya Krushna Mishra (1932), Debakanta Mishra (1939), and Nrusingha Charan Panda (1929). Panda is a renowned writer and his famous novel *Dagdha Golapara Chira Basanta* (The Perennial Spring of the Withered Rose, 1981) deserves mention. It revolves around the difficulties that scientists face and their creations involving the contemporary world. Amulya Krushna Mishra has written two significant works in the genre of SF, a collection of short stories, *Palataka O Anyamane* (The Runaway and Others, 1988) and a novel *Bigyanara Chhanda* (The Lyric of Science, 1963). Mishra wrote a single SF novel, *Krutrima Manisha* (Robot), after which he chose to write essays on subjects of science. Latest developments in the genre of SF are the interests shown by several new authors. The genre has also caught the attention of the critics and has become popular amongst children. A popular work written primarily for the children is *Akashaku Satati Pahacha* (Seven Steps to the Sky) by Shantanu Kumar Acharya, published in two volumes.

2.1.3.7 Science fiction in Tamil

There is a long list of SF films that have been made in Tamil. These include: *Vikram* (1986), *Perarasu* (2006), *An Human* (2011), *Adhisaya Ulagam* (2012), and *Appuchi Gramam* (2014). A popular collection of SF stories is by Mohan Sanjeevan, *Vinveli Nilayam* (Space-Station-9), a collection of 12 stories written in the late 20th century.

2.2 The present state of science fiction in India other than literature

Various film scripts are written based on information drawn from the scientific world. Though the attempt of the script writers is ultimately to show the development in the field of science and technology, in the course of designing the themes and subthemes in the scripts they have tried to touch upon different elements of natural sciences. In order to catch the audience, they have become more selective in using the discoveries in scientific fields, thus trying to focus human brain is much superior to the machines as man makes the machines not the vice versa. In Indian films, these attempts are made at regular intervals, which are more prominent in Hindi and Bengali cinema and some of the films are produced in South Indian languages. Amongst the various mainstream films made in India, some are considered to be called SF. Many of the SF films have also achieved the status of blockbusters.

2.2.1 *Film scripts, television serial scripts in Hindi*

1   *Mr. X in Bombay* (1964) is a Hindi film which featured Kishore Kumar, Madan Puri and Kumkum, and was directed by Shantilal Soni. The heroine, Kumkum's father, is a scientist who regularly performs experiments of different kinds. On one occasion, this leads to the death of one of his employees after they drink a sample of a liquid that the scientist had invented. After the incident, the action of the story unfolds.

2   *Chaand Par Chadhayee* (Trip to the Moon, 1967) is a Hindi film. It features a journey to the Moon, where an astronaut and his ally indulge in a series of fights with aliens from another planet.

3   *Elaan* (1971) has certain elements of SF. The film features an atomic ring, invented by a scientist. The ring is capable of making a person invisible, if it is kept in one's mouth.

4   *Shiva ka Insaaf* (1985) is an SF film directed by Raj Sippy.

5   *Mr. India* (1987) is considered to possess a number of SF elements. What makes it SF is a special watch, which, when worn, renders the wearer invisible. The person can then only be seen through a red glass.

6   *Funn2shh* (2003) is a comedy film, and takes the audience to the 10th century. Time travel is the significant element here.

7   *Koi Mil Gaya* (2003) contains an alien visitation. The plot is similar to Satyajit Ray's *The Alien*. Here, a scientist tries to establish contact with aliens through a computer created by him and sending across the sound patterns of *Om*. He dies in an accident, but his son meets these aliens. The alien gets his power from the sun.

8   *Taarzan: The Wonder Car* (2004) features a car that is artificially intelligent.

9   *Jaane Kya Hoga* (2006) is an SF film that features a human clone created by an aspiring scientist.

10 *Krrish* (2006) is a sequel to *Koi Mil Gaya*.

11 *Ra One* (2011), which is considered to be a technical breakthrough, revolves around a game based on motion sensors. In the game, the villain (G.One) is more powerful than the hero (Ra.One) and it is the villain that always wins here. Hence, the villain must be brought into the real world so that he can be killed by Ra.One.

12 *Creature 3D* is set to be released in 2014 and will be the first 3-D SF film to feature a monster.

13 *Paani* is a SF film in Hindi, which was released in 2015. It deals with the issue of water scarcity and is set in 2040 AD.

Among the most successful Indian SF television serials are:

1   *Space City Sigma*: This television serial appeared on DD National Channel during the late 1980s. It is considered to be one of the first SF serials made in the country. This TV serial involves an encounter with an alien race which is technically more advanced than humans.

2 *Indradhanush*: This is a TV serial meant for children with elements of SF and Fantasy. The serial also aired on DD National Channel between 1988 and 1989. The story revolves around a set of children who encounter aliens and a time-travel machine.

3 *Captain Vyom*: This too is a popular SF TV serial that aired on DD National Channel.

4 *Aasman Ka Raja*: This Indian SF TV serial was launched in 2004 on Sony Entertainment Television channel.

5 *Seven – The Ashwamedha Prophecy*: this too is considered to be an SF TV serial which aired on the Sony Entertainment Television channel in 2010.

2.2.2 Film scripts, television serial scripts in other Indian languages

1 *Ajantrik* (1958) is a Bengali film. There are SF themes in this film, along with elements of drama and comedy. The film includes an automobile as an important character. This is achieved by the use of different sound effects for highlighting the various movements of the car.

2 *Kalai Arasi* (1963) is a Tamil film with components of SF. It is the first Indian film to depict a story which includes a description of aliens.

   The Alien (1965) is a Bengali film, which started work but had to be cancelled. The film was based on a story by Satyajit Ray, "Bankubabur Bandhu," in which a young Bengali boy becomes friends with an extra-terrestrial named Mr. Ang. It is speculated by many that this film formed inspiration for the script of the Hollywood film, *E.T. The Extra-Terrestrial* (1982) by Steven Spielberg.

3 *Karutha Rathrikal* (1967) is considered to be the first SF film in Malayalam. In the story, a doctor invents a certain medicine to take revenge for her uncle's death. This medicine causes split personality disorder. The film is inspired by Robert Louis Stevenson's novella *The Strange Case of Dr. Jekyll and Mr. Hyde* (1886).

4 *Vikram* (1983) is a Tamil SF film. It envisioned inventions such as the development of advanced nuclear missiles, high-technology computers, and security mechanism, which were implemented in the future by the Indian government. The film was the first to present on screen the latest gadgets and technology of the period.

5 *Jaithra Yaathra* (1987) is a Malayalam SF film. The SF element in the film is a locket that is capable of making a man invisible.

6 *Nalaya Manithan* (1989) is a Tamil film. The film is set in the 21st century. Here, a doctor invents a drug that can bring dead people back to life, as long as they are given the drug within two hours of their death. What the doctor did not know was that the result would a zombie, who is immortal.

7 *Adhisaya Manithan* (1990) is another Tamil film. This film is a sequel to *Nalaya Manithan*. Here, the zombie created in the first part is killed, yet he lives and hunts down the humans which trespass an abandoned house.

8   *Aditya 369* (1991) is the first SF film in Telugu. It is about a diamond robbery in which a time-travelling machine plays an important part.

9   *Hollywood* (2002) is a Kannada SF film, which features an android robot.

10   *Patalghar* (2003) is a Bengali SF film, which involves an alien visitation.

11   *New* (2004) is a Tamil SF film, in which, as a part of his experiments on humans, a scientist turns an eight-year-old boy into a twenty-year-old man.

12   *Bharathan Effect* (2007) is a Marathi SF thriller. It is the first Marathi SF film, in which a supernatural coat is invented with the use of techniques of nanotechnology and lightening power. This coat can turn an ordinary man into a super human.

13   *Dasavatharam* (2008) is a SF film in Tamil. It involves the discovery of a virus that combines the Marburg virus and Ebola, and which can be used as a bio-weapon. The protagonist attempts to save this virus from being misused. Chaos Theory and Butterfly effect also form an important part in the film, which led to the Tsunami in 2004.

14   *Enthiran* (2010) is a SF film in Tamil. The protagonist serves the role of both a scientist and an andro-humanoid robot.

2.2.3 Publications: magazines, children's literature, exhibitions etc.

Magazine

A popular SF magazine which publishes stories of SF and Fantasy is *Indian SF: Science Fiction and Fantasy Stories*. This magazine, published bi-monthly and free of charge, encourages Indian writers from all over the world to publish. It publishes various genres within SF:

> aliens, bio-tech, far-future, alternate history, parallel universe, space travel, robots and AI, nano bots time travel, clones, dystopia, utopia, steam punk, mythology, magic, magic realism, monsters, dragons and beasts, fairy tales, parapsychology, dreams and other worlds and a whole lot more.[4]

The editor is Geetanjali Dighe.

Vigyan Katha is another well-known magazine, an Indian SF quarterly published in Hindi. The magazine was started in 2002 and its editor is Dr. R.R. Upadhyay. It publishes stories in the genres of SF and fantasy, along with critical commentaries on them. *Fantastica*, an SF and Fantasy magazine published in Rome, has dedicated a special issue to SF from India, apart from countries such as France, Spain, Greece, Italy, and Brazil.

Exhibition

The University of Hawai'i at Manoa organized an Arts Exhibition titled, "EWC Arts Exhibition: Bollywood and Beyond: Costume in Indian Film" from 29th September, 2013 to 12th January, 2014. The exhibition focused upon the use of costumes in the film industry, which reflects a number of things taking into account different time periods. These time periods are the Mughal era, the period when India was under British rule in the 19th century, post-independence, present-day India and the science fiction future of India.

Research Project

The Indian Foundation for the Arts sanctioned a project for the study of SF in Hindi in 2013. The project was for over a year. It is a project meant for

> research into the construction of the genre of scientific fiction in Hindi by shedding light on how writers have used their own understanding of both science and the potential of science to perceive, comment on and reinvent their past, present and the future. It will also look at how pro-ductions, articulations and manifestations of science fiction influence aural and visual cultures in India.[5]

Portal

IndianSciFi.com is considered to be the first portal for Indian SF. It provides access to stories, including audio stories, a discussion forum where readers and authors can interact. The option of chat is also available. It is operated by Madan Mohan Web Media Pvt. Ltd. This portal also connects the visitor to the latest news of science and technology. Links to related sites are also available.

Journals

The *Indian Journal of Science Fiction Studies* is an initiative on behalf of the Indian Association of Science Fiction Studies. It provides opportunities for SF writers to publish their works.

Texts

Exploring Science Fiction: Text and Pedagogy is a significant text on SF, edited by Amit Sarwal and Geetha B. The book addresses, among other things, the pedagogical problems faced by teachers in India with regard to SF. Dr. Srinarahari, the general secretary of the Indian Association of Science Fiction Studies (IASFS), applauds the book as it encourages study and research in SF at university level.

The IASFS regularly conducts SF workshops which encourage children to write SF stories. In the annual report of the VIth Annual SF Conference held in Pondicherry, Dr. Srinarahari announced the publication of 101 SF stories by children. All of the above offers evidence that Indian SF is becoming increasingly accepted and explored through different mediums, be it films, journals, texts, or workshops.

2.2.4 *The Indian Association of Science Fiction Studies*

The most recent activity in the field of Indian Science Fiction is the 19th Annual/5th International Science Fiction Conference organized by the Indian Association for Science Fiction Studies (IASFS), Bangalore. It took place online in collaboration with Bangalore University from December 7-10, 2020. The theme was "All Roads Lead to Science Fiction." Participants included students, teachers, researchers from 58 departments at the university, 700 affiliated colleges, scientists, editors, journalists, authors, and subject experts from across the world.

The secretary-general of the Indian Association for Science Fiction Studies, Dr. Srinarahari underlined that the association has been successful in organizing fourteen national and four international conferences. These were hosted with the English departments in several universities of the country. A proposal was also put up to the government of Karnataka to consider setting up of a "virtual science fiction study chair with an honorary chairperson, supported by a technical team from the university, so there would be uninterrupted progress in the field of research creative work."[6]

A special session, namely "Narrating Stories of Tomorrow" was also held, wherein the authors could read their stories. Stories were narrated in Hindi, English and the different vernacular languages. At the end of the conference, a proposal was also put up for the upcoming SF conferences in the post-pandemic era, most likely to be held at the end of 2021.

Furthermore, the conference encouraged interdisciplinary research and tried to bring about a mastery in the use of scientific understanding in the process of writing. The conference became a meeting ground for students, scholars, researchers, technically skilled people, scientists, academicians, enthusiastic SF readers and authors, where they could discuss the new and major trends in SF, along with exploring the greater possibilities of SF.

The Indian Association of Science Fiction Studies (IASFS), a voluntary organization, was formed on 2 January, 1998. Its creation marks one hundred years of SF in India. IASFS has been instrumental in providing an opportunity to many to voice their views on SF in the annual conferences organized by it. It also offers opportunity for publication in its journal, the *Indian Journal of Science Fiction Studies*. The organization also provides support to research scholars in terms of research material and guidance in the field of SF. To date, IASFS has organized fourteen National and four International Conferences, in addition to several workshops throughout India. Its founder and president is Dr. K.S. Purushottam. According to Dr. Srinarahari, it was in 1988 that the second wave of the World Science Fiction movement began in India. This was when an Indian magazine interviewed Isaac Asimov through the medium of satellite. A decade later, IASFS was formed. This year also marked the centenary of the Indian SF story, "Agosh" published by the scientist Jagadishchandra Bose.

Many present applauded the recent developments and the progress made in the genre of SF in India over a short period of time. With the exception of SF short stories and novels, movies also became the subject of study. Papers were also presented on SF in Hindi, Marathi, Kananda, and scholars participated from all over the country.

2.2.5 *Indian Science Fiction Writers Association of India (ISFWA)*

The Indian Science Fiction Writers' Association of India (ISFWA) is an autonomous, nonprofit organization, which has 50 active science fiction writers as members. They bring out a quarterly publication, namely, *Vigyan Katha*, which is a collection of stories. The organization along with the Indian Association of Science Fiction Studies, based in Bangalore, continually organizes meets and conferences including the 17th Indian Science Fiction Writers' Conference. This constitutes a golden feather in the hat of ISFWA as it achieved immense response from science fiction writers over India and even abroad. The 17th Science Fiction Writers Conference was organized at Benaras Hindu University, Uttar Pradesh, India from December 15-16, 2018. The conference was arranged jointly by the Indian Association for Science Fiction Studies, Bangalore and Indian Science Writers Association, Ayodhya, MCIIE, IIT, Benaras.

2.3 Indian science fiction: major themes

2.3.1 *Social and environmental issues*

Since the 1990s Indian SF has been concerned with exploring issues that are danger to the environment. The various environmental issues reflected upon by SF writers in their fictions are different types of pollution (water, air, soil etc.), the degradation of the environment, climate change, and the depletion of resources. This also raises concern for the endangered wildlife species and non-renewable sources of energy. Dr. Arvind Mishra's story, "Ek Aur Kraunch Vadh" (2000), concerns the killing of a crane (bird) and the ill-treatment of animals when they are killed for experiments. SF author, Harish Goyal's story "Thakte Daine" (1997) is about the extinction of birds as a result of air pollution. Vandana Singh also holds great concern for the environment and has been part of environment groups since her college days.

Modern SF is at its best when it comes to showing the reader the repercussions of environmental changes in the society and how man would be impacted by them. We are totally dependent on our natural environment and nothing can threaten us more powerfully than a radical degradation in our surroundings. We are vulnerable to this degradation and SF alerts us to it. Contemporary SF writers in India are most concerned about environmental issues and a large proportion of their writing concerns these issues. A developing nation, such as India, is more prone to such issues as compared to developed nations. Environmental issues like pollution is a huge challenge for India. It will be long until India has access to the same environmental standards as a developed economy. Two stories that tackle the issue of pollution and also offer a solution to it are "Aliens se Muthbhed" and "Punaruddhaar". Here, it is shown that pollution caused on Earth after nuclear holocaust can be controlled with the help of nano-technology.

Air pollution is a serious menace to the Indian environment and the major contribution to it comes from fire wood, the burning of biomass, the adulteration of fuel, and emission from vehicles. Air pollution is also responsible for the phenomena, 'Asian brown cloud,' due to which the monsoon is delayed.[7] The burning of fire wood, biomass cake and agricultural waste releases more than 165 tonnes of combustion gases into India's air, both indoor and outdoor. Household stoves used in rural areas which require the burning of biomass cakes are the greatest sources of greenhouse emissions into the environment. This further contributes to climate change. In addition, the burning of crop residues in northern parts of India between October and December contributes significantly to the problem of smog and haze during the winters. Vehicle exhaust also adds to the deterioration in environmental conditions. A SF story that deals with the worsening atmosphere on the streets of Delhi is "Dilli Meri Dilli" by Deven Mewari, which was published in *Jansatta Ravivari* in 1994. It presents a Delhi that is degraded and no longer habitable due to severe air pollution and smog in the city. Harish Goyal's story "Zehreela Dhooan" (2006) similarly deals with the problem of air pollution.

Another major hindrance to a clean environment is solid waste pollution. India generates an annual amount of 226.6 million tons of solid waste and the cities contribute a large share in it.[8] Trash and garbage can be seen along roadsides and this also pollutes water bodies, where garbage is often dumped. Both the Ganga and Yamuna, amongst many other rivers, are increasingly polluted every year by solid waste thrown by people in the name of offerings. Also, the same waste when consumed by animals such as cows or dogs, lead to their death in many cases. Harish Goyal's story "Polythene Kahar" (2006) discusses the abuse of polythene and the adverse effects around its disposal. Related to solid waste pollution is another menace: soil pollution. The inappropriate disposal of industrial waste and its toxic metals is a prime source of soil pollution. In addition, radioactive release from a nuclear power plant causes considerable harm to the soil and hampers plant growth. Natural factors which harm the soil causing soil erosion are rain, wind, etc. In most cases, soil erosion is caused by deforestation and the excessive use of fertilizers, insecticides and pesticides. This also erodes the fertile layer of the soil. Land pollution is undoubtedly a contributing factor to air and water pollution.

Water pollution is a cause of concern because when solid waste, along with liquid waste, is released into water bodies, it affects not only the animals in water but also plants. These are toxic to aquatic life. Certain waste materials take longer to degrade than some, adversely affecting aquatic life. In addition, the unwanted substances in water such as industrial effluents mean that the water is unsafe for drinking. This leads to many diseases. Zeashan Zaidi's SF drama in Hindi, namely *Buddha Future* (2011), is concerned with the different kinds of pollution in the environment, such as water, air, soil and noise pollution. The plot also brings out the need for safeguarding animals against extinction and the challenges associated with the increasing population in India. Harish Goyal's "Fluorosis" (2006) is also focused on water pollution and the various challenges associated with it.

In addition, the phenomenon of global warming has led to an increase in the temperature of water bodies, leading to the death of aquatic life and causing the bleaching of coral reefs in water. Harmful chemicals such as pesticides, insecticides and heavy metals seep into the water as waste and enter human bodies through poultry, agricultural produce, and so on. The majority of these chemicals are carcinogenic. Since there is no limit on the amount of pesticide to be used on crops, these problems recur. It is estimated that around 580 people die in India every day as the result of water-borne diseases. Zeashan Zaidi's SF drama, *Sau Saal Baad* (2002), deals with similar issues as it focuses upon the problem of air and water pollution in India. Harish Goyal's two stories, "Pighalta Glacier" (2002) and "Jal Plavit Kolkatta" (2014), are concerned with global warming.

A disorder in the environment is caused not just by man, but by a misbalance in the ecological system which can also be caused by natural changes. This is the so-called ecological imbalance. These natural changes can be disasters such as floods, earthquakes, volcanic eruptions, forest fires etc. Humans intensify such changes through their disruptive actions such as the hunting of animals leading to their extinction; overfishing; excessive and improper utilization of non-renewable sources; and deforestation. These things are affecting not only affecting humans but also other living species on the Earth. These factors have also led to the loss of biodiversity, change in migratory pattern of many species and change in climate. "Badalta Mausam," a SF story by Zaidi, raises the issue of global warming in India. It was published in *Vigyan Katha* in March 1999. "Dowsing" (2006) by Goyal suggests a mysterious way of solving the problem of water depletion and drought.

The relation between population explosion and environment has attracted the interest of many writers and it is explored in several works of Indian SF. An increased population exerts more pressure on the already reducing resources of the society, such as food supply, which further leads to a shortage of food, hence famine. Excess population also becomes a major reason for pollution in air, water, and solid waste pollution. Population excess is also leads to reduced income and fewer opportunities for employment. Hence, all these factors are interlinked. One story within this genre, "Parivartan" (2008) by Zeashan Zaidi, tackles the issue of overpopulation in India.

To sustain the rapidly growing number of people, natural environments such as forests have to be cleared for farming and accommodation. Deforestation leads to global warming and climate change. Goyal's story, "Aasmaan Mein Surakh" (2006), deals with the depletion of the ozone layer. These factors also drive out animals and their loss of habitat, leading to their extinction. Excess population leads to inflation, because demand exceeds supply. In such a situation, accommodation is a problem as there is increased pressure on the land. Overpopulation leading to poverty is also responsible for the nation's high infant mortality rate. Low birth rates are another result as the mother is unable to get proper nutrition when incomes are low. This challenge is not faced by developed economies. People living in slum areas are more prone to various infections caused by insanitary conditions, and a lack of clean drinking water and medical facilities. Unhygienic conditions result from the depletion of water resources and the discharge of solid waste matter and sewage. Poverty also induces anaemia, rickets etc. due to starvation or malnutrition. Famine is another calamity caused by overpopulation and poverty and a common phenomenon in developing countries. Manjula Padmanabhan's play *Harvest* reflects upon the many problems faced by an overpopulated nation, where there is a shortage of resources and employment opportunities. Om, a jobless man, agrees to sell his organs in order to support his family with money. He becomes a donor to a rich patient in a first world country. In the process, the patient takes complete control over the life of Om and his family through the introduction of video monitoring.

2.3.2 *Cloning*

The theme of cloning, and most particularly human cloning, is popular in SF. The idea of human cloning brings with itself debatable questions of identity. At times, human cloning may be the dominant element in a SF story, but its purpose is to encourage the readers to analyse and probe the meaning of identity. One example of a work of Indian SF that deals with cloning is Deven Mewari's "Antim Pravachan" (1994):

> Human cloning is the creation of a genetically identical copy of an existing, or previously existing, human being or growing cloned tissue from that individual. The term is generally used to refer to artificial human cloning; human clones in the form of identical twins are commonplace, with their cloning occurring during the natural process of reproduction.[9]

Human cloning is of two types: therapeutic and reproductive cloning. In therapeutic cloning, cells from a human are cloned for further use in medicines and transplants. This area is actively being researched, but not in practice. Reproductive cloning deals with the creation of an entire human being through cloning as against just certain cells or tissues. According to Grace Yim in an article, "Human Cloning: Science Fiction or Reality," the idea of human reproductive cloning is something that only happens in SF. It is not possible in the real world as such an experiment would be lethal for both the mother and child. Even if the process is carried out, it would be a risky and dangerous process and it is unlikely that a healthy human child would be reproduced. A story written by Zeashan Zaidi, "The War of Reflections" (2014), uses a mechanism similar to cloning. The scientist in the story invents a machine which divides human cells in two: "These cells form quickly and leave the original body and form a new body which is exactly a copy of the original body. As these cells are connected with each other through invisible waves, the wound that the copy of the body gets, the same wound appears on the original body. As a result, the original body is killed along with its copy."[10] The scientist's explanation is that the human body is comprised of two halves which tend to act in opposition to one another. Both heat and cold are necessary to keep the body alive. The scientist asserts that the human mind stays in a dilemma, when they need to perform a task; whether to do it or not or what is the best way to perform it. This is because every cell of the body has these opposite phases. A machine that the scientist invents divides or segments the cells into opposite phases in two different bodies. Hence the body and its reflection are destroyed in the process of opposing one another. Harish Goyal has also written a few SFs on cloning, *Manav Clone and Tritiya Vishva Yuddh* (1998). This work covers different aspects of cloning. His "Clone Samrajya" (2008) and "Dusra Hitler" (1998) also deal with the same theme.

The theme of cloning, according to Dr. Mishra, may have been inspired from mythological epics such as the *Mahabharata*.

> In Mahabharata the birth of 'Kauravas' – sons of Dhritrashtra, 100 in numbers is described to have been resulted from fetus of premature birth. An imagination what modern cloning technology has made possible! Today's 'test tube baby' is a case in point.[11]

2.3.3 *Mythology and Proto SF*

India has a long tradition of employing the elements of fantasy and mythology in its literature as well as its films. Dr. Srinarahari, in his article "Koi Mil Gaya, India's First Science Fiction Film," gives the example of our Hindu epics such as the *Ramayana* and the *Mahabharata*. He claims that both are replete with myth and magic. These two epics include several instances where magic is visible, for example in the war scenes, or in the use of magical rods and carpets. He adds that in the heydays of film making in India, where fantasy or magic dominated were made by a certain Mr. Vittalacharya. These films were originally made in Telugu and later dubbed in other Indian languages.

Srinarahari explains that the

> Mahabharatha epic is rich in exquisite architectural structures. On the one hand, it describes lengthy floors like glass and water, and these are often juxtaposed one for the other. Conversely, there is the description of a palace built out of wax.[12]

The imaginary worlds depicted in both literature and films have also taken inspiration from the imaginary worlds presented in Indian epics.

> There is: the paradise, the pathala (an imaginary world in the centre of the Earth); the fairy world such as Gandharva lok (lok means world)

Yaksha lok; Kinnara lok; Mathsya lok (an underwater world with aquatic beings that have mermen and women: human bodies in their upper part and lower part resembles the scales of fishes, but usually with divine qualities); Chandra lok (the Moon); Naga lok (the world of snakes) and others.[13]

The idea of air travel, according to Srinarahari, was first mentioned in the *Ramayana*. It is called 'pushpaka vimana' – the earliest record of air travel to be found in history of mankind. This airplane belonged to the wealthiest of the Hindu Gods, Kuber. Other fantastical objects and vehicles used in SF films and literature include magic carpets, a sofa, a cot, and other technical gadgets which have been used to transport people from one world to another. The 'pushpaka vimana' also appears in Ashok K. Banker's SF novel, *Gods of War* (2009) where its portrayal is quite magnificent. Here the five main characters travel in the *Pushpak*, on their way to complete their mission of travelling to the end of time in order to bring peace back to the world. In this mission they are 'guided' by the elephant God, Ganesha. One of the characters, Santosh, asks Ganesha of the *Pushpak*,

> Deva, you called it Pushpak. Do you mean the Pushpak of the legend? The one in which Ravana kidnapped Sita-maa and took her back to Lanka, and in which Rama and Sita and Lakshman travelled back to Ayodhya after the war?[14]

To which Ganesha replies, "Very good. You know your epics well, young man! Yes, indeed, it is the same Pushpak. It is one of the celestial devices created by Vishwakarma, architect and engineer of the devas."[15] We are also told that the Pushpak could take on any shape, size and appearance according to the needs of the user. When asked whether the Pushpak was the creation of magic, Ganesha retorted by saying,

> Pushpak may seem magical, by the standards of your backward technology. But it functions on a completely scientific basis, I assure you… That is techno-fantasy. I mean true science. The kind that was used to create the universe and all that within it. I speak of God's power.[16]

Among many mythic elements, the *Pushpak* and Lord Ganesha are present in the novel. Salim, a socialist trader from Birmingham, observes in the following manner when he first sees Ganesha, the potbellied body and elephant head:

> He had seen images of the Hindu god Ganesha any number of times, was intimately familiar with the deity of auspicious beginnings and scribes, the omnipotent Remover of Obstacles… The being that stood before him now, its head exposed at last after Salim's repeated polite but firm insistencies, was undoubtedly a Ganesha, down to the boyish

plumpness of its human body, and the fleshy bluish grey head with its waving trunk- the head of a baby elephant, according to mythic lore.[17]

As mentioned above, another popular concept in Indian SF films and literature is interstellar travel. Dr. Srinarahari, to show that this too is derived from Indian epics, gives the example of a mythological character, Narada. He is also called 'thrilok sanchari' ('one who could travel across the three worlds, the Earth, Paradise and Hell'). Srinarahari gives the example of a Kannada film *Makkala Sainya* (1964), which shows a journey to Moon and a view of life there. A time machine has also been used along with the elements of magic and fantasy in the Telugu film of 1990s, *Adithya*. In this film, the protagonist travels to the 18th century, at the period when King Krishnadevaraya ruled the empire of Vijayanagar.

> It also depicts war weapons, which could chase the antagonist and instantaneously kill him wherever he might be. The well-known among them is Vishnu Chakra-the circular disc weapon of god Vishnu, the preserver of human beings. Each war scene has special effects in for weapons that could bring rain, fire, and total destruction.[18]

In addition, the concept of tele-viewing can be found in the *Mahabharata*. In one episode, King Dhritrashtra is able to witness the war with the help of Sanjaya, who narrates it as if it was being telecast live.

Dr. Srinarahari further remarks that the use of science and technology in Indian films and literature can also be seen in the use of different kinds of arrows for the purpose of war. Different arrows are used depending on the destruction that is to be caused. For example, when some arrows are used they would cause fire or rain; others could lead to a split in the Earth's surface. These arrows could also be aimed to neutralize the effect of the arrows used by the enemy. All these are inspired by the arrows used in the *Mahabharata* during the war. The arrows used by Lord Krishna and Lord Rama were 'Narayanashtr' and 'Brahmaashtra.' *Muqabla* is a 1996 Hindi-language film in which a man gets transformed into a machine and back, during a song sequence. In fact, there are several examples of the use of technology, what Dr. Srinarahari calls magic technology in Indian films and literature. Magic and biology also play an important role.

Apart from the above mentioned, a common trope used in Indian films and literature is that of the *paaras mani* (precious stone). This particular stone was believed to possess the ability to bring people to life and also to restore youth. A film with the same name was also made in the 1960s. Works that used this trope dealt with the idea of a long life and reincarnation. This aspect of a long life span requires the mention of the mythological character from the *Mahabharata*, Bhishma. He was the eighth son of Shantanu, the Kuru King, and also the grand uncle of Pandavas and Kauravas. He was blessed with the gift of *Ichcha Mrityu*, meaning that he could decide the moment of his death (although he was not immortal). The technology of test-tube babies is also present in the

Mahabharata, in the instance of the birth of Dronacharya. Another example of a magical biological phenomenon is that Hanuman's body could expand or contract according to need. All these examples mentioned suggest that an intermingling of the themes of SF and fantasy can be traced to Hindu mythology employed both in SF literature and films. Dr. Srinarahari labels such Indian mythological films and literature 'Proto SF' because in such works no clear explanation is given for the scientific principles, even though there is a certain closeness to SF. The focus is more on fantasy than on SF. While these Proto SFs carry elements of SF, they do not offer a rational explanation.

Dr. Arvind Mishra also chose to comment on the similarity between myth and SF in a paper written by him, "Mythological Ideas for SF Story Themes: A Novel Approach of Effective Science Communication among Indian SF Audience." He remarks that SF, like mythology, presents a scenario to the reader, which is impossible in the contemporary time and appears unfamiliar. He emphasizes that there are odd and fascinating similarities between SF and mythology. Both introduce strange, innovative ideas and imagery. The important difference is the use of reason in the description and application of technology in SF. Myths do not observe such an approach since the technology of today was not there ages ago, when the myths developed. Ideas, however, continue to hold relevance in both, which have also inspired future discoveries. "Mythological ideas when complemented with modern technology could give rise to wonderful sf themes."[19]

Dr. Mishra also suggests that ideas and concepts from Indian mythological stories can be used to communicate specific scientific ideas and knowledge in a clear manner to the intended Indian audience. He gives the example of an idea that he borrowed from the *Srimad Bhagavatam*. Dr. Mishra drew inspiration from the story of Pradyumna, son of Lord Krishna and Rukmini, who defeated the demon Sambara. In the myth, Pradyumna is made to grow much older than his age through a ritual so that he is strong enough to fight the demon. Mishra also in his story, "Alvida Professor-Good Bye Professor" (2001), accelerates the ageing process of the protagonist.

> I used this very idea in my story entitled "Alvida Professor-Good Bye Professor" (2001) to accelerate the ageing of the main protagonist by imagined technology of growth genes being inserted in man's genome at embryonic stage in order to accelerate his ageing process and face the tough situations of the harsher future world without being dependent on the parents for a very long time. Here the abracadabra of the myth was replaced by a logical and scientifically provable technology…The example may be a guide line in using mythological ideas in similar vein and could invariably be incorporated with technologies taking clues from modern S & T.[20]

2.3.4 *Gender bias*

In a patriarchal structure, women are seen as "the other" and are required to bear the brunt of marginalization and discrimination. Placing men in the centre, patriarchy relegates women to the margins of the society. This has been the case both in the West and in India. The feminist movements started in the West have also inspired movements in India and helped women gain access to rights that were not granted previously. Feminist SF has also played a significant role in challenging the existing status quo of patriarchy where women faced gender discrimination. The authors have contained within their fictions similar issues which they would like to address and be tackled in the society.

Since Feminist SF makes use of an imaginary setting in most cases, the authors tend to critique the injustice done by the patriarchal setup by using unfamiliar, unreal settings. "Consequently, current problems are recontextualized, a technique which is meant to give the reader a new perspective on certain aspects of life they might otherwise take for granted, such as the inadequacies of patriarchy and women's marginality in society."[21]

Many SF authors have also chosen to set their works in a setting that is very close to the real world. For instance, Rokeya Sakhawat Hossain's "Sultana's Dream" is a utopia and set in an imaginary world called Lady land, but this world is very similar to the real world. In such a way, she was able to contrast her present-day world to that of utopia. Her story exposes and also challenges the restrictions imposed upon women by the patriarchal structure. Significantly, the story also puts up alternative measures and ways of dealing or repairing the biased/flawed situation. Similarly, many SF writers have chosen to comment on the gender bias practiced against women, such as female infanticide, female foeticide, and so on. SFs from India draw attention to the declining female population in the country and its effects. India's cultural setup is such that it strengthens gender bias, which has contributed to the preference for the male child in the country. According to the 2011 Census, there has been a decline in population of girls below the age of seven years. An estimate states that nearly 800 million fetuses were aborted in the last ten years. "The 2005 census shows that infant mortality figures for females and males are 61 and 56 respectively, out of 1000 live births, with females more likely to be aborted than males due to biased attitudes."[22] Harish Goyal's story "Bhroon Hatya" is a story on the issue of infanticide. Another story by him on the same issue is "Danav Hamare Beech Hai," published in *Science Times News and Views* in 2007.

Additionally, according to the 2011 Census, there has been a decline in the child sex ratio, these being children between 0 and 6 years. According to the Census, there are 914 females per 1,000 males. This is a drop from girls being 927 in 2001, the lowest since Independence. Many medical practitioners have resorted to the illegal practice of fetal sex determination and sex selective abortion to satisfy the wealthy parents and those who aspire to get sons. Irrespective of this being illegal, the physicians endure the risk of penalties for the financial benefits. Women still lag behind in the field of education in many provinces within India: 65.46% females are literate as compare to 82.14% males.[23] The major reason why fewer women are literate is that parents tend to perceive the education will go waste as the girl will finally go to live at the husband's house. The resources hence invested in her education will not benefit her parents directly. Another area where women encounter bias is the workplace. There often tends to be a difference in wage levels between men and women. Women earn only 64% of what a male colleague would earn in the same position and the same qualifications.[24] Deven Mewari's story "Goodbye Mr. Khanna" is about the exploitation women face at the hands of men at their workplace. This story is published in his anthology, *Meri Priya Vigyan Kathayein*:

> Discrimination against women has led to their lack of autonomy and authority. Although equal rights are given to women, equality may not be well implemented. In practice, land and property rights are weakly enforced with customary laws widely practiced in rural areas. Women do not own property under their names and usually do not have any inheritance rights to obtain a share of parental property.[25]

Harish Goyal's SF stories "Height" and "Clone Princess" (2014) tackle the issue of gender bias in Indian society. "Clone Princess" presents an alternative world which is alone populated by female clones. A similar work by Goyal is "Dam Todti Manavta," where there are no women, only men alive.

2.3.5 Space travel

A journey to outer space is a classic theme of SF. Jules Verne's SF novel *From the Earth to the Moon* is considered to be the first SF to deal with the topic of space travel as a logical engineering concern. He identified that once in space, there would be no gravity; it is also possible that there would be an absence of air. Considering these factors, Verne's spaceship only went close to the Moon, examining it closely and identifying its craters. During this period, it was believed that it is sufficient to dream of the extraterrestrial possibility in space. A movie was also made on Verne's novel by Georges Méliès in 1902.

According to Bruce Sterling, a SF critic, certain disenchantment set in after the first man landed on the Moon in 1969. It was then discovered that life in outer space was not as glorious as imagined. The astronauts who went to space were highly skilled and trained and their main focus was to protect their hardware. They struggled with limited fuel, oxygen, water, power, apart from being in a cramped space, life that was nothing close to being on a luxury starship. SFs which portray the element of space travel with realism are rare. SF tends to cut out the unromantic features of space travel, achieved through the device of faster than light travel. "Although this imaginary technology is no more technically plausible than lifelike androids, it is a necessity for the alien-planet adventure story. Science fiction writers cheerfully sacrifice the realities of astrophysics in the service of imaginary world."[26]

The term 'hyperspace' is often used to refer to faster-than-light travel in SF. Travel is undertaken in the genre to an alternate zone of space parallel to our universe, which can be permeated through an energy field or other means. In hyperspace, travel is often portrayed as faster-than-light travel in normal space. Often times, faster-than-light travel is enabled and described in SF through hyperspace. The protagonist, Anasuya, with the help of scientists from outer space discovers a set of equations to make faster-than-light travel possible in Vandana Singh's novella *The Distances*. Detailed discussion on this will follow in the next chapter.

A subgenre of SF which shows travel to outer space or life in outer space is space opera: "Space opera is a subgenre of science fiction that often emphasizes romantic, often melodramatic adventure, set mainly or entirely in outer space, usually involving conflict between opponents possessing advanced abilities, weapons and other technology."[27] Dr. Arvind Mishra's story "Antariksha Kokila" concerns female space travelers from another planet who come to Earth to steal children from their mothers. These women from space have lost their maternal instinct and unable to raise their own children. Hence, the action of the story unfolds.

According to K.S. Purushottam, the SF critic and author, most stories of Indian SF are about aliens and space travel. Nellai Muthu, a space scientist in the Indian Space Research Organization (ISRO), also writes SF. Space travel, along with alien civilization, constitute his favourite themes. Muthu's novel *Maakol Maindaragal* (The Inhabitants of Planet Maakol) is about a civilization whose residents are composed of silicon, in contrast to those on Earth, who are essentially made of carbon. Dr. Arvind Mishra's story, "Guru Dakshina," is about Asimov Robotics.[28] Here, a space visitor comes to India to conduct research on Indian culture and stays back, refusing to return.

Related to space travel is the trope of time travel, which is employed quite commonly in SF. Instances of time travel go back to the *Mahabharata*, as indicated by Dr. Arvind Mishra in his article "Mythological Ideas for SF Story Themes: A Novel Approach of Effective Science Communication among Indian SF Audience."[29] He is of the opinion that this concept was also found in Indian mythology. Dr. Mishra cites the example of King Raivat, who travels to heaven to meet Brahma, the creator. When he returns to Earth, King Raivat is amazed to find that a long time has passed, in fact several generations. According to Dr. Mishra, the ancient writers worked with a prophetic rich vision and envisioned advanced technologies that could be realized and also form an interesting SF theme. The concept of time travel has also been used in Indian SF films, such as *Aditya 369* (1991), *Funn2shh* (2003), and *Action Replayy* (2010).

2.3.6 Technology in science fiction

The presence of technology in SF investigates the practicability and consequences of innovative discoveries. In their fiction, SF authors have adopted or generated new technologies and also offered elaborations on what these might be and how they can be used. At times, the technology is mentioned for the first time in SF, after which it becomes a reality, an example being space travel. At other times, the technology is already there, it has been invented and the task of SF writer is to speculate about its use and effect on humans and their living conditions. The technology in SF can be portrayed in different ways. It may be an existing technology, or at times a realistic portrayal of a far-fetched technology, or just as a simple plot device that appears scientific, but has no foundation in science.

Examples of SF from India where technology has inspired innovations in real life or explores the consequences of an already existing technology are *Chandra Lok Ki Yatra* (1900) by Babu Keshav Prasad Singh and *Baisvee Sadi* (1924) by Rahul Sankrityayan. *Chandra Lok Ki Yarta* illustrates a journey to the Moon sixty years before it actually took place. Also, the story discussed the topic of space travel and moon a hundred years before *Chandrayaan*, India's first lunar probe began to explore Earth's satellite. Babu Keshav Prasad Singh was inspired by Jules Verne's *Voyages Extraordinaires*. The story proved to be futuristic.

Futuristic SF in Hindi gained a strong hold with the coming of Rahul Sankrityayan's *Baisvee Sadi*. The novel, which is set in 2124, depicts a world in which advances in technology also lead to improvements in the political and social arena. The protagonist, Vishwabandhu, lives in 1924; one day, however, he wakes up to find himself in 2124, 200 years later. Such a world is governed by a world government which means that while the president is Indian, the prime minister is Japanese. A single language is spoken by all. Absolute law and order is restored and hence there is no need for police. The protagonist exclaims that scientific progress has attained its climax. Farming is done with the help of biotechnology and farmers genetically modify the crops according to their needs. In Sankrityayan's time, no one could have imagined that food could be genetically engineered. In the futuristic world of 2124, one village produces only one kind of crop; for example, there would be a village that grew only apples, and another would grow only oranges, and their fields would extend to miles. Animals were kept only in zoos and do not roam on roads or in residential areas. Citizens communicate with one another through a device that resembles the modern-day Internet. Additionally, there is a radio phone, much like the modern video phone. Sankrityayan envisioned many things, some of which we see realized such as genetically engineered crops, video phones etc.

Many SF authors and critics also believe that advances in technology were also predicted in the *Mahabharata*. Although the epic provides no scientific explanation about how the advances can be realized in future. "Every science fiction imagines a world beyond the current. Science fiction is often predictive because what it contains as fantasy became reality sometime in the future."[30] Along this model, the *Mahabharata* has been given the status of being the most imaginative SF of all.

It visualized the impossible (at the time) technologies and human studies. Most science fiction imaginations have a few decades before their visions become a loose and then defined reality. The technologies dreamed in the Mahabharata probably took thousands of years to become reality – but reality they have become.[31]

Among the predictions made in the field of medical sciences that have become reality are In-Vitro Fertilization (IVF) and test-tube babies. It is said that Kunti's children were "gifts of Gods." The six boys were born through what can be called as a precursor of IVF in which a sperm (that does not belong to its father by law) is required to fertilize the mother's egg, contributing to the birth of a child. It is well known that the Kauravas were not born of their mother's womb, but nurtured in jars of ghee. The mechanism of test-tube babies where the embryo is developed outside the mother's womb is actualized in today's world. This idea can also be seen in Dr. Arvind Mishra's story "Dehdaan," in which a woman from another planet takes sperm from an Indian space traveler in order to repopulate her planet, where the entire male population has been exterminated.

Several weapons were also imagined in the *Mahabharata*, such as atom bombs, biological and chemical warfare. Although this was created at a time when combat did not exceed the use of bow and arrows, swords and spears, yet the imagination was such that the author could think of unsurpassable technology.

2.3.7 LGBT themes

LGBT[32] is a popular theme of speculative fiction which means the inclusion of lesbian, gay, bisexual, or transgender themes in SF, fantasy and interconnected genres. In practice, works of SF can include an LGBT character as the protagonist or simply undertake the investigations of gender or sexuality that makes a deviation from the heterosexual norm. Speculative fiction allows the writer to imagine societies that are unlike those which exist in real life. Speculative fiction enables an atmosphere of freedom which is useful for probing into sexual bias. The author achieves this by challenging the reader's heteronormative cultural assumptions. According to Nicola Griffith, a British American novelist, the LGBT readership tends to identify closely with the aliens and mutants in speculative fiction. The protagonist in Vandana Singh's *Of Love and Other Monsters* is bisexual, who later learns that he is an alien from a distant planet and his special powers were destroyed when he came on Earth.[33]

Before the 1960s, there was little or no mention of explicit sexuality in SF, as the publishers believed that it would affect the market of young male readers. However, as the demand for SF and number of readers increased it was easier to include homosexuals without the need to camouflage them. Yet these characters played the role of villains and the lesbians received no representation at all.

In the 1960s, science fiction and fantasy began to reflect the changes prompted by the civil rights movement and the emergence of a counterculture. New wave and feminist science fiction authors realized cultures in which homosexuality, bisexuality and a variety of gender models were the norm, and in which sympathetic depictions of alternate sexuality were commonplace.[34]

It was from the 1980s that homosexuality achieved greater acceptance. Authors went beyond exploring just a presence of homosexuality to particular concerns pertinent to the LGBT community. By the 20th century, the homophobia was dismissed in SF and fantasy. Hence, LGBT themes also figured in television, films, and comics.

While many works of SF in the West with LGBT themes have been produced, there are only a few such works in Indian SF. For instance, Dr. Rajeev Ranjan Upadhyay's "Ek Aur Sikhandi" deals with the theme of homosexuality. Here, two close female friends lead a homosexual life. One of the girls later changes her sex and becomes a male, rather transgender.

2.3.8 Love

SF with LGBT themes tends to foreground the significance of love, irrespective of the prevalent social norms. Homosexual love is portrayed in its true form in such SF. There are a few examples within Indian SF to mention but some, such as *Of Love and Other Monsters* by Vandana Singh, describe same-sex love, along with depictions of lesbian and gay characters. There is also no mention of homophobia in the novella. An SF story that includes the theme of love, not necessarily homosexual love is "Antim Sanskaar" by Dr. Arvind Mishra. It is the story of a woman from a distant planet who falls in love with an earthling. Tragically, however, their consummation of love results in her death. She was programmed in such a way that an intimate connection with humans would destroy her and she would also be contaminated to enter her native planet. Zeashan Zaidi has also written SF stories featuring the love theme. "Vaigyanik Rajkumari" (1999) carries the idea that age does not matter when it comes to love and great friendships. "Qaidi Urja" (2000) also discusses an aspect of love, that there is no place for greed in the emotion of love. Of course, these stories mentioned also carry an overarching theme of technology.

2.3.9 Spirituality

Apart from dealing with aliens and spaceships, the issues of homosexuality, love and many more, SF can also be seen as a means through which the author raises serious questions relating to other aspects of human existence. These questions could be about religion, faith, the meaning of life, destiny, and what exactly it means to be human. SF allows the writer an ease with which they can discuss these questions which may not be so easily discussed in other genres. The setting, plot and scope of most SFs support the exploration of such themes, which have troubled human beings since times immemorial. These themes could also have to do with religious texts and scriptures such as the *Ramayana*, the *Mahabharata* and the Bible.

The most apparent way in which spirituality is portrayed in SF is through the assessment of the human spirit under challenging or even alien circumstances. SF has the ability to ask intense and probing questions unlike any other genre. It raises questions such as: how should one maintain dignity and humanity when faced with invincible odds and danger to human life? Many works of SF have shown how humanity can be very loving and supportive when faced with insuperable odds. In Ashok K. Banker's *Gods of War*, individuals from different parts of the world come together to save the world from apocalyptic destruction. Each of these individuals comes from different countries, backgrounds and religions. It is the love for humanity and need for peace in the world that unites them.

Notes

1 Gupta, Sagar Mal. "Development and Evolution of Science Fiction in India and the World". *Science Fiction in India: Past, Present and Future*. 2011, p. 63
2 Mishra, Arvind. "Mainstream and Genre SF: emergence and Trends in Hindi vis a vis Western Literature". *Science Fiction in India: Past, Present and Future*. 2011, p. 162
3 *SFE: The Encyclopaedia of Science Fiction*. SFE Content, 2011. Web. January 17, 2013. http://www.sf-encyclopedia.com/entry/bengal.
4 *Indian SF: Science Fiction and Fantasy Stories*. March 1, 2014. Web. April 8, 2014. http://indiansf.in/about/
5 Dugal, Simrat Kaur and Charu Maithani. *Indian Foundation for the Arts*, 2013. Web. 2013. http://www.indiaifa.org/simrat-kaur-dugal-charu-maithani.html
6 SF in India: The 19th Annual/5th International Science Fiction Conference by Srinarahari Mysore. April 2, 2021. Web. April 25, 2021 https://locusmag.com/2021/04/sf-in-india-the-19th-annual-5th-international-science-fiction-conference-by-srinarahari-mysore/#:~:text=The%2019th%20 Annual%2F5th%20International%20Science%20Fiction%20Conference%20 was%20organized,December%207%2D10%2C%202020
7 The Editors of Encyclopaedia Britannica "Asian brown cloud". *Encyclopædia Britannica*. November 21, 2018. Web. December 27, 2018. https://www.britannica.com/science/Asian-brown-
8 Nathonson, Jeremy A., *Encyclopaedia Britannica Inc.*, July 30, 2019, https://www.britannica.com/technology/solid-waste-management.
9 Thomas, Isabel. "Science Daily. Should scientists pursue cloning?" *Science Daily*. Raintree, 2013, https://www.sciencedaily.com/terms/human_cloning.htm.
10 Zaidi, Zeashan. "The War of Reflections". July 8, 2014. Web. August 11, 2014. http://zeashanzaidi.blogspot.in/2014/07/the-war-of-reflections-part-6-last-part.html#more.
11 Mishra, Arvind. "Science Fiction in India". January 13, 2012. Web. December 2012. http://indiascifiarvind.blogspot.in/2012/01/mythological-ideas-for-sf-story-themes.html.
12 Srinarahari, M. H. "Koi Mil Gaya, India's First Science Fiction". 4 September, 2014. Web. 10 September, 2014. http://www.concatenation.org/articles/koire-vised3.html.
13 Ibid.
14 Banker, Ashok K. *Gods of War*. 2009, p. 102
15 Ibid., p. 102

16 Ibid., p. 106
17 Ibid., p. 61
18 Srinarahari, M. H. "Koi Mil Gaya, India's First Science Fiction". September 4, 2014. Web. September 10, 2014. http://www.concatenation.org/articles/koirevised3.html.
19 Mishra, Arvind. "Science Fiction in India". January 13, 2012. Web. December 2012. http://indiascifiarvind.blogspot.in/2012/01/mythological-ideas-for-sf-story-themes.html.
20 Mishra, Arvind. "Science Fiction in India". January 13, 2012. Web. December 2012. http://indiascifiarvind.blogspot.in/2012/01/mythological-ideas-for-sf-story-themes.html.
21 Gilarek, Anna. "Marginalization of the Other". *Gender Discrimination in Dystopian Visions by Feminist Science Fiction Authors*. December 4, 2012. Web. January, 2013. http://www.degruyter.com/view/j/texmat.2012.2.issue-2/v10231-012-0066-3/v10231-012-0066-3.xml.
22 Hausman, Ricardo, Laura D. Tyson et al. "The Global Gender Gap Index 2013". http://www3.weforum.org/docs/WEF_GenderGap_Report_2013.pdf.
23 Ibid.
24 Hausman, Ricardo, Laura D. Tyson et al. "The Global Gender Gap Index 2013". http://www3.weforum.org/docs/WEF_GenderGap_Report_2013.pdf.
25 Ibid.
26 Sterling, Bruce. *Encyclopaedia Britannica*. August 8, 2014. Web. September 10, 2014. http://www.britannica.com/EBchecked/topic/528857/science-fiction/235730/Space-travel.
27 Chandler, Otis. "GoodReads". *GoodReads*, February 2015, https://www.goodreads.com/topic/show/1757873-what-is-space-opera.
28 ASIMOV Robotics Pvt. Ltd is a solution and services proving company to address all needs or robotics and automation.
29 Mishra, Arvind. "Science Fiction in India". January 13, 2012. Web. December 2012. http://indiascifiarvind.blogspot.in/2012/01/mythological-ideas-for-sf-story-themes.html.
30 Garimella, Sujata. "The Mahabharata: A science Fiction". *India Opines*, October 2013. Web. December 2015. http://indiaopines.com/mahabharata-science-fiction/.
31 Ibid.
32 LGBT themes refer to lesbian, gay, bisexual and transgender themes in speculative fiction.
33 This will be discussed extensively in the next chapter.
34 Google Books, May 15, 2014. https://books.google.co.in/books?id=vShYfiP_6s AC&printsec=frontcover&dq=LGBT+themes+in+speculative+fiction.

3 Contemporary Indian science fiction writers and their works

3.1 Writers in focus

3.1.1 Rokeya Sakhawat Hossain

Family background and education

Rokeya Sakhawat Hossain is popularly known and referred to as Begum Rokeya in Bangladesh and as Rokeya Sakhawat in literary circles. She would largely identify herself as (Mrs.) R.S. Hossain, Roqyiah Khatun or even Khatoon. Her family members called her Rokeya and others close to her would even call her Ruku, depending on how close they were to her. Her name was spelled either as Roqyiah or Rokeya; both names were used, can be linked to the idea that "like women their names were also thought to be *purdanasin* (secluded/private) at that time."[1] Rokeya, in her work *Aborodhbasini*, said that a record of women's complete names was only made at the time of marriage. Hence, if one had access to her marriage certificate, then one could ascertain the exactness of the facts.

Rokeya's father, Zahiruddin Mohammad abu Ali Haider Saber, was a landlord and a polyglot, who was able to speak in seven languages. Hardly anything is known about her mother, Rahatunnessa Sabera Chowdhurani, except that she maintained a strict purdah practice. Rokeya had three brothers, Mohammad Ibrahim Abul Asad Saber, Khalilur rahman Abu Zaigam Saber and Israil Abu Hafs Saber. The first two excelled and flourished and went on to do government service. Little is known about the third brother, who died a premature death. She also had two sisters: Karimunnesa and Humera. It is said that Karimunnesa was "the first known modern Muslim woman poet of Bengal."[2] While the father was very concerned about the education of his sons, he refused to provide his daughters with any formal learning, fearing the social stigma attached to female education at that time. Hossain, in "The Begum's Dream,"[3] has said that during that time in India, "girls with education were regarded as being abominable as without purdah."[4]

The notions of child marriage and purdah were predominant during Rokeya's time among Muslims as well as the Hindus, which resulted in the absence of girls from any formal institute of learning. Furthermore, Muslims in colonial India were treated with discrimination, and this also impacted on women's education. There was no proper institute where Bengali Muslim women could study. It was only in 1939 that the Lady Brabourne College was set up as an institution where Muslim girls could attend college on an equal footing with Hindu girls, for the first time. Students from all religions could attend, yet some seats were reserved for Urdu-speaking girls, of which most of them were Muslims.

Even though Rokeya was only permitted to read the Qur'an in Arabic, and was taught at home, in later life she was proficient in five languages: English, Bangla, Persian, Urdu and Arabic. Being deprived of formal education, she was able to learn Bangla from her sister, Karimunnesa and English from her brother, Ibrahim, who would give her secret lessons at night. As recognition of her brother's role in shaping her, Rokeya has dedicated her only novel, *Padmarag*, to Ibrahim.

Karimunnesa had to endure more challenges during her self-education. She had to carry out the task in complete secrecy under harsh control by her father and challenging conditions. As the eldest, she also could not take support or help from any older sibling. When her study plans were discovered, she was immediately married off for fear that education would spoil her prospect of getting married and she would also not be a good housewife, in case she was educated. At the time of her marriage, she was not even fifteen years of age. However, she remained invincible and continued to school herself by reading the books in her marital home. The books belonged to her husband's younger brothers, who had attended school. At the same time, she continually encouraged Rokeya to continue her education despite opposition from her relatives. Rokeya commemorated her sister by dedicating her essay "Lukano Ratan" (Hidden Gem) to Karimunnesa.

Hossain was married at the age of sixteen to a progressive Bengali Muslim in 1986. He fortunately supported women's education and encouraged her to learn English. Rokeya's short story, "Sultana's Dream," came out in 1905 while her husband was away on a business trip. She wrote the story to impress her husband with her newly acquired skills. He was most impressed and exclaimed upon reading the story: "A splendid revenge!" By "revenge" he meant that through her writing, she had avenged the ill-treatment of women, because of the practice of zenana, also known as *purdah*.[5]

Considered as the earliest work of Indian science fiction, certainly of Indian science fiction in English, Rokeya Sakhawat Hossain's short story, "Sultana's Dream," was first published in the *Indian Ladies Magazine* in Madras in 1905, where it was well received; in 1908 it was republished as a standalone book. In her writing, Hossain clearly incorporates science fictional elements with the social issues. There is a constant emphasis on the idea of science and the power of the intellect to deal with the various challenges as the Queen says if women are lacking in physical strength they should "try to do so by brain power."[6] Rokeya's primary concern was with the issue of formal education for women. She wanted women to be self-sufficient. For her, activism and writing were intertwined.

The short story became immensely popular among the highcaste women readers, those privileged enough to read and write in English. However, it is believed that her ideas would have filtered down to less privileged Indian women through magazines such as *Swarnakumari Debi*. Women, at that time engaged with social reform and female education read this magazine. So one can say that Hossain's ideas were accessible to one and all, be they rich or poor.

Literary, political and educational activism

Although a prolific writer, Rokeya Sakhawat Hossain remained undervalued and neglected by literary scholars for a long time. There were a number of reasons for this. Bengali Muslim women were not the subject of research because of the overarching rendition of Hindu women writers by literary chroniclers. Secondly, feminist literary criticism tended to valorize western heroines and relegate those from other cultural settings.

Rokeya made an outstanding contribution towards the elevation of women's position in society. Although she has had many predecessors and successors among Muslims in Bengal, no one was able to challenge patriarchy as successfully as she did. As quoted in Hasan's article, Rokeya like her other women counterparts in India "was doubly 'Other' - as woman and as a colonized person,"[7] according to Tharu and Lalita. Hasan, in his essay "Commemorating Rokeya Sakhawat Hossain and Contextualizing her Work in South Asian Muslim Feminism," remarks that Rokeya was in fact "triply Other: woman, colonized as well as being Muslim."[8] He laments that Rokeya did not receive the deserved attention even in her own country. Jahan Roushan, in his book *Inside Seclusion: The Avarodhbasini of Rokeya Sakhawat Hossain*, says that, "No full-length critical evaluation of [Rokeya's] works... has appeared in Bangladesh... So far she has been neglected by students and researchers alike."[9] Jahan made this remark in 1981, and it led to a number of works being published in Bangladesh and elsewhere on Rokeya's life, but the magnitude of works is still insufficient considering her contribution.

Ray, one of the editors of *Women Writing in India*, remarked about Rokeya that:

> I was amazed and almost shocked. How could a Bengali woman, a Muslim woman, in the first decade of the [twentieth] century have written like this?... It was revolutionary thinking even by the standards of the late twentieth century. The more I read, the more fascinated I become.[10]

Rokeya's work received critical attention from 1973, 41 years after her death with the publication of *Rokeya Rachanabali* (Complete Works of Rokeya). This compilation was made by the famous poet and critic Abdul Quadir (1906–1984) and published by the Bangla academy in Dhaka. This publication encouraged research on Rokeya. Until 1973, the only exceptional works on Rokeya Sakhawat Hossain were Shamsunnahar Mahmud's

Rokeya Jiboni (The Life of Rokeya [1935]) and Moshfeka Mahmud's *Potre Rokeya Porichiti* (Rokeya in Letters [1965]). These works give us biographical details about Rokeya, but only sketchily, and all were produced by her family successors. As a result, Rokeya is now revered as an iconic figure and as one of the foremothers of feminism. She is widely acknowledged and appreciated for her efforts towards achieving women's rights and their social upliftment.

Rokeya's literary career began with the publication of her essay "Pipasha" in 1902 in the Calcutta-based magazine *Nabaprabha*. One can notice a gap in the literary works she produced between 1909 to 1914 irrespective of "her tremendous creative talents, insights and energies."[11] This vacuum can be ascribed to the various hardships she suffered due to the deaths of her loved ones; her parents, children and husband. She spent a large part of her short married life taking care of her ailing husband, who was some 16 years her senior. At an early age, Rokeya faced the death of her two daughters, who died at the ages of just five months and four months, respectively. Rokeya also strove to set up her school, against the misdeeds of her step-daughter and step-son-in-law resulting from a feud over property. Yet we know that Rokeya wrote inexorably for entire three decades, starting from 1902 and ending only with her death. She "produced foundational literary works of different genres and subject matters, predominantly women's issues."[12] The last essay she wrote, "Narir Adhikar" (Women's Rights), remained unfinished on the night she died due to a heart attack. It was published posthumously in 1957, twenty-five years after her death in a magazine called *Mahe-nau*.

Rokeya worked very hard to find a platform where Muslim women could voice their views and be a part of the public sphere. In British India, there was no League or Association of which women were a part. Muslims did run some political and educational organizations, such as the All India Muslim League, the All India Educational Conference and the Central Mohammadan Association. These were run by men and meant exclusively for them. Rokeya struggled to establish a branch of Indian Muslim Women's Organization (Anjuman-i-Khawatin-i-Islam) in Calcutta in 1916. The central branch had been founded in Aligarh in 1914. To bring the women in Bengal out of their cocooned existence, their seclusion, was an arduous experience for Rokeya. She motivated and coaxed them to cherish the value of being part of activities of Anjuman. Rokeya had to teach them a lot many things, as the Bengal women had no experience or understanding of organizational tasks. Rokeya was persistent in her efforts to alert Muslim women of the importance of being active and educated, and brought them to Anjuman meetings. As a result, the All India Muslim Education Conference opened its branch in Bengal and Rokeya played an instrumental part of the organization. In 1926, she was even elected the President for one of its sessions in their conference and made a valuable speech. Her aspirations with respect to Anjuman are depicted functionally in her novel, *Padamarag*. Here, she renders for the readers a home called the Tarini Bhaban (the House of the Rescuer) where oppressed women seek refuge. Within the house is present the Nari-Klesh

Nibarani Samiti (the Society for the Prevention of Women's Sufferings). Tarini Bhaban is a shelter house for those females who had been cast out from society; they were able to create a world of their own on the site.

The focal point of Rokeya's activism was to encourage female education. In the British India in which Rokeya lived, even the social setting was antagonistic to women's education. This was the case to such an extent that the great leaders such as Sayyid Ahmed Khan (1817–1898) refrained from including the cause in their influential movement for Muslim education, fearing that it would flout their project of advancement. However, Rokeya did not succumb to such pressures; she continually pursued her scramble for female advancement through education and in the process she braved the social norms and obstacles that came in the way.

Rokeya drew attention to the cause of female education at a consequential period in the history of Muslim Bengal. The Muslims had realized that due to the long-lasting colonial struggle, they have suffered economically, politically and culturally. As a result, they started working to put an end to this atrocious condition, under the guidance of Sayyid Ahmed Khan. But Rokeya identified the flaw in their working as the Muslims worked industriously to set up multiple organizations and leading various movements. She pointed out that what they left behind – female education – was the most important issue. Rokeya questions the regressive attitude of the Muslims, made available to us through the translations made by Hasan: "Can a community, that has locked half of its population in the prison of ignorance and seclusion, keep pace with the progress of other communities that have advanced female education on a full par with men?"[13] She regretfully refers to a time in history when the Muslim religious leaders opposed Muslim education, the repercussions of which they were now reaping. That injudicious stance adopted by the Muslims kept them away from the large resource of knowledge and the prosperity that would result from it. She attempts to warn the Muslim community of the consequences, in case they do not heed to her advice to pay attention towards women's education. She warns that their generation will lag behind as compared to children of other communities as they were being raised by educated mothers. For children to be intelligent, the mothers must not be ignorant. When Rokeya began her school, she invested her soul and mind into it. The work occupied her mentally and physically, which, towards the end of her life, also affected her health drastically. She would go personally to the doors of students and persuade the parents to send their girls to school. She assumed full responsibility for the girls; she looked after them and paid careful attention to their tutoring. She also let the girls study free of cost, and they did not even have to pay their travelling cost.

Rokeya was highly radical in her thinking, considering the circumstances in which she worked to set up her educational movement, and she did not discriminate between the instruction for men and women. Even the more progressive scholars of the period restricted the teaching of women to socially accepted disciplines. In his article, Hassan quotes from Srabashi

Ghosh's article "Birds in a Cage: Changes in Bengali Social Life as Recorded in Autobiographies by Women." Ghosh tells us:

> Even long after women's education was accepted by the society, women were considered inferior to men in intelligence. They were not given the opportunity to study science. Perhaps it was thought what was not needed for household chores… unnecessary for them. Sarala [Devi Chawdhurani] and Shanta [Nag] were students of Bethune College which was founded in 1849 exclusively for girls. No science subject was taught there.[14]

Victoria College, which was run by the well-known Hindu philosopher and social reformer Keshub Chandra Sen (1838–1884), also did not include any science subjects on its curriculum. He felt that the purpose of education was to enable them to run better households. Rokeya differed in her opinion; she saw no disparity in the education of males and females. She campaigned so that women could have access to subjects such as botany, chemistry, horticulture, health care, personal hygiene, gymnastics and so on. In "Sultana's Dream," we see that the character, Sister Sara, is competent in fields such as history, military strategy, politics, science and education. Her novel, *Padmarag*, shows an ideal set-up for female education where almost all streams of knowledge are taught – such as geography, history, science, mathematics, literature. Hossain may not have been able to implement in the practical world all that she envisioned in her imaginative world, but she included other things in her curriculum, apart from the regular courses in English, Urdu, Bangla, Arabic and Persian: sewing, nursing, cooking, home economics, gardening, physical education and handicrafts.

Rokeya, for all her efforts in literature as well as her endeavours for women's emancipation against the unfavourable and hostile conditions of her period, is revered as the most distinguished writer of Bangladesh. She struggled against a society that was not ready to accept her revolutionary feminist ideas. Her ideas and strategies for female emancipation and advancement are relevant even today. Her influence can be strongly felt in the Indian subcontinent.

3.1.2 Manjula Padmanabhan

Family background and education

Manjula Padmanabhan was born in born in Delhi in 1953 into a family of diplomats. As a result, she grew up in many countries of the world, such as Pakistan, Sweden and Thailand. She received her education at Bombay University.

Padmanabhan likes science fiction the best, which is associated with her sense of "not belonging" – being a sort of alien. There is a feeling of not belonging to her "home country" which encouraged her interest in "otherness." It is this "otherness" that drew her to speculative fiction since her father was a diplomat, she got chances to stay out of India most of her life.

She still flits between her mother's home in Chennai and her own 'home' in Newport, Rhode Island in the US. Finally, Padmanabhan moved to India only when her father retired. This led to a sense of unhappiness, a sense of being a misfit, accompanied by the desire to be one. Her "otherness" or alienness is characterized by her having been away from India most of her life, that she could not speak Hindi, or conform to the traditional dress codes. Hence, speculative fiction is an easy outlet and allows her imaginary worlds, where being alien is the norm. There was no country where she could actually feel "at home."[15]

Literary, political and educational activism

Manjula Padmanabhan is a multifaceted personality. She is not only a novelist, a children's book author, journalist, playwright, short story writer, but also a comic strip artist. In her writings, she also deals with the key issues of alienation and marginalization. When Padmanabhan writes, draws or paints, she does not conceive of herself as a feminist. The author refuses to be put into the tight boxes of being a 'male' or 'female' writer. She resists such tight definitions. She simply believes in creating work that is honest and believable.

Padmanabhan's cartoon strip, which is titled *Suki*, appeared regularly for many years in the *Sunday Observer* (Bombay, 1982–1986) and later in the *Pioneers* (New Delhi, 1991–1997). She has produced 24 illustrated texts and written a number of children's books. Her plays comprise of *Lights Out!* (1984), *The Artist's Model* (1995), *Sextet* (1996), *Harvest* (1998), and *Hidden Fires* (2003). One of these, *Harvest*, won the Onassis Prize in 1997; it was elected from 1470 entries in 76 countries. *Harvest* is a futuristic play about organ selling and the exploitative exchange that occurs between developed and developing countries. The play has been filmed by Govind Nihalani. Padmanabhan's books comprise *Hot Death, Cold Soup* (1997), *Getting There* (1999), *This is Suki!* (2000), *Mouse Attack* (2003), *Mouse Invaders* (2004), *Kleptomania* (2004), *Double Talk* (2005), *Unprincess!* (2005), *I am Different* (2007), *Escape* (2008), *Where's That Cat* (2009), and *Same and Different* (2010). Padmanabhan's novel, *Getting There*, becomes significant because it is part autobiography and part fiction; it may be termed autobiographical fiction. The novel itself is humorous. The protagonist moves around the world, much like the author. The central character closely examines her own life – by defining her relationships, romance, love, spirituality and self-perception. The underlying idea is that one is responsible for their actions and that one is in charge of their fate; every action is a choice. The novel, *Escape*, her first book for an adult audience, was shortlisted for the Vodafone Crossword Book Awards 2008. It is also credited for being one of the first few works of modern Indian science fiction in English. It centers on the issue of declining sex ratio in country due to the strong social bias directed against the girl children.

In her science fiction works, Padmanabhan explores the autocracy of those in domination in a technologically advanced future awaiting modern nation-states likes India. Within this framework, she also explores the equation of the female citizen to the nation state. As has been quoted in Chapter VI, "Charting a Vision for the Future", Shodhganga INFLIBNET:

> According to Ania Loomba, national fantasies (colonial, anti-colonial or post-colonial), play upon the connections between women and the land. The nation-state is often imagined literally as a woman. As national emblems, women are usually cast as mothers and wives, and are called upon to literally and figuratively produce the nation.[16]

The article also quotes Radhika Mohanram:

> Women are the state in that they reflect and embody its power yet also function as the site upon which the state confirms its identity... in the process of naming itself, the state has to exclude her... Thus the nation-state takes the place of patronymic in its positioning and definition of women.[17]

Padmanabhan uses an eco-feminist perspective to explore the relation of woman to the nation-state. She reacts strongly against social and environment issues in her works, whether it is against illegal trade of organs, rape or female foeticide. Her works draw the attention of readers to alarming issues, which are being ignored. For instance, her novel *Escape* can be read as a post-modern dystopia. It foresees for the readers and the nation a dark future if the current limitations are not ameliorated. The underlying message in her works is that reality can be fashioned out of dreams and that hope is not an empty fantasy. She conveys the idea that there is a lot of power in imagination; it has the ability to propose and bring about a change. Speaking about why incidents such as riots occur repeatedly, Padmanabhan identifies religious constraints as a reason.

Padmanabhan has a blog, namely "YES!," where she writes regularly on topics that are close to her or worry her. Her cartoon strip, *Suki*, forms part of her blog. Padmanabhan's articles are also published in the online, fortnight issue of *Hindu Business Line*. The column is named "BLink". She writes on her life in USA and the various experiences she had while living there. Similarly, her columns dealing with her life experiences appear online in the blog *Rediff on The Net*.

3.1.3 *Vandana Singh*

Family background and education

Vandana Singh was brought up in a middle-class family and sent to an English-medium school for her education. She learnt English at the age of four, meaning that both English and Hindi come naturally to her. Both her parents had graduate degrees in English literature, so she was as familiar with Shakespeare and Keats as she was with the great Indian epics or Premchand.

Singh grew up in a large family consisting of her brother, sister, parents, aunts, uncles, cousins and her grandparents. Vandana is the youngest of the three children. In her childhood, she had the privilege to listen to the *Ramayana* and the *Mahabharata* from her mother and grandmother, and many folk tales and village lore from others in the family. During her teenage years and her adulthood, she became associated with environment and women's movements, which had a significant impact on her. At the age of seventeen, straight from school, she went to the Himalayas on a trek as part of a newly formed environment group called Kalpavriksha (which later became one of India's larger environment groups). She was part of a loosely formed group of students who wanted to study the Chipko movement. There she learnt a great deal about the village poor, and their attempts to save their forests. The expedition was an eye-opener as she leant that "feminism was not an exclusively Western phenomenon," that we could have our own indigenous feminism. She learnt this as she saw the village women fighting to protect their forests and also taking steps to prevent men from drinking and hence destroying their lives in despair. Another thing she learnt was that these poor and illiterate people were capable of lifting themselves out of poverty and environmental degradation without the help of rich and literate. These ideas contributed in a larger way in changing her view of the world.[18]

Singh continued to work with environment and women's movements groups during her college in India until she moved to the USA for her post-graduate studies in physics. Since then she has been in the USA, where she now lives with her husband, daughter and dog. Singh holds a PhD in theoretical particle physics and teaches physics at Framingham State College in Massachusetts, USA.

Literary, political and educational activism

Vandana Singh is a writer of speculative fiction, a genre which includes both science fiction and fantasy. Her love for the genre is because of

> its imaginative richness, its vast canvas, and the sophistication with which its best practitioners wield their pens... no other genre asks deeper questions about the human condition or sets up literary thought experiments about our interaction with the physical world including other worlds and new technologies.[19]

Vandana Singh, in her article, "Alternate Visions: Some musings on Diversity in SF," in her blog *Antariksh Yatra*, emphasizes that SF must be diverse in nature. She states that:

> The best speculative fiction, like travel... takes you to strange places, from which vantage point you can no longer take your home for granted.[20]

Singh asserts this reason for the need for diversity in speculative fiction. By diversity, she means fiction produced by authors from "different countries, cultures, races, genders, sexual orientations, physical abilities and experiences."[21]

Even until now, the origin of SF is placed in the West and the 'norm' is defined according to it. However, writers who live in the East, or people who are blind, or bisexual, or transgender, tend to experience the world that is different from the normative. Singh asserts that if speculative fiction deals with difference, with otherness, then the voices of these people should not be relegated to the margins, but considered a fundamental and innate component of the corpus of speculative fiction.

Singh cites the example of an anthology of SF stories, *So Long Been Dreaming* (2004), edited by Nalo Hopkinson and Uppinder Mehan. One of Singh's stories is also included in it. She feels thrilled to be a part of it because in it she could read stories of writers from different backgrounds, from Caribbean to Native American. She remarks, "I got to see the universe through multiple lenses that boggled my mind, made me at times uncomfortable… and expanded my imagination."[22] Singh stresses that we need to be more imaginative and to look at things from multiple perspectives. This can also help us understand things better and she gives us the example of climate change. She refers to the practice of unending malls and highways being built in India. Though this may be generating employment for a section of the population, it is also destroying the livelihood of many people. Speculative fiction provides multiple perspectives, when it is written by authors of diverse backgrounds. This way the problem can be assessed in the best possible manner. She implores us to take off our blinkers and our tinted glasses and to explore the world "in its variegated, dizzying, kaleidoscope richness."[23] We need to assess a situation from multiple angles for a fuller understanding. No genre other than speculative fiction, science fiction and fantasy have realized their transgressive potential.

As a writer who emphasizes on diversity, Vandana Singh resists being labeled. She feels that labels are limiting, that they are an attempt to put one in a box. She recounts being described at times by others as a 'multicultural' writer and a postcolonial writer. She says that labels are true in certain circumstances, but that they cannot confine her, nor can they be relevant in all aspects. Her writing is informed by her background, but her background is also inclusive of things such as her subject of study, physics. She remarks in her article, that on an occasion a successful SF writer felt threatened when he learnt of her physics background. Singh encourages discussion of physics aspects in her stories, being open to constructive criticism. But she is put off when she comes across ideas such as: "You're female. What do you know?"[24] Part of her disapproval of being labeled as a 'multicultural' or postcolonial writer is that they are expected to write only about their backgrounds or be spokespersons for their cultures and countries. Singh argues that if "science fiction is to be truly liberating, and if part of its freedom is to allow us to step into unfamiliar shoes,"[25] then a writer's story need not have anything to do with his/her background. It should not be necessary for Vandana Singh to write solely about India and Hindus. In fact, Singh tells us that her forthcoming story will comprise characters from different cultures.

Singh remarks that identity is a strange thing. It is important not only to own an identity but also to acknowledge its multiplicity, and the context which determines it. She highlights why diversity is necessary in SF and why many authors from the Third World write SF. She says,

> We need to be comfortable with moving our coordinate systems around so that we can see the world, the universe, from multiple gazes and perspectives... SF allows us to question, to challenge, to bring into visibility our belief structures, our assumptions about ourselves and the world; for writers from post-colonial nations to imagine their own futures, their own alternatives, is a deeply revolutionary, freeing act.[26]

She adds:

> We need new paradigms, new ways of relating to the non-human universe, if we are to survive the climate crisis. SF gives us the tools to write those other paradigms into being.[27]

By writing speculative fiction:

> We can reconnect with... the oldest works in the world-in which humans interacted with rocks, trees, stars, animals, demons and tree spirits,... Modern literature's obsession with the exclusively human is a sign of a deep malaise, apart from being utterly boring and unrealistic.[28]

Lastly, "SF's mandate to extend the imagination,... allows us to wriggle out of categories and pigeon-holes."[29]

Singh stresses the need to write SF in one's own language to realize its revolutionary potential. Works written in English cannot compensate for works written in original languages of authors from multiple linguistic origins. Hence, it is important that people write and publish in their own languages. Vandana Singh, however, does not dismiss the importance of writing in English. She refers to it as cross-pollination, which is important as English is the dominant language of the world. Hence, one should practice writing both in English and one's own language. There is a necessity for a global SF conversation.

Vandana Singh opines that one's first language is a personal and essential thing. Hindi is her first language, and she makes it a point to read and write in Hindi, from time to time, even if it is solely for herself. She writes mainly in English and feels discomfort at not experimenting too much with Hindi. She has, however, sometimes used Hindi words in her works, when the situation demanded it. Singh does not feel that there should be a glossary for the Hindi words. People who come across difficult words or an unfamiliar language would undertake the exercise of finding out the meanings through the context. This can also be seen as an attempt on the part of the author to familiarize the reader with a new language. Exploring words in foreign languages could give rise to a thousand worldviews; they are not merely "window-dressing," but could stand for much more.

Singh is ecstatic to share that there has been a marked improvement in the number of people writing SF from the time she started getting published, in the early 2000s. The diversity has grown significantly: "There are new writers from what were once far-flung places changing and enriching SF, rebuilding the Edifice, with new tools and sensibilities – a contingent of writers from Asia and the diaspora." [30] Singh shares that there are so many works produced by writers from different backgrounds that it is difficult to keep up with them. Yet these writers and their works are not enough, they remain marginalized.

Vandana Singh argues that the diversification of SF need not happen at the expense of the canon, comprising of Anglo literature. She says one could easily make space for SF, that there is plenty of room and each of the literature is significant in its own way. In her article, Singh celebrates the diversity in SF and all the further work that will be done in the field. She implores the readers that we must continue writing. She adds that it works as medicine in a world where there is hatred, war. Words could make a meaningful difference, even in the case of heartache.

In addition to writing speculative fiction, Singh also writes poetry and children's fiction. Her short story collection for children, *Younguncle Comes to Town*, was widely appreciated, and her *Younguncle in the Himalayas* is in fact a book. With reference to *Younguncle Comes to Town*, Ursula K. Le Guin said, "Vandana Singh is a most promising and original young writer," [31] hence, her audience is not limited to adults. Her stories have appeared in magazines such as *Polyphony*, *Strange Horizons*, and *Rabid Transit*. Her story, "The Wife," was featured and reprinted in *The Year's Best Fantasy and Horror # 17* and "Delhi" appeared in the 22nd volume of *The Year's Best Science Fiction*. Singh's background in physics and her teaching job form an inspiration in her writings as much as other factors. Her teaching directly assists her in writing science fiction as she gets new ideas, when she is explaining something or if the students ask thought provoking questions.

However what aroused Singh's interest in reading science fiction, to a great extent, was Ray Bradbury's *Fahrenheit 451*. She was eleven years old when she read the book. She describes the effect as "a whole universe dropped at my feet." [32] His books opened up a whole new universe to her - the multiple capacities of imagination - the art of creating societies, worlds, universes out of whole cloth and also questioning the human condition. One would continue to remain in that world which Bradbury had created, even after closing the book, she says.

Although Vandana Singh read and enjoyed writers such as Asimov, Clarke, and others, she experienced a feeling of disenchantment and they could not hold her interest for long. It is only when she landed in America in her twenties for her Ph D that she started reading science fiction again. The reason being that there was no other literature that she could relate to, feeling like an alien in a faraway land. Away from her culture, she began to feel that the world (even the one she came from) was a strange place to be in, and science fiction provided her a comfort that other genres did not. She could find identification for her alienness in it. The second factor which triggered Singh's interest in science fiction was the works of Ursula K. Le Guin. Until she had read Le Guin, Singh felt that there was no place for third-world people in the future of science fiction. If so, they were only presented as "faceless unwashed masses… or the occasional caricature."[33] She calls it as an 'Exclusion Principle'. However, Le Guin's writing broke that barrier and put the Third Worlders among humans instead of the aliens. This factor spurred Singh to find her place in science fiction.

Vandana Singh has been writing both in English and Hindi since she was about five years of age. To capture a larger audience, she writes in English. She remarks that it forms her base of communication with the world. However, when Singh writes for herself to satisfy her personal aesthetic and emotional needs, she writes poetry in Hindi: "Hindi to me is the primal element, the first air I breathed." Both Hindi and English literary figures have inspired and influenced her writings. She mentions some of them: Premchand and Sanskrit poets like Kalidasa and Jayadeva,; Ghalib and Sahir. In English she took motivation from Shakespeare and Charles Dickens, Ursula K. Le Guin and Ray Bradbury, Keats. She also draws from the storehouse of the rich Indian tradition of folk tales, lore and mythology which she heard from her grandparents, aunts, cousins, and uncles.

Vandana Singh holds great concern for Nature, the physical world and a deep sympathy for species other than human beings, dogs and cats. She finds it most unfortunate that most of her contemporaries are least concerned about Nature, the climate change and living beings. She in fact writes a blog on climate change named *Climate Change: Learning, Communicating, Acting*. In her article, titled "If You See Something, Say Something: The Scientist as Activist," she espouses that a scientist is also an activist and can work towards bringing about a change. To know that the environment is degrading and still waiting for it to happen is not the task of a scientist or a credible moral stance, she asserts.

> It is time for scientists to emerge from their laboratories and offices and speak of what they know about climate change, and join their fellow citizens across the world in confronting the powerful vested interests that stand between us and a sustainable world.[34]

Her stance is that all scientists have a responsibility to society since their discoveries and predictions can change the society for good or bad.

In addition to writing and upholding the cause of nature and other living species, Vandana Singh holds interest in Indian classical music and she has been a student of vocal classical. Other than that, she enjoys old Bollywood songs, Sufi music, Persian classical to name a few. She also enjoys listening to the Indian singer and musician Rabbi Shergill and Pakistani singer Abida Parveen.

Achievements

One of Vandana Singh's stories was published in The *Year's Best Science Fiction*, Volume 30, edited by Gardner Dozois. In 2013, she was successful in having published three short stories ("With Fate Conspire", "Cry of the Kharchal" and "Peripateia") and one novella (*Sailing the Antarsa*). Additionally, her story "Tetrahedron" was reprinted in Romanian language in a Romanian SF magazine. In the same year, she wrote an experimental *novella*, which formed part of *Hieroglyph* anthology. Edited by Ed Finn & Kathryn Cramer, it was published in 2014.

3.1.4 Priya Sarukkai Chabria

Literary, political and educational activism

Priya Sarukkai Chabria is a poet, novelist and translator. Her works include *Dialogue and Other Poems* published in 2005 by Sahitya Akademi, and reprinted in 2006. The work is a two-in-one volume, with one volume carrying the poetry of another poet, namely Anna Sujata Mathai, the other volume containing her poems. Chabria's poems, book reviews, essays and short stories have been published in various journals, both in India and abroad, such as *Quarterly*, managed by the India International Centre. Her works can also be found in *Adelphiniana*, *The Little Magazine*, the *Journal of Indian Literature*, *L A B*, *New Quest* and *Aphrodite's Garden*. Her novels include *The Other Garden* (1995), *Generation 14* (2008). Her other works are *Bombay/Mumbai: Immersions*; *Not Springtime Yet* (2008); an anthology, *All Poetry is Protest* (2003); *Love: Stories* (2003); and a short story "Ice Wine". She has translated the works of the eighth-century Tamil poetess Aandaal. Chabria tells us that Aandaal, the Tamil divine poet, is celebrated for being the only woman among the Alwars, the twelve Vaishnava saints. The Alwars were devotees of Vishnu, called Tirumal in Tamil. It is believed that Tirumal demanded to be taken as Vishnu's wife. The legend says that

she, a foundling, was caught wearing the god's sacred garlands signifying she was his bride and chastised before her father – also an Alwar – realized her divine nature. When she was about sixteen she merged with her god at his temple in Srirangam, Tamil Nadu.[35]

Chabria has translated verses from *Naachiyar Tirumoli* (*The Sacred Songs of the Lady*), which is Aandaal's second work, and also in fact her last. Aandaal wrote it when she was around fifteen years of age. Aandaal used poetic devices of the Sangam period (2BCE–4CE) in the hymns composed by her, such as the *eraichi* (parallel meaning) and *ullari* (hidden inset meaning). These devices ask for multiple explanations. Chabria says that "Each verse is like a verbal hologram."[36] Hence, she has worked to provide the readers with three forms for each verse; the first is a close rendering; the second explores mythological aspects; the third versioning seeks a possible third nuance.

Chabria has edited the anthology *50 Poems 50 Poets* (2006). In addition, she edits the website *Talking Poetry*. She takes care of the literature section of the portal managed by the NGO called *Open Space*. The aim of this NGO is to manifest change via the arts. Chabria also plays an instrumental role in promoting the cause of poetry, as an activist. She has organized poetry workshops and sessions for the NGO. The Indian government has awarded with the Senior Fellowship to Outstanding Artists for Literature (1996–1999) from the Department of Culture, Ministry of Human Resource Development, Delhi. She was credited with the honour of exploring the foundation of classical *rasa* theory of aesthetics in present-day works in English. This also spurred the production of a typescript, *Out and In: A Book for Lovers Past and Present*, in the form of a dialogue with late medieval Sanskrit and Prakrit poetry.

Chabria has played an instrumental role in many multimedia programmes. *Vipinam: The Grove* is one of her productions which debuted in Delhi in 2005. This production is part of her experiment in which she projects artworks on screen using digital imaging, accompanied with her poetry, music as well as classical dance by Malvika Sarukkai. Another experimental endeavour is *Srinkala*, which synthesizes image, classical dance and contemporary poetry in English. A multimedia production which she scripted and narrated is *Fireflies*. It combines poetry reading in English, classical dance and small paintings. The production was presented at the Asian Arts Festival in Singapore in 1994 and major Indian cities. Chabria has a multifarious personality; she not only writes and creates multimedia projects but has also co-founded a film society, *Friends of the Archive* along with Malvika Sarukkai, a classical dancer. Furthermore, Chabria collaborated in the script of a short film, *Dhaara*. The film was screened in the Oberhausen Film Festival in Germany in 1989. In fact, the film inaugurated the Critics Section and one of her first stories, "The Cloud Quilt," received special mention in *The Asian Age Short Story Competition* in 1995. Her article, "Priya Sarukkai Chabria: My Many Ramayanas," was published in *Muse India* and was commissioned by *Open Space*, Pune for an upcoming publication on *The Ramayana*.

On being a writer, Chabria said, "a writer reflects in your personality, how one understands life... One tunes one's self to hear what people want to say, what lies between the words... what people don't get to say."[37] For her, the ability to write is a privilege. "When you write, you can assume multiple personalities, be it a tree or a bird, a man or a woman. Like the French novelist Gustave Flaubert said about the character, Madame Bovary, 'I'm her.'"[38] She feels that unless one is curious or uncomfortable with the situation around them, one would fall short of what to write about. An urge to say something or a quest for the self and the world is a must for being a writer. According to her, it is the writer's surroundings which determine the style of a writer. "Were I in New York, I would write in a different way than I write now," she explains. "Even if you use the same language, English, the difference would be visible in the choice of words, use of grammar and so on."[39] On what inspires her, she remarks: "The creative process is rather mysterious. You don't know where you find it. But there is always a search involved."[40] She too, like Manjula Padmanabhan, resists the practice of labeling a writer. Imagination in itself is the greatest attribute of a writer, which allows one to assume any character or role, Chabria feels. She feels that one can write freely, while being morally correct, if one possesses imagination, passion and the capability to experiment.

3.2 Introduction: writers and their works under investigation

3.2.1 *Sultana's Dream*[41]

"Sultana's Dream" (1905), a short story by Rokeya Sakhawat Hossain, is considered a classic work of SF in Bengali and among the first few works of feminist SFs in India. The story is a 'feminist utopia' where women are in charge of the affairs of the state and men are secluded to the *zenana*,[42] referred to as *mardana*[43] in the story. This can be seen as a reversal of the traditional practice of *purdah* observed by women. In the feminist utopia, Rokeya confronts the so-called supremacy of men over women and lays bare the worthlessness of the claim made by men that they preside over the domain of work. In "Sultana's Dream," through the satirical reversal, Rokeya lays bare the deplorable condition of women during the colonial period in Bengal and also constructs an ideal world where the women can live an independent life after educating themselves. By doing so, Rokeya was able to criticize the prevailing conditions in the Muslim community of India which condemned a section of the population in *purdah* and a state of helplessness. In her essay *Motichur*, Vol. I (1904), Rokeya blames the patriarchal system followed by the Muslims and for not giving equal rights to their women; at the same time she holds the women responsible for sacrificing their self-respect due to their own inaction.

The writing style of "Sultana's Dream" is very basic. It is the first work she tried after learning English. From her childhood, Rokeya showed an inclination towards education. Being a girl, however, she was not allowed to go for any formal education. However, her husband supported women's education and it was from him that she learnt English. Her husband enthused in her the interest and courage to write her story in English, "Sultana's Dream." After he read it, he remarked, "A splendid revenge!"[44] By this he meant that Rokeya through her writing had taken revenge upon men for their gender discriminate system of *zenana* (*purdah*). The story demonstrates remarkable possibilities and future of women and how these can be employed for the social and political betterment of a nation. By showing that women could be superior and enterprising in various fields, such as expertise in law making, formulating political ideas, utmost dedication and commitment, Rokeya established that women could be equal contributors to the liberation movement of colonial India. This would be possible if women's inherent skills and abilities were to be encouraged, sharpened and exploited. A similar message can be found in her stories, "Gyanphal" and "Muktiphal".

The short story, "Sultana's Dream," chronicles the experiences of Sultana, the narrator as she falls asleep while thinking about the condition of Indian women. In the dream, she meets an amicable personality, Sister Sara, who describes to her how her world works. It is in fact a world opposite to that of Sultana's and referred as Ladyland. In Ladyland, the *purdah* system exists; but here it has been reversed and it is the men who are placed in the closed quarters of the home and deprived of any rights. The women here are educated and possess a scientific bent of mind. They have harnessed solar power to work to their benefit. They can also extract water from clouds when there is a scarcity in Ladyland. The women are so industrious and skillful that the day's work can be done in just a few hours. Working hours have been reduced to two as against seven. The reason given is that men would waste five hours in smoking. Plus, there is no crime in Ladyland as the men were held responsible for it. The widespread religion is that of love and truth.

In Ladyland, the secluded Muslim heroine is delighted to find no men outdoors and is scolded for her mannish shyness. Sultana, after being teased, of course, starts to behave confidently. Walking through Ladyland, Sultana is exposed to the affected bravery of the men of her country, who consider women as an inferior breed. The story is hence an exploration of the issues of gender, religion and social politics as an inquisitive Muslim women moves around freely in all the places to which men no longer have access.

While the traditional gender roles are reversed in Ladyland, they still exist. One gender continues to be forceful, intelligent and logical, and the other gender is still fragile, stupid, and irrational. As Sister Sara tells Sultana, the former gender is female and the latter is male. The reader also gets a sense that the existing order is perfectly natural. The idea emphasized here is that these attributes are endowed culturally, rather than biologically. "Sultana's Dream" presents the reader with a strong and clear picture of a world which is turned upside down. The story clearly indicates that change in the real sense is possible, if the ones who are ill-treated (here, the women) unite and firmly believe in the fact that they are the ones who are forceful, intelligent and logical. Gender roles are obstructions and are in existence as long as we recognize them as such. There is a need to question them to create not just a disparate but more suitable world.

The tendency to create a community for women with a utopian vision for improving and enriching women's lives was first observed in Margaret Cavendish's novel, *The Blazing World* (1666). This idea is further articulated in Charlotte Perkins Gilman's *Herland* (1915). Yet these mentioned works were limiting and failed to offer an agenda with respect to women's rights and their freedom. In *The Blazing World*, for example, a young woman reaches another planet where she becomes the Empress. This world is run on the principles of natural science and philosophy. Despite this, the path the Empress chooses to follow is that of a colonial British and the Queen is ultimately established as a guardian of male ideology. A large portion of the utopias produced during this period was reformist rather than revolutionary until the appearance of *Mizora* (1881) by Mary Bradley

Lane, culminating in Charlotte Perkins Gilman's *Herland*. Gilman's *Herland* shows three men with a different attitude and mindset in pursuit of women, when they arrive in an affluent land which is entirely managed by women who are attractive, strong and healthy. "Sexual interaction, idea of marriage, fear of rape, problem of parthogenesis and possibilities of natural child bearing-all these issues are addressed in the text in which... Gilman replaces religion with sacred motherhood and eliminates sexuality."[45] By contrast, "Sultana's Dream" is not a story of pursuit of men by women, but about rising from a happy dream. Here, religion is not entirely done away with. In fact a universal religion is followed and motherhood and sexuality are not talked about at all. Towards the end, we see Sister Sara as emblematic of powerful women of the land, who gives a victory speech that conveys an unwritten picture of women as strong and asexual, who have assumed control over man, science and nature.

"Sultana's Dream" was written during the Bengal Renaissance broadly between 1775 and 1941, which entailed both harking back to ancient traditions for influence and also strive for growth and modernity. While Hindu writers and philosophers looked towards and reinterpreted their Vedic philosophy to deal with social deterrents like *sati* and the caste system, the Muslim literati began to self-examine by looking to the ancient Islamic texts and traditions for inspiration.

Muslim intellectuals such as Abul Kalam Azad[46] expressed the desire to remodel the Madrassa method of education, like Rokeya. On the topic of education, Rokeya once remarked:

> The opponents of female education say that women will become wanton and unruly. Fie! They call themselves Muslims and yet go against the basic tenet of Islam, which gives women an equal right to education. If men are not led astray once educated, why should women?[47]

This idea is also voiced by Sister Sara in "Sultana's Dream." Rokeya has also expressed, "Allah has made no distinction in the general life of male and female- both are equally bound to seek food, drink and pray five times a day."[48]

Rokeya's feminism is largely indigenous, although she is considered by many to be a contemporary of Mary Shelley and Virginia Woolf. Hossain's work of raising consciousness was mainly centred on Bengali Muslims. Her corpus of writing is mostly written in Bengali and it focuses largely on issues that affected the Bengali Muslim upper and middle class, such as *purdah* and *zenana*. As such, her writings were not intended for a western audience. It must be emphasized that although Hossain was more radical than her Bengali counterparts, she was still rooted to the Bengali social and literary scene. Her religion was integral in her feminist approach. She opposed the *purdah*, but supported the wearing of the veil. She advocated universal education - as long as there was a separation between sexes and Arabic was part of the curriculum.

3.2.2 *Escape*

Escape raises the issue of the declining sex ratio in India, that is mainly the result of the strong social bias against girl children and the large-scale misuse of the cheap and widely available technology of sex-determination tests to identify female foeticide. According to the 2011 Census, India's current child sex ratio was 914 females per 1000 males, the lowest since the 1961 Census. Additionally, the fall in the child sex ratio in rural areas is more than four times of that in urban areas. Padmanabhan, talking about her novel, remarked that:

> In the case of *Escape*, the idea presented itself originally as a newspaper 'middle' which would take the form of a page from the diary of the last Indian woman left alive… I kept thinking that despite all the positive stuff going on, it seemed more likely that women – Indian women anyway - appeared to be on the decline. So that was the context… around 2006 I began to think of turning that idea into a novel.[49]

The novelist presents a horrifying vision of the future, in which women have been completely exterminated. The novel uses the science fiction mode to give a strong warning about the unthinkable terrors that humanity would have to face if the violence against women is not stopped.

Manjula Padmanabhan's 2008 novel *Escape* (2008) is set in an unnamed country, possibly India, where women have been exterminated. Through hints it is clear that the country is India. There are no surviving members of the female species, except for a twelve-year-old girl named Meiji who has been saved and kept secretly by her three uncles, Eldest, Middle and Youngest. The three uncles strive to protect Meiji from the Generals, who rule over the nation-state. These Generals are clones of one another, since natural means of reproduction have been overturned by technology. The result is a highly advanced country achieved through the use of nuclear power and technology, but the resources of air, water, land as well as the ecosystem have been deeply damaged by pollution. In the novel Padmanabhan also finds a metaphorical correspondence between the use of chemicals to suppress Meiji's growth and cosmetic surgeries used by many women to alter their appearances. Padmanabhan explores all these issues as Meiji travels with Youngest to a place which will be safer for her and where she could find more like herself.

As it opens, the novel conveys a sense of shocking fear and secrecy. The custodians of Meiji are extremely conscious of the immense risk they are taking. Meiji is always seen either dressed as a boy or concealed in veils in public. She does not have much awareness about her own sex. The exact situation is found to be mirrored in Indian society, where the women are made to either abort or secretly get rid of their female progeny due to the pressures of the society to give birth to a male child. The scarcity or absence of women builds a hopeless craving among normal young men who are willing to forego anything to gain a female partner. Meiji's suitors are brought in a highly confidential manner, after being blindfolded; they are constantly monitored and only allowed to look at the girl very briefly since her Uncles dread that the suitors may reveal the presence of Meiji to the Generals. This reminds of the social and psychological difficulties that are an integral part of the various communities in North India observing the illegal practices of infanticide and foeticide, causing a serious gap in the sex-ratio so much so that men of marriageable age are unable to find brides for themselves.

Meiji's life can be likened to that of a prisoner as she has been kept indoors since her birth. This also impacts her growth and development, both physical and emotional. She often grapples with her emotions and her isolation. She is ignorant of the presence of an outside world. Meiji's uncles dispense unto her hormone suppressants in order to stunt her normal growth and she looks like a child even at the age of sixteen. As she grows older and reaches her teenage and adulthood, she is perplexed by the changes occurring within her mind and body. She does not understand what it is to be a woman and its implications, for she has never seen a woman. Through her sixteen years, she has only seen men, her three uncles. The three uncles worry as Meiji matures and discuss amongst them if they should reveal the truth to Meiji. Again, we can say that his reminds us of the conventional Indian society in which women like Meiji are prohibited from access to knowledge and freedom, denied self-awareness, and also the right to take their own decisions and determine on their own what course their lives will take. It is the man or the male-dominated society that decides the fate of the female.

The world described in *Escape*, in which the man has become default and woman, is a relic of a past world that is extinct, and forces Meiji along with her uncle Youngest to undertake a journey. The journey is both inward and outward. The inward journey is, interestingly, more exciting than the outward journey for both of them. Having only vaguely heard of women, Meiji comes close to self-loathing when she realizes that she is the last of a tribe that has been destroyed. At a time when it is difficult for her to even visualize a world where women existed, she must also deal and come to terms with the changes happening in her own body and also understand that womanhood brings with it some unique abilities.

The inward journey of Youngest is also unique, as he not only plays the role of Meiji's escort and protector but also strives to understand and control his own sexual impulses. He feels sexual attraction towards Meiji at a few instances, but he fights it. Yet, in a world that has killed women, Youngest emerges as a symbol of hope, for him Meiji is an amalgamation of mother, sister, wife, lover. His feelings for her are quite risky and difficult to understand because this kind of feelings considered shameful and indecent to for family members however he calls them "too pure, too beautiful, to be snuffed out."[50] Thus, Youngest can be seen as the prototype of the new male, a faint ray of hope and indicates a possibility for change and freedom from the male dominated system that determines the fate of women.

Furthermore, Manjula Padmanabhan in her novel makes an attempt to criticize the functioning of the State, how the ruling class dominates others below them; in this way Padmanabhan is able to indirectly satirize the rulers of the present times. Women and Nature are envisaged as threats by the ruling class. In the present scenario in India, there is a serious need to assess the responsibilities of government organizations towards the safety and protection of women against violence and abuse. In that sense, assessing the role of the police department also becomes extremely significant, whether they are able to fulfill their duties in safeguarding women or not. Also, are there strict measures of law to prevent pre-natal sex-determination? Are the government agencies really in favour of providing women their rights or not? Just as Women, Nature is also seen as an enemy to be subjugated and utilized for the benefit of the patriarchal institutions such as multinational industries. The novel, *Escape*, abounds with references to eco-feminist concerns, enabling the reader to understand how women and nature are simultaneously obliterated, ruined by the power-hungry elite.

As Meiji undertakes the journey which is both inward and outward, she gradually realizes who she really is, and how valuable and worthy she is, being the sole survivor of her species.

> She comes to know what a 'woman' is. Even as she struggles to control the powerful forces within her body, she hears horrible tales of how women were killed by the Generals... the women were not allowed to survive because their minds could not be controlled. In one of the many manuals written by the Generals to guide the citizens, there is this quotation: "The drones are what the Vermin Tribe (women) should have been: servile, dumb and deaf." Meiji also comes to know that her own mother had publicly immolated herself in order to divert the attentions of the Generals from little Meiji. She is angry with her mother for leaving her alone in a male world... She vows to keep on fighting for survival as a vital link in the precious chain of life.[51]

Manjula Padmanabhan's novel accentuates the concomitant annihilation of both Woman and Nature.

In her article titled "Ecofeminism in India: Disappearing Daughters in Padmanabhan's *Escape*," Rupali Palodkar foregrounds that in Indian society,

> the ownership of women's body and sexuality and that of land (nature) has continued to vest with men since ancient times. Of all places in the world, it is in India that sex-selective abortions are practiced on a wide-scale... There is a need to find an alternative to men's exploitation... and to discover an ecologically sound way of life that would not threaten the existence either of the earth or of women. That is why women writers like Manjula Padmanabhan are turning to ecofeminist thinking and are writing about the consequences of degradation of nature and woman.[52]

Manjula Padmanabhan in *Escape* has tried to awaken women to realize their living conditions, their circumstances, the injustices they are subjected to, and this can be recognized as the first step to putting a full stop to the violence committed against women. Padmanabhan provides an outlet, a means of expression to the marginalized women of a patriarchal society. Woks such as that of Padmanabhan display, become active participants and seek to improve the social, political and economic circumstances of the period which tend to sustain the unfair treatment and violent abuse of women. The novel commences an action that impels the readers to be mindful of those whose voices are hushed and offers to stand out as a guiding light and hope for them.

3.2.3 Generation 14

Generation 14 by Priya Sarukkai Chabria is set in the 24th century. The central protagonist is a clone, named Clone 14/54/G. She is the fourteenth copy of an "Original" who changes genetically by recalling memories-has "visitations," as she narrates them of incidents that occurred in the past. She is a part of a stratified global community, where she lives along with Originals, Superior Zombies, Firehearts, and other clones. She is treated as an object of suspicion by the ruling powers until it dawns on them that she could be helpful in solving a complicated mystery. In the story, we are told that the clone's Original was a revolutionary anthropologist, whose life was terminated shortly before she was going to divulge an important secret. The rulers believe that they may be able to extract the secret through Clone 14/54/G, and so they start to indulge her in various ways. There is resistance to the rulers but not on the surface and those who form part of this group contact Clone 14/54/G to secure her confidence too. According to Chabria, we are moving towards an era of cloning, and in her novel she has explored the idea of cloning. She contemplates questions like: "What is the relationship with a human clone going to be like? Will we have problems with him/her, will we treat her like an independent being?"[53] She makes use of the clone as a symbol for a world that is bound to result in communal violence.

> As a society governed by fear and terror, we are not thinking for ourselves. A clone's mind is controlled – she cannot think for herself and she is not allowed or incapable of pondering about certain facts of life. Clone 14/54/G has a default memory chip that takes her into the prohibited world of memory and emotions.[54]

Chabria describes the novel as an amnesiac journey into the past of the clone and it took the author to go for eight years of research to put the novel together. As Chabria says, "I explored history from 2500 B.C. to the 24th century."[55] The historical information helped her better contextualize the main characters' journey into the past.

The novel devotes a section to the meditations and contemplations of Original until the time of her address at the great Celebration and before her murder. This kind of an elaboration helps the reader to understand the plight of Clone 14/54/G. Chabria has carefully interwoven into the narrative, a number of detailed anecdotes which are referred to as "visitations" in the novel. These stories have been acquired from India's past and narrated in the first person. These include the story of a parrot in a Lucknow household of nawabs, a fish that is tossed in a flood in Kashi and has a meditative bent of mind. These are accompanied by anecdotes of a mother who grieves the loss of her son to Asoka's Kalinga war, and a wolf-dog who accompanies his master who conquers local tribes. Nearly all of them have a moralizing end where the main character has to reap the effects of their penalties or violent acts. The author's attention is to establish plurality through these digressions.

Chabria believes that the novel is concerned with the philosophical question of internal identity and that of the nation. The novel also raises the question whether we will learn from the mistakes we have made in the past and rethink our identity and motivation. The reason the clone has visitations from her past is to show that even memory that is forbidden and not being permitted to deliberate upon it is impacting us at a time when there is too much information available. Chabria asserts that her attitude is not one of cynicism in this futuristic dystopia, in fact that the novel is rooted in faith and it is through the writing that she can exhibit that faith to the readers. In the novel, Chabria also appears to be concerned with the political scenario of the world as well as with the behavior and the treatment of its citizens.

3.2.4 Of Love and Other Monsters

The novella *Of Love and Other Monsters* is the story of Arun, who has the unusual ability to form a meta-mind, that is bringing together minds of many people at a time. He can also manipulate these minds. The novella begins when Arun is seventeen years old, and his first memory is that of a fire and being rescued from it by a woman called Janani. She gives him an identity and work in her shop, since he has no memory of his past. She educates him; from her he learns his letters and arithmetic. She also makes sure he learns little about history, geography and the rudiments of the English language. Arun, during this period works at the shop and forms meta-minds in his free time.

Janani warns Arun of another man with the same extraordinary ability to form meta-minds, and wishes that he never meets or finds Arun. Then, one night, that man finds Arun, who feels some kind of attraction towards him, and he begins to walk towards him. Janani however, is less affected by the power than Arun and pulls him back. This man whom Janani calls dangerous is named Rahul Moghe. She fears him so much that she sends Arun to the neighbouring town, while she moves to Rishikesh. According to her, the present place is no longer safe for either of them. Janani's agitation arises from the fact that Rahul Moghe's appearance can be deceptive, he can take on different looks and he drags at one's mind without warning.

Through Janani's aid, Arun gets a job as a clerk at a computer training institute. Here, he improves his English and also helps the system administrator with computer maintenance work. Janani continues to help, and send money for computer classes which help Arun realize that he has a knack for programming. He also develops a voracious appetite for reading in both English and Hindi. Soon Arun receives a job offer from Delhi and he moves there. In the meantime, Janani keeps sending Arun his belongings from before the fire; but they make no sense to him, things like photographs, pieces of abstract ceramic sculpture, and remains of etchings. It is during his stay in Delhi that he gets ample time to explore his ability to form meta-minds.

After spending a few months in Delhi, Arun moves to America. He is encouraged by Janani to do so as she gets to know that Rahul Moghe has been seen in Chandigarh, a few hours from Delhi and she urges Arun to move to "the land of milk and honey."[56] His first destination in the USA is California, from where too he is forced to move after Moghe finds him. Arun moves to Boston where he meets Sankaran, a post-doctoral researcher from south India. Arun feels attracted to him, yet helpless since he cannot marry Sankaran. While in Boston, Rahul Moghe again tries to get to him and this time the pull is stronger and he is drawn to him. Moghe creates a meta-mind in which he leads people to jump from a building window. Arun successfully enters this meta-mind and breaks it. In the process, however, he loses all his energy and Moghe takes him to a dingy hotel room, where Moghe tries to tell him that Janani burned him and took away his memories; Moghe cannot resurrect Arun now. Moghe tells Arun that they are originally aliens and that Arun has lost all its memory; they can build brilliant meta-minds together. Moghe offers to train Arun on using his power. Moghe explains to him that Janani is his murderer, that she burned Arun and hence he can no longer change form, like Moghe. He asserts that they owe allegiance to a different star – *Sapta Rishi*. Looking at the things Janani sends to Arun, this makes perfect sense. Arun can now realize why he feels like a stranger in the world he inhabits, and that is why he feels the urge to travel constantly in search of his identity. He strives to build connections with people to achieve the completeness he lacks.

Arun, in a baffled state, escapes from the hotel and goes to India in search of Janani, who last heard of had gone to Thailand on an adventure. In India, Arun learns from Rinu, Janani's partner, that Janani was part of a network of those who could sense aliens. They burn these aliens, take away their power and turn them into humans. After getting to know the truth, Arun searches for Moghe, whom he successfully finds. But Janani's accomplices learn of this and they organize the burning of Arun and Moghe. Although Arun escapes in time, he is unable to save Moghe. Moghe lives but is confined to an asylum.

3.2.5 Distances

Distances is a novella about Anasuya, a foreigner living in a far future desert city, the City.[57] She is here on exile and has been summoned to work at the Temple of Mathematical Arts. Anasuya belongs to Sagara, the distant sea, and she drifts away on a raft to the City as she was sleeping. The City is a stark contrast to her homeland. Things for her seem upside down, and all things are artificial, as opposed to the abundance of nature in Sagara with its underwater caves, salt water marshes, cliffs and seaweed forests.

Another factor which makes Anasuya distinct from others at the City and also adds to her feeling like an outsider is her skin colour. Anasuya has a "slender green body,"[58] unlike the brown skin of others. It is the presence of soliforms in her body, which gives her the green colour. Besides, Anasuya has a unique gift; a gift by the sea, namely the *athmis*, her mathematical precision, which she alone possesses in the City. The *athmis* also gives her an understanding of the harmonies of the world, especially mathematical, that came to her at the age of five. Her method of performing mathematical operations is very different from that of others in the City. When Anasuya came to the City, she felt both joy and frustration. People could understand her, but they used an awkward language for it and she had to learn to use it. People at the City, until they met her, had only heard of people as Anasuya. She was for them a legend. At the City, she learned the mathematical language in use, the various rules and methods to create mathematical art and became skilled in mathegraphia.[59]

An amnion is specially built for Anasuya at the Temple for her to immerse herself in the liquid and perform mathematical operations. The spiroforms give their best results in water. She had never been out of water for so long until she came to the City and being in the amnion feels no less than a homecoming for her. The Temple had a reputation of solving the most complex of mathematical equations and this renown grew with the presence of Anasuya, who is considered to be their best.

The Temple of Mathematical Arts is visited by a team of mathematicians from the Lattice of Tirana. They have travelled on a ship for eighteen years, with a purpose. We are told that they are eight in number and speak a tongue different from that spoken in the City. The ones that Anasuya can register are Vishk, Kzoric, Hiroq and Nirx. Vishk is short, thin, and shy with a stooping back. Kzoric has a broad build, loud voice, ties her hair in a large bun, and possesses a sharp gaze. Hiroq is tall, long face, deep voice yet a shy person. Nirx is short and slim, and her face is wrinkled, conveying as if she is keeping a secret that will be difficult to find out. Nirx has discovered a geometric space, referred as *sthanas*. The set of equations formed are complex and hence Nirx and her team have come from Tirana to seek their help. This job then is assigned to Anasuya, considered the "best rider" at the Temple, most sacred and famous institution for the solution of mathematical poems. As she works on this *sthanas* in the amnion, Anasuya realizes that the Tiranis have come with a much larger project, which they are trying to keep a secret. Both she and the Master suspect that the *sthanas* represents a physical system that has not yet been discovered. After much exploration and many sittings in the amnion, Anasuya finds that it is the map of hyperspace, which can make possible faster-than-light travel, which they had been trying to hide. The temple chemists and Anasuya confront the Tiranis on this deceit. The project is stopped and it is only once that the City officials decide on the importance of it that they allow work to be resumed on it. The terms are that the Tiranis must share all their information and keep nothing secret. As time progresses and Anasuya comes nearer to creating the map of hyperspace, she finds that she is turning brown. She associates this change in color to losing her mathematical insight, her *athmis*. Towards the end of the story, she turns completely brown and becomes unable to work on a mathematical poem like she could earlier. She decides to return home to Sagara, and warn her people about the discovery that was made.

3.3 Rokeya Sakhawat Hossain: *Sultana's Dream*

3.3.1 Genre: feminist utopia

Feminist utopia is classified as social utopia SF. In most cases, a work of feminist utopia imagines a world which is diametrically opposite of patriarchal society. A feminist utopian novel visualizes a society which is devoid of gender discrimination, envisages a future scenario or an alternate world where men and women are not restricted to perform the traditional part in an unequal structure.

3.3.2 Issues and concerns

3.3.2.1 Education

Rokeya was an active proponent of change and she sought to do so through education. She saw education as the foremost means for bringing about change. She wrote extensively on educational topics throughout her life and established the Sakhawat Memorial Girls' School in Calcutta in 1911. While Rokeya advocated for a change in the way men regarded women and how women viewed themselves, she was concerned about one's sacrifice of the Muslim identity. Her work was mainly aimed at Bengali Muslims, Rokeya was also an important member of the Anjuman-i-Khawatin Islam, an All India Women's Movement, which took its roots in Aligarh in 1914.

Rokeya chose to portray the most vigorous and unswerving of women in her writings as a slave. This is how she went about her enterprise of liberating Muslim women. In her works, the recurring idea she projects is that women are not allowed freedom of choice and treated insignificantly, just as a piece of furniture in a male dominated setup. One of her works begins by alerting the readers about women's real position, when she says - "I hear that slavery has been abolished from the face of the Earth, but does the slavery of women still not exist?"[60] Through these lines, Rokeya is trying to emphasize that once a girl reaches womanhood and gets involved in the relation called marriage, she begins to get enslaved by her husband to such an extent that he controls even her right to have a voice of her own. Rokeya also chose to comment on the word *swami*, commonly used to refer to husband. She defines that this word confers to the husband a status of lord, master, a ruler, an employer, an owner and a saint. Yasmin Hossain, a critic, has also chosen to comment on this as

> man's unfettered and uncontested *swamitta* over the body, mind and intellect of women is the most significant manifestation of his author-ity, completing the image of male supremacy, for on accepting a *swami* women automatically relegate themselves to the status of *dasi* or slave.[61]

Rokeya was extremely critical of jewelry and she determined it to be the chief image of slavery. She drew a parallel between the iron chains with which a slave is tied and the gold chains with which a woman is decorated. Rokeya saw the precious jewels as a means of beautifying the slavery of women. The heavy anklets and bracelets for her arms are compared to hand cuffs and different items put on animals to control them for instance:

> The *cheek*, a tightly fitting ornament for the throat, is compared to a dog collar; the large elaborate gold necklaces falling over the chest and down as far as the stomach are likened to harnesses worn by ele-phants… Hence the image of well-born, well-married women as crea-tures laden with the precious evidence of a forced servitude.[62]

The newly wed adorned with heavy jewels and make up is the voiceless and invisible woman, considered to be an ideal woman. She carries the burden of prestige and honour of her family and has to be a role model for the other women in *zenana*.

Rokeya held strongly in her position that education is the key factor which can lead to an improvement in the position and circumstances of women. Rokeya praises the western women, who have made the best use of education and become professionals, hence being equal contributors as men to the making of a thriving nation. Rokeya regretfully tells her readers that no such woman (like the West) can be found in India and more so amongst the Bengali Muslims. Even though Rokeya does not see women as victims in the larger sense, but she is aware that women tend to suffer at the hands of existing norms and order due to which women are given an unequal status, and termed as 'slave.' The 'slave' status is conferred on to women by the male power.

During the same period, women who belonged to the *bhadra lok* (edu-cated middle class) began to express the need to be treated earnestly as individuals. With adequate motivation, they also began to assert their sense of personal identity which was distinct from male identity and that stereotypical image of women defined by men. Rokeya too voices these sentiments and she encourages Muslim women to realize the flaw in their position and pose a challenge to these by highlighting their prerogatives and wants. Rokeya wanted to universalize the agenda of women's emancipation. By pointing the likeness between women everywhere, Rokeya wishes to encourage a feeling of empathy among them and a need to take action, not just for them but for the women world over, coming from different countries, religions and cultures. This camaraderie can be seen in the women in "Sultana's Dream." Sister Sara is empathetic towards Sultana, and encourages her to not be afraid and move around freely when she is in Ladyland. She explains to Sultana that it is unfair to shut the women in the *zenana* and let the men loose. Sister Sara explains to Sultana that men may be stronger physically but that should be no reason why men can dominate women, she gives the example of a lion which is physically stronger than man but cannot dominate human beings. She locates the cause of subservience of women within them when she says, "You have neglected the duty you owe to yourselves and you have lost your natural rights by shutting your eyes to your own interests."[63] Sultana is able to understand the power dynamics and feels the urge to see the developments in Ladyland, in her country too. She learns that women are capable of not only household work but also office work. Women in Ladyland are adept at more work than the men in Sultana's land. Sultana learns that with sufficient efforts and self-realization, even the women of India could attain freedom from their men.

In her attempt to demonstrate that women's liberation was possible, Rokeya did not turn to the examples of western women but she looked to the Indian subcontinent or Muslim community in her search for an inspiration. She refused to spend time in arguing that women faced lesser problems, or they had lesser obstacles to fight against in the West, as compared to the women in Indian subcontinent. However, Rokeya did give examples of women who contributed significantly to the society individually, and made places for themselves. She referred to a doctor, namely Miss Cohen, who took responsibility for girl's health in schools, and also quoted from an article by Annie Besant and their attempts to secure their place in public life, it is indicative that their works, their views or thoughts about women in general and their views about their concerns not directly related to women could receive recognition. Another significant idea that becomes evident is that it is not impossible that women can attain a successful professional career side by side with the men. It goes without saying that Rokeya is also mindful of the contribution of her own works towards the advancement of female emancipation and women's education.

The lady characters in Rokeya's fiction serve as role models. For instance, in *Padmaraga*, Siddiqua is an independent professional woman who provides inspiration. Strong, independent and lively women can be found in her other fictions, such as *Saura Jagat*, *Bhrata Bhagini*, and "Sultana's Dream." In "Sultana's Dream," the powerful and inspiring women are Sister

Sara, the Queen and Lady Principals. They serve as role models for not only Sultana but also the readers. They are strong, independent, educated and empowered women. All the changes in Ladyland happened when the Queen inherited the throne and introduced many changes. Before the Queen, the women were in strict *purdah*, however:

> Our good Queen liked science very much. She circulated an order that all the women in her country should be educated. Accordingly a number of girls' schools were founded and supported by the government. Education was spread far and wide among women. And early marriage also was stopped. No woman was to be allowed to marry before she was twenty-one.[64]

Education liberates women in Ladyland.

Rokeya argued that the life of women in Muslim *zenana* was that of mental and spiritual lethargy. They suffered from a lack of confidence and had very little sense of identity or self-worth. She stressed that seclusion coupled with ignorance resulted in mental stagnation. Sultana is too shy to walk in daylight or in the presence of man-servants, feels that harm may be caused unto her.

In this environment where women were expected to be in strict *purdah*, girls who were educated were eyed as loathsome. Women could only educate themselves and acquire knowledge through their brothers, husbands and in-laws. In case of Rokeya, it was her oldest brother, Ibrahim Saber, who introduced and inspired her towards education. Of her brother, Rokeya remarked:

> I have never been inside a school or college. What little education I have is due to the kindness and enthusiasm of my eldest brother. My other relatives far from being encouraging were openly hostile, constantly making fun of me. But I was not dissuaded neither did my brother lend his ear to these criticisms, or lose his enthusiasm, for that matter.[65]

The second large influence on Rokeya was that of her sister, Karimunnessa. She set an example for Rokeya and aroused in her mind the questions which she explored and dealt with throughout her life. Karimunnessa was vocal about her defiance of social norms. "It was the older sister who taught her to intellectualise the issues and… to question the very nature and purpose of existence, and push forward her quest for self-identity."[66]

The topic of education and struggle for the same remained a sensitive issue for Rokeya throughout, just as it did for her sister, Karimunnessa. This feeling was shared by other women in *zenana* too, who were keen on acquiring an education. It was with her husband's death in 1909 that Rokeya left the domain of domesticity to walk on the path of her ambitions. In her work Sugrihini, Rokeya advocated setting up of a Zenana Medical College, considering women were encouraged only to learn about basic health and hygiene. By supporting education for women in the *zenana*, Rokeya did not ignore the importance of formal education for women. She pressed for all the entitlements and rights which were possessed by men for women, but at the same time she did not support co-education. In her entire career as a writer, she insisted on segregated education as superior. In *Burkah*, Rokeya asserts that women should not undertake formal education till they have access to universities meant specifically for women, staffed with female teachers. As mentioned earlier, in Ladyland, the Queen forbids women to marry till they attain the age of twenty-one; besides they must educate themselves by attending schools and universities before they proceed for their marriages. Sister Sara apprises us that it is in accordance with the number of girls that schools were built and the government gave full support. It was this way that education could be spread among women, far and wide. Her views on education of women "emphasizes an unresolved tension between Islam and the claim of a basically secular world in which women have jobs, status, and economic power independent of the family unit."[67]

Rokeya also espoused religious education and this was due to the fear of conversion, more specifically conversion to Christianity. Even though, while in Bengal, Rokeya was actively engaged with active women from other faiths, she laid emphasis on quintessential Islamic values. She feared that attending a Hindu or Christian educational institution would lead to wearing away of the Muslim identity and Islamic values, and subsequent conversion to another faith. Hence Rokeya emphasized on teaching the Qur'an to Muslim girls from their primary school years. In her fiction, Rokeya makes a strong argument in favour of only Islamic education for girls. In *Saura Jagat*, the character Zaffer is afraid that his nieces by attending a missionary school are prone to the danger of converting.

Rokeya was successful in establishing her own school for girls in Calcutta in 1911. The strength was limited to five girls when the school was instituted but within the span of ten years, she could attract many more students and could witness with her eyes their success and completion of graduation from Calcutta University. Rokeya struggled to fight against the opposition of public and Muslim community's lack of faith and acknowledgement of the importance of education and its results. Through her own struggle and that of Karimunnessa, she realized that she needed popularize female education and its benefits. She toiled to raise the consciousness of Muslim women, more specifically of those restricted to the *zenana*. She was also instrumental in bringing about the Bengali division of the Anjuman-i-Khawatin Islam in 1916. The organization aimed to work for *zenana* women.

3.3.2.2 Gender

In the feminist utopia, "Sultana's Dream" by Rokeya Sakhawat Hossain, the situation of men placed in *zenana* in Ladyland, Sultana in colonial Bengal and women in Ladyland is comparable. While the men in Ladyland are restricted in *purdah*, Sultana resides in a secluded Muslim family in India, and women in Ladyland lead a common life, in a seclusion, even though a perfected one, in a moribund, utopic world. Sister Sara can only come into view in Sultana's dream, because within the limits of her country's foreign policy no trade is possible with countries where the women were kept in the *zenanas* and they do not like dealing with men because of their lack of moral values. Hence, Sister Sara has to abstain from entry into Sultana's world which is blemished because of patriarchal authority. Then, one can say that the sudden denouement of the dream and the wakening up of Sultana from her dream works to remind the readers that women's emancipation which appears in the dream sequence, is not yet realized in colonial Bengal for the Muslim women. It is also suggested that this utopian model of an ideal society is tainted by the patriarchal dogma. Such dreams would appear again, but vanish until the women decide a way to empower themselves. Without that genuine and permanent change is not possible.

Rokeya is extremely critical of the gender norms of her society and how they become apparent in male–female relationships. Rokeya uses the element of satire and presents playful inversions such as women fight the war and confine the men to *zenana*, giving the reason that someone must maintain the *purdah* and in this case, the men.

> There's obviously an element of gender essentialism here: women are productive, virtuous, and like gardens and cleanliness, while men are either making weapons, going to war, or wasting time and smoking charoots... Early in her visit to Ladyland Sultana is told that she looks "mannish"- They mean that you are shy and timid like men." The text suggests that men's temperaments, whether as lazy warmongerers or timid homebodies, might be the result of socialization. We're told that the men complained at first about their confinement, but by the time the story opens appear to have become used to it.[68]

The concerns expressed in "Sultana's Dream" regarding gender roles in India become exceptional when applied to the private space. Men in Ladyland are secluded to *purdah* and commodified like the women of colonial Bengal. Men are shy and timid now and perform all of women's works like cooking and taking care of babies. This way, Rokeya tends to undermine gender.

Gender suppression appears as a major issue in "Sultana's Dream." One can use the motif of colonialism to refer to the gendered oppression which is successfully reversed and as a result the new nation is under the rule of female occupants who emphasize their feminist doctrine to Sultana, a guest from colonial Bengal. Sultana finds that the order is entirely different from colonial Bengal where women have no hand or voice in the management of social affairs. In India man is lord and master, he has taken to himself all powers and privileges and shut up the women in *zenana*. The man is "lord" and "master" who colonizes the Bengali woman just as the British who took over the authorities and rights of Indians. Yet, as mentioned above the colonization of women by men in Ladyland is overturned. There is a marked reformation in women's lives such as, "There are girls' schools, later marriage at the age of 21 and no purdahnishin women."[69]

"Sultana's Dream" satirizes the ethics of patriarchal society of colonial Bengal to point out how ridiculous it can be, by giving justification for the creation of *mardana*. Just as the women of colonial Bengal are informed that their rightful place is in *purdah*, the men in Ladyland are kept indoors. When Sultana asks Sara about this situation of men, she explains men are not trained properly, therefore, they do not know the ways to live in a civil society and may cause harm to women if allowed to move freely; she compares men to wild animals and justifies their captivity. Men in Ladyland are equated with animals, similar to the way women are treated in colonial Bengal. Besides, when the war took place with the neighbouring country and women decided to take charge of it, the Queen insisted that before women take charge of the war all men must occupy the domestic space which was earlier occupied by women. This statement is satirical too, where two contradictory ideas appear. In order to attain freedom, a section of the population must be trapped and Bengali men done precisely the same thing, "in a similarly absurd configuration, they have entrapped women into symbolizing the nation's honour and true spiritual essence."[70]

While satirizing the role reversal, Rokeya at the same time wants the Bengali female reader to view the implications of it in their own context. Rokeya wants the women to note that by secluding the men in *purdah*, the women in Ladyland have gained access to power. Hence, the Bengali woman can take note of what is missing in their case and what could it be replaced with. Surely, we also learn that Sultana is quite eager to return back and detail the lives of women in Ladyland and is encouraged by Sister Sara to tell other women about Ladyland. Sultana thinks her friends will be surprised to know about Ladyland, a place where women are the rulers and men are kept inside to take care of domestic affairs. Rokeya targets to alienate the female readers from their familiar environment; she wants to make the familiar as other-worldly and arouse in those women a sense of confidence for modifying their current circumstances. Truly, it is the process of defamiliarization[71] which shakes Sultana into an awareness of the incongruity and inconsistency of many things which she took for granted. The main purpose of doing so is to awaken the readers and make them conscious of the capabilities and potentials of their deep private yearnings - which is familiar but due to constant repression and subjugation have become unfamiliar.

Rokeya uses the tools of defamiliarization from the very beginning of the story. As the story begins, we find Sultana placed within the *zenana* as she lounges in her bedroom deliberating on the condition of Indian women. The narrative is such that the reader gets the same feeling with Sultana and moves with her. Very soon, the reader and Sultana are taken away from the seclusion of her bedroom to the crowded and busy outside world. In fact, once Sultana is in Ladyland, everything seems different and unfamiliar, and the reader experiences the same. Rokeya creates a situation in which everything that the narrator and the readers believe or determine is not the actual reality, hence the familiar becomes unfamiliar.

The planned approach of defamiliarizing Bengal and the coincident metamorphosis of Ladyland in contrast is carried forward to its stark comparison with the indoor of homes in colonial Bengal. The projected aesthetic contrast is attempted to make the Bengali women realize how unpleasant their captivity is? Rokeya achieves this by accentuating the luscious outdoors and the bounty of nature in comparison to the lifeless, moribund way of life of the purdahnishin women in *zenana*. Sister Sara's kitchen is described to be no less than a Queen's bedroom. In comparison to the inky, coal-fired kitchens in colonial Bengal, Sister Sara's kitchen is fitted with all the modern gadgets like solar cooker and it is situated "in a beautiful vegetable garden... no smoke, nor any chimney either in the kitchen — it was clean and bright;... There was no sign of coal or fire."[72] The flower gardens are also described as flower garlands in a certain version of "Sultana's Dream." The outside world becomes one with the home, and nature is interspersed with the indoors and has decorated the home in such a way that tomato plants and creepers are like ornaments.

Upon entering Ladyland, Sultana finds that it is a beautified place and nature appears in its most pleasing manner that she mistakes a patch of green grass for a velvet cushion. Even the street flowers appear ornamental. When Sultana compliments Sister Sara on the expertise, she says your city can become equally beautiful if people want to make it so but Bengali Men may think it useless because "they have so many other things to do"."[73] Rokeya saw these "other things" not as important as sustaining a green environment.

> What would have seemed like a ridiculous statement at the beginning of the story becomes plausible due to a continuous buildup of aesthetically pleasing descriptions of the outdoors as women's true home. Female readers would have reacted strongly to these descriptions when seated in their dark, crowded interiors.[74]

As a matter of fact, we find that nature is established as a means, in "Sultana's Dream," through which the negative aspect of Bengal can be controlled or over powered. The effect is such that since women have become interested in horticulture, they are "all very busy making nature yield as much as she can." The women "do not find time to quarrel with one another as we never sit idle." It seems quite a positive development. Nature and its importance in the eyes of the Queen and other women in Ladyland is continually emphasized. Knowledge is seen as an ocean which is inaccessible to the *purdahnishin* women. In addition, women used nature's force of solar heat for cooking and also utilizing it in time of war to defeat the enemy. They also successfully exploited rainwater for creating artificial showers, in turn adding to their comfortable life. Finally, we also see that Rokeya highlights the issue of women's freedom using the tool of defamiliarizing the gender roles assigned to Bengali women as the norm in this regard Mukti

Lakhi says, "Rokeya demonstrates that women should not be confined to a set of model of womanhood, as the nationalists have done in colonial Bengal."[75] As a result, we find that in Ladyland the women do not confirm to any pre-assigned roles or behave according to a stereotypical image of women. Hence, in Ladyland women are not timid or dull, and their brains are not smaller than the men as Bengali women are taught to believe. In fact, Rokeya associates shyness with men so much so that what is considered as an essential trait of womanhood in Bengal is referred as "mannish" in Ladyland. Sara tells Sultana, "You are shy and timid like men."[76] While Rokeya emphasizes how fluid gender roles can be to signify the potential of women, she thrusts on the men certain biological roles. In Ladyland, men are equated with lunatics and animals; they lack patience, "a man has not patience enough to pass thread through a needlehole even!"[77] Men are not depicted as trustworthy, they waste working hours in smoking and fighting with others. On the surface the description may seem contradictory, but Rokeya does not believe that men are, biologically, by nature as animals or lunatics. In fact, by giving men such negative attributes in the same manner as the men do to women, she tries to stress that women are treated with discrimination. Rokeya here also gains an opportunity to prove that it is by inverting the oppressive patriarchal ideologies that gender roles are generated. Rokeya by doing so is able to foreground the prospects for women. Hence, the technique of role reversal which seems contradictory in "Sultana's Dream" is a clean literary tool used by Rokeya to convey many ideas.

Furthermore, Rokeya acquaints her female readers to the fact that even women can participate in disciplines traditionally meant for men. In Ladyland, we find that women are teachers, scientists, coming up with inventions like the use of solar heat for multiple purposes etc. The women scientists even invent air-cars, artificial showers, use of electricity for farming and cooking by solar heat. This ideal state of affairs is attained because in Ladyland, education aims at providing women all-round development of their personality and not just making them able home makers, unlike colonial Bengal. Rokeya builds up a case to pinpoint the importance of women's work and intelligence as against the men before she embarks upon the topic of education. In fact, Sara asserts that women may not be as physically strong as men, but "Women's brains are somewhat quicker than men's."[78]

3.3.2.3 Struggle against religious suppression

Rokeya in her utopia imagines an idea of "modernity" that is free from religious tyranny. The religion in Ladyland "is based on Love and Truth."[79] Sister Sara affirms, "It is our religious duty to love one another and to be absolutely truthful," to which Sultana exclaims, "I see purity itself reigns over your land."[80] Anyone who fails to follow the religion in Ladyland is asked to leave and never to return. There are no specific religious laws which govern Ladyland. In contrast, many Muslim nationalists have implored Islam to clearly define the roles for women, by secluding them to *purdah* and bounding their education to only the reading of the Qu'ran. Rokeya voiced her views quite forcefully against such a mishandling of religious power. It is believed that due to her radical views in her article *Amader Abanti* (Our Degradation [1908]) that certain lines from it were deleted by the publisher. The article was published in *Motichoor* and the lines effaced were:

> whenever a woman has tried to raise her head, she has been brought down to her knees on the ground of religious impiety or scriptural taboo... What we could not accept as correct, we had to in the belief that it had the authority of a religious dictum... Men have always propagated such religious texts as edicts of God to keep us women in the dark... the scriptures are nothing but a set of regulating systems prescribed by men. You hear that the prescriptions were laid down by saints. If a woman could have become a saint, perhaps she would have prescribed opposite regulations... We must not allow ourselves to bow down to the undue authority exercised by men in the name of religion. It has been seen time and time again that the stricter the religious restrictions, the more severe is the women's victimization.[81]

The image of bringing a woman on her knees by religion grabs attention because Islamic prayer is done by coming on one's knees. While this refers to the act of prayer, it is also seen as a mark of submission and begging. Rokeya sees prayer in the nationalist age as suggestive of decadence and in a radically profane argument she argues that "religion is a male construct. Her worlds divide the world up into opposing gendered camps, with religion belonging solely to men and being forced on women."[82] Here, Rokeya is not placing an argument against a single man assuming control over a woman through religion, but the attack is on men's "regulating systems" prescribed for women. According to Mukti Lakhi, another reason why Rokeya emphasizes on a religion based on love and truth, that is neither Hindu nor Muslim, is because of the prevailing context of 'divide and rule' policy of British by which Bengal was divided by them on October 16, 1905 into Muslim and Hindu areas. The aim was to heighten tensions between the two groups and strengthen the British rule. The presence of one religion which is informal and organic in nature and scope and is based on "universal principles of goodness, means that there cannot be conflict between religions in Ladyland; divide and rule cannot work."[83]

3.3.2.4 Struggle against political suppression

"Sultana's Dream" also makes a strong case against the political suppression which colonial Bengal faced at the hands of British. Rokeya shows Ladyland to be a free nation-state as compared to colonial Bengal. Ladyland could attain its freedom by defeating foreign armies, which they achieved through women's "brainpower"[84] and not military power. The women exploited the heat of the sun and used it as a weapon to defeat the enemy. This can be seen as an answer or a solution to a colonial Bengal that has been overpowered by outside forces, which, according to Rokeya, can be vanquished. She indicates that the stupidity of Indian men is responsible for their country's subjugation. It is significantly emphasized by Rokeya that women in Ladyland are no less nationalistic than the people of India. This nationalism refers to a state of patriotism where the citizens are faithful and overjoyed at the state of their nation-state, where justice is the primary virtue. The Queen declares that she will commit suicide if the land and my honour are lost. The idea of justice is more valuable to the Queen than her life, which is as important to her as her soldiers' lives. Rokeya makes a suitable contrast between the Queen and local Indian princes who brought about the colonization of Bengal by selling their allegiance to the East India Company. Rokeya clearly demarcates the difference between Ladyland and colonial Bengal and suggests that Ladyland does not accept the British colonial policy as the government of Ladyland does not conquer anyone's land. It can be clearly noted that here a contrast has been drawn between Queen Victoria and the Queen of Ladyland who is extremely generous and stays away from any desire to covet another's wealth.

Undeniably the Queen, like the British, allows and encourages her citizens to trade with other nations except the nations where women are exploited. This can be noted as a rejoinder to the British who justified their mission of civilization by placing attention on the deplorable condition of women in India. Lakhi has quoted from James Mill who also justifies their civilizing mission:

> The history of uncultivated nations uniformly represents the women as in a state of abject slavery... A state of dependence more strict and humiliating than that which is ordained for the weaker sex among the Hindus cannot be conceived.[85]

The focus of attention on the women and their condition made by the British was definitely a political strategy. It was a necessary move adopted by the colonizers to manifest and claim a moral superiority over the colonized. Rokeya brings out for the reader the hypocrisy of the claim made by the colonial rulers, also clarifying what morality means in the real sense; the political and economic subjugation of India by the British cannot be justified by the fact that Indians are morally weak because of the way they treat their women. On the contrary, if the British believe in the idea of morality they should decline any relation with such a country.

3.3.2.5 *Scientific inventions in SFs*

Towards the beginning of the story, we learn from Sister Sara that the Queen of Ladyland likes science and carries a scientific bent of mind. Hence, she encourages the study of the same amongst women. This is linked to her mission of educating women far and wide. Emphasis is on educating women and making them self-reliant. Many interesting scientific innovations have been introduced and successfully followed for the conservation of nature amongst many benefits. For instance, there is no smoke, nor any coal or fire cooking is done with the help of "solar heat." Curiously Sultana tells us that Sara shows her "the pipe, through which passed the concentrated sunlight and heat"[86] and cooks something to show her the entire process of cooking with solar energy. One can note the effective employment of science and its principles here.

The topic of education in the story is tied constructively also to show how women were able to leave the *zenana* and took control over the nation-state. This is seen as the events unfold. The Queen sets up two universities for women in the capital of Ladyland. These two universities came up with their own inventions contributing to the advancement of the nation; for instance, one of them

> invented a powerful balloon, to which they attached a number of pipes. By means of this captive balloon which they managed to keep afloat above the cloud-land, they could draw as much water from the atmosphere as they pleased. As the water was incessantly being drawn... the ingenious Lady Principal stopped rain and storms.[87]

Sultana wished to receive more explanation as to how this invention became possible, but she could not understand it well, as her scientific knowledge was limited. One can then ascertain the fact that the invention was of a high scientific order.

The second university was not far behind and due to their radical thinking and approach, they invented an instrument with the help of which they could collect "as much sun-heat as they wanted. And they kept the heat stored up to be distributed among others as required."[88] These scientific achievements, however, did not receive appreciation from the men who simply mocked them and called their inventions a romantic imagination. To this, the women chose not to reply with rage; instead they waited for the right opportunity. Soon after, a war was declared by the King against the Queen and her country owing to a dispute. The military men and forces of the Queen were slowly losing at the hands of the enemy. When defeat was near, the Queen and a few wise ladies assembled to decide the plan of action. The Queen advises to use the brain power to defeat the enemy.

It was the analytic mind of the women, and especially the Lady Principal of the second university, that suggested recourse. Yet before her plan could be executed she implored the Queen to order that all men should enter the *zenana* only then they will go on war against the enemy. The men accepted it as they were wounded and tired of fighting. They held no confidence in the women and, hence, felt sure their country would lose. But the Lady Principal of the second university had modern gadgets for warfare and along with her students she prepares for the war; however, instead of opting for direct war they opt for indirect war and with the help of modern gadgets they "directed all the rays of the concentrated sunlight and heat towards the enemy."[89] The heat and light were unbearable for the enemies and they ran away in state of panic. Hence, the women in Ladyland were able to save their country through the use of "brain power", their education and the multiple gifts of science they had invented. They could do all this without any help of the men of their country. We are told by Sara that since this war, their country was never attacked.

When speaking of the scientific innovations, it is essential to mention that they have photovoltaic electricity with the help of which "the fields are tilled... which supplies motive power for other hard work... and we employ it for our aerial conveyances too."[90] Besides, citizens of Ladyland do not suffer from any need of rain water as the "water balloon" stores rain water, which can be drawn at their need. Additionally, in Ladyland there are seldom any floods or thunderstorms. Besides, if the weather becomes too hot, they "sprinkle the ground with plentiful showers drawn from the artificial fountains. And in cold weather we keep our room warm with sun heat."[91]

Another scientific development is that the roof of the bathroom is detachable. It can be removed as per desire. Sultana is told that they "could enjoy a shower bath whenever she liked, by simply removing the roof."[92]

The Queen is described to be sagacious and far-sighted and in her land a unique thing is invented to make travel easier and faster. It is interestingly called an air-car and Sister Sara takes Sultana to meet the Queen in the same vehicle. This air-car is described in detail and by following the given procedure it is possible to manufacture a similar working air-car. This air-car is made up of:

> Hydrogen balls, and they were used to overcome the force of gravity. The balls were of different capacities to be used according to the different weights desired to be overcome. She then fastened to the air-car two wing-like blades, which... were worked by electricity. After we were comfortably seated she touched a knob and the blades began to whirl, moving faster and faster every moment.[93]

The air-car can be brought to the ground by reversing the mechanism by which it came into motion. So, by visiting the Queen and her capital, Sultana could also visit the famous universities, along with the manufactories, laboratories, and observatories. When Sultana and Sister Sara get into the air-car to return back, Sultana is awakened to consciousness with a fall.

Use of electricity to create the motive power to enhance the hard work, 'water balloon' for rain water harvesting, new ideas on disaster management, development of skills for the creation of artificial rains, use of new techniques in house architecture and, finally, the invention of the air-car are few examples of the signs of scientific developments mentioned in the text.

3.4 Manjula Padmanabhan: *Escape*

3.4.1 Genre: feminist dystopia

A work of feminist dystopia can be seen to possess the characteristics of a dystopia. Dystopic SF visualizes a world where things have taken a bad turn, putting before the readers the probable repercussions of the current evils in society. In a feminist dystopia, the subjugation or ill-treatment of women is magnified or over stated to point out the need for the revision of existing practices in contemporary society.

3.4.2 Issues and concerns

3.4.2.1 Setting

Escape is set in an unnamed country. It is a nation-state which has experienced many significant changes, and is on occasion referred to as The Change. The nation-state is run by military Generals who are clones of one another and exercise complete dominance over the lives of citizens through the Drones, which are also referred as Boyz or human robots. There is no concept of democracy or freedom available to the citizens and the land is run by extremely advanced science and technology. The entire ecosystem has been destroyed by the Generals' atomic bombs.

Youngest foregrounds, "They believed they were improving the world."[94] Furthermore, along with destroying the city, they exterminated the species of women from their world, what they refer to as "the Vermin Tribe."[95] All references, words and pictures related to women are forbidden. For this very reason, the three Uncles have secretly protected their young daughter, Meiji, from the eyes of the Generals. Yet the Uncles worry about her safety and want to send her with Youngest on a perilous journey to save Meiji's life. The novel is concerned with this journey, which is a daring attempt to cross the boundary monitored by the Generals.

As the novel opens, the atmosphere is tense. We become aware of the fear and secrecy observed in a barren country populated with half-human robots that lack emotions and work mindlessly. In contrast, the three brothers possess distinctive personalities and traits; while Eldest is mature and has a prophetic vision and insight, Middle is sharp and conscientious, whereas Youngest is affectionate, empathetic and the closest to Meiji. Meiji is always kept in the underground dungeon meant for her, which is equipped with the latest gadgets for surveillance.

Even in this confinement, where she spends her entire time, the Uncles have provided her ways and means to both educate and amuse her. Meiji was kept secretively as she grew speculating the risk. She may be discovered by the Generals any day and killed. The Uncles fear the worst for her and ponder over their situation of powerlessness in an autocratic state. They realize that sending Meiji and Youngest amidst all the danger will be an extreme path, yet they understand that it is inevitable. While Eldest seems optimistic about the plan to send Meiji away, Middle appears worried and calls it a nightmare of uncertainty. He is skeptical about whether or not they will succeed as they will encounter many missteps and pitfalls.

Until the Great Change, which was brought about by the Generals, the Uncles were already wealthy landlords. After the change, they built a vast estate that includes farms and mansions furnished with modern and updated technology. They also built a dronery where they manufacture drones for their use as working hands. Since reproduction was out of the question, this was the only means of producing human-like forms. These drones were devoid of emotions, often deaf and dumb, manufactured only to follow set orders.

Unaware of her own sex, Meiji's life is in complete control of her Uncles, who are also her protectors. They are worried that they may be doing her more harm than good, instead of giving her the normal life they would like for her. Eldest stresses that she should know the whole truth about herself, including the circumstances and the state of the world at the time of her birth. He also wants it to be revealed to her that they themselves are responsible for her stunted growth. He wants to provide her some choice in determining her own future. As a growing child, she definitely has many doubts and queries which she keeps to herself. In the course of the story, we learn that she is given hormone suppressants to delay her growth. She is visited by suitors arranged by her Uncles, who react with desperation and violence when they see her. This further adds to Meiji's feeling of being confounded.

Meiji's inner turmoil can also be found mirrored in the lives of citizens of the world portrayed in *Escape*. The people in the novel have lost touch with a normal life. There is no freedom and everything is prescribed by the rulers; hence, despite their luxuries, the citizens are unhappy and are leading a static life. Even those Uncles who appear detached and unconcerned seem to be affected by the lack of any feminine affection. Youngest, the most emotional of the Uncles, resists being attracted to Meiji. He is teased by Middle who says, Youngest "is still at the mercy of his… glands."[96] Despite this, Youngest seems most worried about Meiji's safety. As time passes away and the risk for Meiji increases, the three brothers arrive at the decision to finally send away Meiji in order to save her life. Hence, she is accompanied by Youngest on this strenuous journey away from the periphery of the land of Generals. It is a tough decision for them, yet they feel they have little choice.

3.4.2.2 *Female foeticide*

Escape, a dystopia takes a raw fact of our present world – declining sex-ratio – and turns it into a present of the future. It is a powerful novel that studies "the socio-cultural, political, psychological, intellectual, emotional, spiritual and other aspects related to the imbalance in the sex-ratio."[97] According to B. Parvathi, the author belongs to that generation of Indian women writers in English

> who have boldly stepped out of conventions that define respectability to address issues of gender, woman, her body and its behavior, its exploitation in a family and social setting… Manjula Padmanabhan has opened a fresh dialogue on a new angle of feminist concerns.[98]

Female foeticide and infanticide are twin epidemics that have a distorting impact on Indian society. They are considered as crucial Human Rights issues. Over the last twenty years, these issues have remained unchecked and unbridled in certain territories, causing severe damage. A few of the detriments could be preventing girls from getting an education and increase in crimes against them. A well-defined way to prevent the practice of illegal sex-selective abortions is to enlighten men and women with regard to issues concerning women's rights.

In order to learn about the prevalent child sex-ratio, the following can be observed about the declining number of women in India:

> According to UNICEF, in 1991, the figure was 947 girls to 1000 boys. Ten years later it had fallen to 927 girls for 1000 boys. A decline of 20 girls among 1000 boys should set alarms ringing. In 2001, India's male population (age 6 years and below) was 84,999,203 according to the Government of India's census data. Hence, between 1991 and 2001, nearly 1.7 million girls have disappeared. 1.7 million girls might be 2.16% of the female population (0–6 years) of India in 2001, but the effects of this will be seen in many years to come. UNICEF also reports that this problem is not isolated to the country's rural areas but it is more prevalent in certain geographical areas and is spreading, across economic strata.[99]

This alarming situation is what Padmanabhan draws our attention to. She presents a scenario where the species of women have been exterminated and only a single female child survives, Meiji. Meiji is hence so precious and unique that she has to be kept secretively and protected not only from the Generals, who consider them sentimental and also the breeding ground for fear and sorrow, but from others, who see women as agents of mortality. However, the Generals are not the only cause of worry for the Uncles as they feel they must also safeguard Meiji from the line of suitors who arrive to see her, when they get to know the slightest about an alive female. These suitors could also expose Meiji's presence to the Generals. The unavailability, in fact the extinction of women, has made young men desperate for female company, to the extent to which they are even ready to risk their lives. At the beginning of the novel, we learn that a suitor is brought into the Estate by the Uncles, where he is kept under surveillance for six days to make certain that he means no danger. He has to go through a high security check before he sees Meiji. She is also asked by her Uncles to speak very little so that the suitor is assured of her sex. However, the suitor is quite desperate to see Meiji and, even when denied permission, he leaps upon her with his arms in the air. At this, the trained escort-drones broke the suitor's neck. The suitor had crossed his bounds despite the warning given unto him. Meiji is shocked out of her wits and left trembling at the suitor's violent ways. Yet she has been trained by her Uncles to control her emotions. This situation, in which men are left despairing for female companionship, can be seen mirrored in many states of North India. Namrata Poddar, in her report, 'Female Foeticide and Infanticide is the cancer that slowly kills us', takes the example of Haryana to illustrate the idea. Due to the shortage of women in Haryana, there are fewer brides available to marry and men have no option but to move 3000 kms away from their land to bring suitable brides and, on occasion, to pay a substantial fee for doing so. Poddar adds that women brought for marriage from other states and provinces may find it difficult to adjust in a culture and society which is different from theirs, considering that Haryana is a patriarchal society. This has led to a higher number of divorces and increased occurrences of domestic violence.

The dearth of women has also led to an increase in crimes against women, such as molestations, rapes, indecent behaviour and treatment meted out to women in both cities and rural areas. Women's groups have demanded that the terminology which denotes the verbal and physical molestation of women be changed to '*sexual harassment*' from simply '*Eve teasing*.' Additionally, the fewer the number of women, the lower is their representation in places of power like the judiciary, parliament, the civil service, and so on. This is happening because girls are not allowed to come out of confinement of their homes for fear of being harmed. This will result in women being unable to achieve their goals, and what they truly deserve, because they are not given access to opportunities because they are denied basic human rights.

The basic right of a mother to give birth to her child is taken away from many in India, where society pressurizes her to bear a male child and forcibly abandon the female offspring. They are denied their right as a mother and gradually they become conditioned in such a manner that they follow the dictates of the patriarchal society. Similar is the case of Meiji, who from the beginning is not encouraged to make her own choices and gets used to it to such an extent that she does not even feel the need to decide things for herself. Freedom of choice is less of a concern for Meiji.

Meiji is reluctant and does not want to even guess things, but simply be told. This is exemplary of the fact that the faculty of reason is suppressed from developing in Meiji to such an extent that she does not even consider it an option to question things around her. A similar situation is confronted by women in present-day Indian society, who often accept the dictates of the patriarchal male due to constant conditioning and counseling from childhood that women must obey their fathers and then, in adult life, their husbands. Women are also burdened with the weight of being the bearers of culture; in that respect they are unable to put up much resistance and must acquiesce, allowing others to make significant choices for them. This leads to a situation of ignorance, low self-confidence and indecisiveness amongst women, who accept their disgraceful conditions as their fate. It is possible that Meiji imagines that each of the Uncles also have encounters with suitors. It is because she doesn't know that she is a woman and that she is also the only remnant of the female species. The extermination of women has not only caused hopelessness amongst men for a female companion; it has also raised the danger they pose to, in the case of the novel, Meiji. The General's comment is also pertinent in this regard: "the loss of the Vermin Tribe causes a general breakdown in the will to survive!"[100] It is evident in the novel that the young suitors are willing to risk their lives for women and that they are unafraid to do so. With respect to female foeticide and infanticide, the eventual dearth of women and the associated rise in crimes against them, Sneh Lata Tandon and Renu Sharma have remarked:

> The twin process of 'elimination of unborn daughters' and the 'slow killing' through neglect and discrimination of those that are born has become a matter of concern... Legally infanticide amounts to homicide... yet law alone cannot root out this social problem. The girls are devalued not only because of the economic considerations but also because of socio-economic factors...[101]

India is a site where some of the most inhumane crimes are committed against women, such as rape, dowry deaths, domestic violence, honour killings, and sexual harassment at their places of work. According to an estimate by the National Crime Records Bureau (NCRB), crimes against women have shown an annual increase of 1.6% in the registration of cases (50.7 lakh cases). The crime rate shot up from 383.5 in 2018 to 385.5 in 2019 for every 100,000 people.[102] According to a report of the *Deccan Chronicle*, a case of a bride being burnt for dowry is reported every 58 minutes, and a case of rape every 22 minutes. The brutal case that occurred in 2012, in which a young student from Delhi was gang raped, was accompanied by national (indeed an international) outcry. The prevalent system of law and order even to date remains inefficacious in controlling such acts of violence, exploitation and subjugation. Government organizations display an extremely prejudiced outlook with respect to women. The partiality of politicians protects criminals from any substantial form of legal punishment. The patriarchal society is rigid enough to not consider women as individuals in their own right. Old and traditional institutions of control which prescribe 'what is right and proper for women' are still prominent and this works to emphasize and encourage the continuance of the use of brutal ways to discipline women who refuse to comply.

Namrata Poddar has advanced some ways and means by which the fast-disappearing girls and the mayhem caused by the incessant crime against women in India can be checked and brought under control. If this is allowed to continue, the situation could be similar to that encountered in *Escape*. Poddar points out that it is imperative to abolish dowry and make strong laws for the offenders. The Dowry Prohibition Act of 1961 is insufficient as it restricts the maximum sentence for anyone demanding or accepting dowry, to only five years, irrespective of how grave the crime may be. Poddar asserts that this punishment must be increased to strongly prevent the practice of seeking dowry. Another area that deserves attention is, according to her, the right to inherit property for women, notwithstanding the religion. Poddar shares that it was not until the 2004 amendment to the Hindu Succession Act that daughters were granted an equal right in the family property. The right, however, is not granted to women from other communities in India. Poddar maintains that there must be a common law that covers all religions and which provides and extends equal rights to all women. If every woman is given a share in the inheritance, whatever their religion, this would provide all women with the status, self-respect and strength to make their own decisions. Accordingly, she would then no longer be a subject of pity.

In addition to these observations, Poddar pronounces that doctors and their pre-natal clinics who offer illegal facilities for sex determination tests and sex-selective abortions must be banned and debarred. Larger initiatives need to be taken and also examined to end the practice of aborting a pregnancy due to gender discrimination. Despite the advanced times we live in, the general public in India is largely uninformed about the evils of female foeticide and infanticide. There is also a dire need to educate the youngest generation about these issues. Furthermore, not just women but also men must be a part of the discussions surrounding women's rights. This will promote openness. An environment needs to be built in which women's rights are not met with resentment and in which their choices are appreciated and encouraged. This, in fact, is an idea upon which Poddar lays a specific emphasis.

3.4.2.3 Ecofeminist perspectives

In *Escape*, Manjula Padmanabhan not only advances a strong opposition against the victimization of women, but also focuses on ecosystems devastated due to the indiscriminate use of technology. Padmanabhan offers an ecofeminist perspective of the same issues. In recent years, feminist and ecological movements have exercised increasing influence on shaping changes to traditional frameworks of society.

> The ecofeminist ideology originated in the West and is rooted in an analogy of the biological, procreating and the maternal roles of woman and nature. It advocates that until women are freed from male domination and nature is freed from industrial and societal assault, equitable and sustainable development would remain an empty rhetoric.[103]

According to Pramod Parajuli, "ecofeminist movements challenge state dominance and articulate alternate forms of governance that focus on safe and inclusive development. They transform politics through revival of civil society and subalterns."[104]

Escape, an ecological novel, takes up the issue of nature's destruction and deterioration at the hands of the contemporary ruling order. Ecological issues are often given little priority in developing countries such as India, where economic issues take priority. Nonetheless, in recent decades tremendous urbanization and industrialization have caused substantial damage to the environment, leading, for example, to different kinds of environmental pollution, deforestation, climate change, radioactive and pesticide pollution and the depletion of natural resources. Nature has been disturbed to frightening levels, posing a risk to entire populations and ecosystems. Several

NGOs and similar groups continue their efforts to raise awareness amongst native communities about an environmentally-friendly ways of living. In *Escape*, the Generals have not only terminated the species of women, but also ravaged the ecosystem to further their personal interests. We are told by one of the Uncles, Youngest, that what was once an enormous city, the capital of their world, and populated by 25 million people, had been destroyed by the Generals' atomic bombs. The seeds of this devastation had already been sown by the citizens through their neglect of their environment even before the Generals assumed power. The Generals justified their actions on the grounds that they were civilizing the world. This is similar to the explanations given in the real world by the patriarchal institutions, such as multinational firms,. who try to exploit the already scant resources for the good of the society. They are serving their own means and ends, yet justify their projects in terms of the benefits to wider society. Here, Padmanabhan is making a comment on how the State functions, along with drawing attention to the ruling class which subjugates those below it. She makes a case to critique the rules of the current times who view both woman and Nature as threats.

The Generals value people less than they value either stone or rock. Hence, they consider what they have done as worthy. They have mercilessly annihilated two-thirds of the population of the country, which they describe as "drain-clearing."[105] Their explanation is that "Our world was suffocating in its own excrement!"[106] They removed such a large percentage of population in order to get rid of the idea of individuals and individuality. The Generals have not only annihilated the entire species of women, but also ruined the ecosystem. Nature is seen as excessive by them and often the metaphor of a plant is used to describe women. The Generals are representative of the power-hungry elites in society who regard women and Nature as enemies to be destroyed simultaneously. Manjula Padmanabhan foregrounds the severe contamination of Nature caused by the Generals. After this contamination of nature, the grassy savannah devolved into desert. Dunes of grey slag, putrefying red brick and the white arcs of broken crockery marked the site of small towns. There was no evidence that there were once thriving communities in this area.

The radioactive and chemical pollution caused during the Change was such that as Youngest and Meiji travel towards the affected area that they encounter a featureless wasteland, with no cultivation to be seen, no farms, no villages. The ground there is so contaminated that Youngest and Meiji avoid any direct contact with soil. The affected area supports no life and the air is so contaminated that even the birds die while flying above this area.

Once Youngest and Meiji approach the first boundary post of the "Waste," they find themselves unable to breathe without the aid of their "tall cylindrical radiation helmets" which are equipped with a "built-in air filter."[107] Further into their journey South, Youngest and Meiji meet a gypsy who not only helps them, but also supplies useful pieces of information. This is another repercussion of the "Change." The trains no longer run and the train tracks are used for a variety of odd purposes.

Hence, the rail lines are useless and deployed for other work than running trains. With the destruction of the ecosystem owing to the cement rot, the railway tracks were also ruined. We are told by the narrator that before the "Change" there had been two rail lines, which became buried at least two feet under grey grit during the cement plague and the period of the "Change" after that one line had been cleared for use by the private operators. After the Change, there are no heavy industries and no currency. A barter system was in use to buy things. The Generals have brought about by an erasure of things of the past, and made the future redundant.

The Generals not only erased women from their world, but also obliterate the ecosystem little by little, from the birds to animals and the soil to water. This was made possible due to the work of like-minded individuals who came together and accepted "money from foreign governments in exchange for storing nuclear wastes."[108] This strategy, as the General informs us, was planned by his "foresighted ancestor," who became, in his words, "a highly paid garbage collector." He was joined by "other citizens who would help him realize his vision. Industrialists, bankers, politicians."[109] These people were not clones, but the ancestors of Youngest and the like. They fell into the trap of Generals who wanted "to clone a race of supermen." Many more Generals were produced as a result, along with the Boy Warriors. The supporting members, such as industrialists and politicians, were given an option to join forces or be destroyed. Those who agreed were given an estate and the technology to produce drones, who would then serve as their servants.

Gradually, the Generals also exterminated women and this process was hastened by the already reduced number of females in their world. What was actually the intent of the ancestors of Youngest, to produce clones of some of the great personalities amongst them, was subverted by the Generals, who used the technology to clone themselves and take control of their world. Yet, this was not always the case. Youngest tells Meiji that the Generals cannot be entirely blamed for the most terrible things happening in their world. Youngest reveals to Meiji that the "insiders," the people of their world, are equally to blame for the degraded state of their world, their ecosystem. The "insiders" accepted money in exchange for the importation of toxic waste from other parts of the world. This brought immense prosperity, wealth and commercialization. This process caused not only the destruction of the environment, and a dying out of species in all places but also enormous public anguish and lamentation. It was all blamed on outsiders; however, the source was within and it happened at a time of great prosperity. Accordingly, no one could sense that anything could possibly go seriously wrong while so much money was being made. Hence, corrective steps were not taken by the citizens when they could have prevented the decadent state of the world. The ignorance of some became power in the hands of others.

The result was that in the "radioactive wasteland" streams could no longer be used as direct sources of water; the water there was unsafe to drink. It is not only that the rivers became contaminated, but everything else that the water came into contact with that became polluted. The rich people joined hands with outsiders, who approached the richest of the rich in order to trade their radioactive waste for money and this was happening even before the Generals emerged. Padmanabhan is again focusing attention towards the role of the State, the ruling class and the policy decision-makers. It was these people who collaborated with the outsiders, and subsequently with the Generals, determining the fate of the larger public that is vulnerable at their behest.

The Generals were opportunists and used their chance to sneak in as the citizens were preoccupied in dealing with the radioactive effects. Generals extended false promises and gave the illusion of providing a better world, one free from disease, poverty and hunger. Their plan was instead a complete takeover of the world. This strategy can be likened to the propaganda of certain political parties in the modern world, which advance a false agenda in order to lure people to fulfill their ulterior motives. At the cost of their larger interests, those of the common man are ignored. In addition, the hypocrisy of the Generals' plan was not exposed until rumors began to emerge about large-scale water contamination and deprivation. People were shocked to learn about genetic mutations and wildlife extinction. Initially, it was just the two brothers, but they began mysteriously to multiply. It was by this time that the residents realized the horrifying dimensions of the Generals' glorious and bold vision.

3.4.2.4 Cloning

The theme of cloning runs through the novel. In one of his interviews one of the Generals discloses that "Our ancestor had generated a powerful collective of identical-that is me, us, my clone-brothers – and of course the armies of Boy warriors. Together we make a vitally invincible team."[110] Hence, it is known that reproduction is carried out by cloning in this land. This land where there is no sight of women is an abominable sight, where men have lost their interest in life and roam aimlessly like ghosts. The few men who survive, who are not clones would also die soon. There would then only be clones left who have no minds or souls of their own. It is an extremely barren and infertile land, and the citizens deal with the consequences of nuclear radiation. They live in a semi-conscious state where they are not much aware of the happenings of the outside world. Because of the scale of crimes committed against humanity, the name of this world has also been struck off from its records by the United Nations. In fact, the rest of the world has also cut off all modes of communication with this land.

There is nothing unique about two Generals and they are hardly distinguishable from one another because "today we can duplicate and standardize anyone, anything."[111] They assert that an individual may stop breathing, but his/her brilliance will continue through their replications into tens and hundreds by cloning. According to one of the many manuals written by the Generals, "Everyone and everything is replaceable. No-one is uniquely precious."[112] Being clone-selves, the Generals "reject individuality."[113] They find all such details irrelevant.

The Generals also took blood samples of the men alive so that they can keep copies of them as clones. But they would also mix these samples with those of pigs or sheep. Windseeker, the gypsy, refuses to give Youngest his blood sample as he knows the truth of the cloning process. He is aware that the process will take place through some animal, if not a pig or a sheep then through an ape, a horse or a cow. This is an utterly ruthless process carried out by the Generals.

According to the Generals, theirs is a glorious achievement and they revel in the fact that there is nothing else as remarkable to compare with. The ancestor of Generals not only cloned Generals and created Boy Warriors, but also manufactured half-human robots called drones. A drone Youngest and Meiji notice on their journey is long-armed and has sturdy features, with the characteristic bony hairless head, loose lipped expressionless face and semi-naked body. These drones are mostly deaf and dumb, only perform roles which are programmed into them. The drones are, in fact, compared by the Generals to women, as "The drones are the… servile, dumb and deaf."[114] The extinction of women from this world is suggestive of the fact that they did not allow women to survive because the Generals were unable to control their minds. In fact, the Generals could find no means to control women other than to exterminate them. This is also made clear by the fact that Meiji's mother had the power to save her child from the Generals. She immolated herself by diverting their attention from Meiji. At the end of the novel, Meiji comes to an understanding that her mind is the most powerful weapon she possesses. She also attains the strength to strive for survival and vows to continue the struggle.

3.4.2.5 Scientific elements

A significant element of SF that figures in the novel is a "Desert Chariot" which has been invented by Middle and would be used by Youngest and Meiji to cover a large part of their journey. This is a vehicle with giant wheels that are side by side, joined together by an axle. In addition, Youngest and Meiji would wear radiation suits to escape from being noticed by the satellite.

In order to provide concealment from being detected by the satellite in the daytime, Middle devises another mechanism which he calls "mirrorskin" that has four slender struts extending down from it and it unfolds to reveal a long, curving surface supported on a frame. Within a few moments of being stretched on its frame, it disappears from sight.

Another scientific element present in the story is the "sleeping patch" which, when pressed to a person's forehead, induces sleep. In order to make sure that Meiji gets rest while on the journey, Youngest applies the "sleeping patch" at her forehead."[115] Additionally, we learn that at times instead of food, both Youngest and Meiji "ate concentrated energy capsules."[116]

Apart from the above-mentioned elements of SF in the novel, Youngest also carries weapons, such as a set of six tiny poisoned darts, a hand-mounted laser called a Ruby, which qualify it to be called as science fiction.

3.5 Priya Sarukkai Chabria: *Generation 14*

3.5.1 Genre: dystopia

Dystopia as a genre of literature is often used in SF. It enables the author and reader to investigate social and political ideas. Dystopian fiction depicts a society that is debased and decadent, and hence headed toward destruction or dystopia. Dystopia is the creation of a society that tends to focus on the negative ideas, such as suffering, environmental crisis, despotism, exploitation etc. Authors through these issues put in front of the readers reasons why things might be that way, asking the readers to take heed of the negative scenario and take necessary action. The alternative world becomes a metaphor for the real world. Details about dystopia and dystopian fictions have been discussed in Chapter 1, and hence do not require further elaboration here.

3.5.2 Issues and concerns

3.5.2.1 Cloning

Clones in the novel *Generation 14* are of different kinds and fall into different categories. The 'Z' category Clones are nicknamed as "Terror Bearers because they are lobotomized Clones acting on robotic command."[117] The Superior Zombies have been "cloned with python and venus flytrap genes."[118] They are very sensitive to any movement around themselves. Other clones freeze when they sense a Superior Zombie. Another set of clones are of the R-series, the talkative ones used to disseminate information and head orison meetings. In addition, part of the system is Type-X Superior Zombie (Low IQ), also the boss of Clone 14/54/G at the Museum. These zombies are in charge of bureaucratic work. The Global Community is referred to as an open society with where the Originals, Superior Zombies, Firehearts, and Clones exist side by side. The clones can also perish while on duty; Clone 14/54/G considers this to be an easier method of being withdrawn. In the Global Community, camaraderie is encouraged between 'Same-Batch Clones.' They are exact replicas of each other, as Clone 14/54/G[119] remarks:

> my replicas stood about in identical green uniforms… our voices were of one pitch, our eyes brown-black, our hair cut the same length in pageboy style, the widow's peak on our foreheads dipping exactly.[120]

Also, as mentioned above, clones live until they are useful to the community, after which they are withdrawn. They 'exist' for a longer time, if they exercise themselves at a slower pace. The case is different with the

Originals,[121] "use up their existence, Originals are forever lost though their Clones continue without their 'freed consciousness.' Superior Zombies and Clones exhibit different orders of preordained consciousness."[122] There is no limit to the consciousness of Firehearts, but they remain dependent on the genes of bees and elephants for their extraordinary memory. The poetry produced by them hence is marked with truthfulness, and that is the reason why they are used as interrogators.

Clones in the Global Community undergo a regular examination at the Local Testing Lab where they are scanned. It is a time-consuming process. Clones are not supposed to mate. It is only meant for the Originals.

> The Colony of Originals is kept segregated and pampered for the purpose so that fresh Originals and their blueprints are available for societal betterment.[123]

Clones of the Originals are also suspected of producing cloning malfunctions after the thirteenth generations as the blueprint of the Original weakens subsequently. The narrator, Clone, is a fourteenth generation clone of an Original. Her lot is the first to be examined and tested for any faults. Clone tells us, "No dysfunctional case has been reported yet-except it is I, Clone 14/54/G, generation 14 of 54 Clones of batch G. I have an instinct to keep it secret. I recognize this 'instinct' is primordial survival."[124] We are told that Clone's Original was a writer living in the 21st and 22nd centuries. Upon detailed research, Clone learns that her Original was a writer with specific interest in ancient Zensubaltern studies; and was part of a bhakti-sufi-rebel sect called 'The Universalists.'

Although Clone leads a life determined for clones by the Global Community, she seems to be experiencing strange thoughts, ones which are uncommon for a clone. She lives in Clone Towers in a cell where she is supplied with the comfort of a call-on bed and dry rations dispensed regularly. A sign of being regularly taken care of by the Global Community is the weekly bathwater that has been recycled for a minimum of hundred times, as stated by Clone. Irrespective of following a set routine, Clone experiences unusual urges such as the wish to take a bath at an undesignated time. She worries because she can remember, feels lonely at times, and there is no one with which to share that memory. In fact, the prologue of the novel begins with her declaration: "I am a fourteenth generation Clone and something has gone wrong with me."[125] Her dreams are referred to as 'Visitations' in the novel. Clone ponders that if they are not supposed to carry memory traces beyond the second cloning then she carries traces of memory up to the fourteenth generation, this has something to do with transmutations in her neurological circuitry perhaps something was overlooked in the cloning process.

3.5.2.2 Social issues

Clone develops a mole and is also growing hair, which is quite unusual for a clone. Clone suspects that she may be mutating into a human. At the same time, she is afraid of being caught and worries if she will be able to keep a secret. Yet the realization gives her a feeling of release, of being free, even if it is an illusion. There are possibly others who are also mutating, although in secret. Clone is even approached by her replica, Clone 14/53/G, who confirms that she is mutating and this change is part of a larger movement against the Global Community. They want to change it for the better. Clone asserts, "As I am a mutant I think more, feel more... even pain."[126]

Clone, however, comes to the attention of the Global Community and is held to be dangerous. They believe that she will reveal a secret, which her Original was to give out before she died. Considering that her Original is manifesting herself through Clone, she is taken away for interrogation, where she learns that her original was pushed from the high throne while she was midway through her speech during the celebration. Clone learns that the Original who is in charge of interrogating Clone intends to present her at The Celebrations so that her Original, namely Aa-Aa, can speak through her. He promises to protect Clone from any danger.

It is concurred that Aa-Aa speaks through Clone in the form of 'visitations,' also referred to as "Historiographies."[127] Clone is asked by the Leader of the Global Community to join them in the 'war against untruth' at which she begins to question the nature of this war. Feeling a sense of new power, she recites a poem which voices her thoughts. She names many famous wars and recounts the suffering they have caused.

By naming the wars that took place in Hiroshima, Iraq and even in Kurukshetra, Clone feels all these were wars against the Earth. Her contention is that everyone is a loser in war and that no one wins. Ultimately, wars cause "Blood. Death."[128] She says the enemy lies in you, the one whom you should really fight against.

> Your war against life
> with battle lines drawn
> against the enemy:
> Yourself.[129]

Clone's words seem to be applicable to all times, as she recounts the wars in different times and spaces, from Hiroshima to Kurukshetra to Iraq and to New York.

The Supreme Commander interprets that Clone is referring to the situation of the 21st century, where nations are waging pointless wars against one another. In reality, they are waging a war against the hatred embedded within them. The wars are unnecessary and hence need to come to an end. Wars only cause bloodshed, loss of lives, atrocities and destruction. The author is making a plea to reconsider the situation, and to rethink our identity and purpose; or else everything will be destroyed in these mindless wars.

Aa-Aa, in her personal diary, referred to as her 'Pillow Book', attributes the present state we are in, after the two Great Wars. The first war, known as the Clash of Civilizations, happened due to the neglect of their ancestors, who abdicated their responsibility. The second great war is called the Trans-Species Epoch, or 'The War against the Earth.' This is referred to as the last nail in the coffin. These wars caused large-scale destruction and havoc in the world. These wars seem to allude to the two great World Wars of the 20th century. They had similarly changed the face of the world. Yet Aa-Aa writes in her diary that no lesson was learnt, those who outlived the wars forgot what helped them survive, and they abdicated responsibility. Millions were killed. Aa-Aa says, "We became better and better at suppressing our histories and ourselves."[130] She herself confesses to have become a victim to the system at one point, though not consciously. When Aa-Aa was sixty, which was considered to be young as far as the lifespan of an Original is concerned, she enrolled herself in the Lost Ark Project. This required those who volunteered to travel to the Netherlands to search for any life forms so that they can be captured and then cloned by the Global Community. They wanted to add to their shrunken biodiversity. For that purpose, the team brought back with them a few chigetai. Aa-Aa begins to doubt her own work of cloning these species, Aa-Aa, however, in contrast to the others, raises her voice and it was her feeling of tenderness, care and concern for others that led her to be cast out from the Global Community.

Connected to this idea is Clone's question to Couplet toward the end, when she finds that her lover, the Leader, is dead and has been killed by the regime. Furthermore, considering the damage that has been caused to the world by humans, either by creating endless, barbaric wars for selfish motives or by polluting the environment, Clone, in her speech at The Celebrations, takes her argument further and asks, "Where are we heading?[131]

The idea of endless grief is also conveyed at the very beginning of the novel when Couplet and Blank Verse come to the Museum to research 'grief' in order to compose an epic poem. The Education Module in the Museum offers a relic that belongs to Ashoka's period to harp upon the idea of grief that tells the story of Ashoka who killed lakhs of people to conquer lands. Later on, however, he converts to Buddhism, which is apparently passive but practices conversions actively. In the Museum, there is also an exhibit called 'Woman in Grief,' a palm-sized model of a personage curled in a foetal posture. About her, Fireheart says, "She has lost everything, the poor woman."[132] Such thoughts induce in Clone a 'visitation' of the *Dumb Madwoman of Dauli* (Dhauli). She is a mother who has lost her son in the battle of Kalinga. She questions Ashoka about her son's death, Ashoka's conversion to Buddhism and his newfound compassion which spurted only after killing so many people.

Towards the end also, Clone 14/54/G recalls the soundless grief of the *Dumb Madwoman of Dauli* as she wandered in the killing fields searching for her son. The woman had asked Ashoka, what is the source of compassion and could it not arise from a source that is not sorrow, resulting from bloodshed? The novel ends with the Clone's declaration, "I should love tremendously and way beyond myself. This is the only way."[133]

3.5.2.3 Environment and environmental pollution

Just as Aa-Aa produced more volumes of her writings and also voice-tombs, it became even more difficult for her to disguise her displeasure with the Global Community.

Upon investigating histories of the subcontinent at the different time periods, Aa-Aa comes upon many discoveries that were both alluring and poisonous at the same time, since such studies were not encouraged. Aa-Aa felt that with each finding, she was gaining something. For instance, Aa-Aa learns that there used to be different seasons, which she has not observed in the Global Community. There have been no monsoons in this region since the last 200 years. She learns that May was the hottest and the driest month of the year until the pre-monsoon showers came and cleared away the dust from the trees that grew in abandoned regions of the countryside and those which covered the hillsides. The rains would also satiate the dry earth sprouting grasses and weeds just overnight. The rains no longer happen as they did each year.

Other instances where dangers to the environment are reported can be found in the 'visitation' of the Vidya-Shakti-Matsya, Power-of-Knowledge-Fish, also called meditative fish. This particular dream is placed in Kashi, on the ghats of Ganga. The fish tells us that pilgrims pollute the river. The fish, throughout the anecdote, draws our attention to two very important ideas. One is that life is an illusion, this world is *maya* and that there is a great deal of damage that mankind is causing to its own surroundings. This must end, lest humanity itself would come to an end.

Vidya-Shakti-Matsya remarks that Kashi is the Lustrous city that casts light upon Truth and uncovers Reality. As a fish, he affirms it is quite easy for him to stay grounded in the belief that this world is *maya* (a big illusion) and what may seem like the truth is itself a metaphor for the truth. Fish suggests that one must be careful of the attachments which curtain the mind. He refuses to stick to mob mentality and does not want to chase the food or transient pleasures of life. The river of life is merely the chance one is given to seek Eternal Knowledge. Hence, the name Vidya-Shakti-Matsya, Power-of-Knowledge-Fish.

The fish opposes all kinds of wastage, and his reference is to the endless offerings cast away into the Ganga, not only polluting it but also preventing it from being eaten by those who need that food.

Pilgrims who visit Kashi tend to throw dead bodies in the water. The waste, according to the *matsya*, is enough to feed twenty shoals of fish. The vegetable and fruit *prasad* offerings are meant to alleviate the giver's misdeeds. The pilgrims cast these offerings into the water only to gain spiritual benefits, *matsya* says. However, redemption cannot come from carrying out these simple, monetary rituals, he adds. The pilgrims visit the bathing ghats of Kashi on numerous festival days, such as on *Amavash, Poornimas* and during the cold month of *Kartik*. Vidya-Shakti-Matsya exposes the reality behind the illusion. He says that the tradesmen and courtesans flock to *ghats* in order to extract money from the pilgrims. Whereas the sportsmen, astrologers, scholars and artisans come looking for patrons.

The fish, unlike the pilgrims follows a spiritual path to knowledge. His understanding is that "this world is *maya*, a gigantic illusion."[134] He condemns pilgrims who remain fixated on one image, one idol of God, being caught in the illusion of Form. Vidya-Shakti-Matsya faces many risks while being in the river, from the Big Fish, in order to gain knowledge. He even resists desire, resists falling in love with a beautiful fish. He affirms the mind must be controlled, however tough it may be. Vidya-Shakti realizes that the *atma* must undergo many rebirths, to go through several incarnations before illumination arises. He is positive that all *maya*, all illusions, will clear and dualism will vanish. As a fish, he will become part of the *Brahman*, the Eternal reality, by following a path of knowledge. This seems to be a message to all those pilgrims who visit Kashi with hopes of expiating the worst possible sin. Yet, in reality they are wrapping the veil of ignorance tighter around one's self.

The fish further reports that on account of the large number of pilgrims visiting Kashi, the King has ordered expansion of the burning and the bathing *ghats*. For this purpose, the wild elephants have been driven farther away from their wallowing spots by the sound of hammers, drums and axes. Panthers and boars have also been compelled to leave their habitat. Only the deer and peacocks can be seen roaming the public parks and close to the ghats.

The fish believes in the idea of goodness and also tries to spread it among his shoal. He does not loathe, and hence feels no disgust. He does not ascribe to the idea of being highborn, like his uncle who threatens to excommunicate the fish from their caste for adopting the habits of the "distant delta-dwelling scavengers." The fish refused to accept the *prasad* offerings and instead eat the crocodile's leftovers from dead bodies. *Matsya* looks at this situation from Shankaracharya's philosophy of dualism.

Shri Adi Shankaracharya (788–820), also known as the first Shankara, is known for his extraordinary reinterpretations of sacred Hindu writings such as the *Upanishads* which had a deep impact on the development of Hinduism at a period when disorder, myths and discrimination were on the rise. Shankara supported and prescribed the importance of the Vedas and became the renowned *Advaita* philosopher. He also reinstated the Vedic Dharma and *Advaita Vedanta* to its immaculate clarity and renown. The precept of *Advaita* says that:

> the True Self is Brahman (Divine Creator). Brahman is the 'I' of 'Who Am I?' The Advaita doctrine propagated by Shankara views that the bodies are manifold but the separate bodies have the one Divine in them. The phenomenal world of beings and non-beings is not apart from the Brahman but ultimately become one with Brahman. The crux of Advaita is that Brahman alone is real, and the phenomenal world is unreal or

an illusion. Through intense practice of the concept of Advaita, ego and ideas of duality can be removed from the mind of man.[135]

A similar idea is voiced in the 'visitation' of Dhampadda, an acolyte. When Dhampadda prays with the other *bhikkus*, the words echo and he feels as if his chest were the cave wall and all the *bhikkus* were inside him, chanting with him. He is taught that goodness, or *dhamma*, is everywhere, it is a matter of 'Inner Vision.' Dhampadda speculates that it could be anyone, either a sick man who comes to the monasteries to seek free medical aid, he may be pretending to be sick. A Peepul tree may also be a *Bodhisattva*; it gives so much shade and a place to live for monkeys, birds and squirrels. Or it could be a fish which does not mind if it is caught and eaten; just the way Buddha allowed himself to be killed in so many *avatars* to help others. Dhampadda learns from his teacher, the virtue of kindness, which should remain uniform throughout, unlike the changing seasons. It should also be extended to one and all. He learns that pride is bad, and that he must not tread on the path of others or trample earthworms, centipedes, frogs, snakes, and the like. Just the example of hopping frogs, who leap out of his way when he is running, teaches him that the frogs, however small, can leap high. Hence, he being larger in size than them must not treat another being condescendingly without realizing their potential.

3.5.2.4 Treatment of women

Priya Sarukkai Chabria, in her novel *Generation 14*, presents the reader with the issue of women and their treatment in different time periods. The 'visitation' of a parrot is set in Lucknow, the capital of Awadh before the Indian Mutiny of 1856. The parrot is a pet of the third Begum of the prominent Khan-Sahib. The parrot is in love with the Begum and refers to her as 'My Love.' In this case, the parrot, being a female, is denied her sexuality by the Begum. 'My Love' refuses to acknowledge that the parrot is a female and insists on calling it a 'He'.

The parrot adds that the eunuchs who guard the *zenana* are worse off than her, "trapped as I am in a false sexuality. They have none."[136] The parrot seems unhappy that, "My own body had become my cage. Soundless. Immobile. I am within it."[137] Not only is she made to accept a false sexuality, but the parrot has always been a captive, hence no freedom. The parrot says, "I don't remember ever being free."[138] Her claws have been capped, and each of them is wrapped in a piece of velvet so that she does not scratch 'My Love.' Her wings have been clipped so that the parrot always remains a captive. On Khan Sahib's orders, the outer layer of the parrot's tongue is peeled, so that it speaks prettily. The experience is one of extreme pain and humiliation as the parrot is passed through different hands. The state of the parrot is compared to that of the singing woman, Bi-Jan, who is invited to entertain My Love. Bi-Jan remarks that both she and the parrot are well trained in courteous speech through the use of the whip. The parrot sees the marked difference between herself and Bi-Jan is that the courtesan can leave the world of *zenana* to return to her world of music and entertainment. This emphasizes the parrot's captivity even more as she has never seen the outdoors.

3.6 Vandana Singh: *Distances* and *Of Love and Other Monsters*

3.6.1 *Genre: speculative science fiction*

The term 'speculative fiction' was coined by Robert Heinlein in 1941. It is an umbrella terms that refers to works that encompass the genres of science fiction, fantasy and gothic. Interestingly, the term 'speculative fiction' is also used to refer to works that is not purely science fiction, fantasy or gothic, and do not fall in any specific water-tight categories. According to a critic, David Bowlin,

> Speculative fiction is a world that writers create, where anything can happen. It is a place beyond reality, a place that could have been, r might have been... Speculative fiction goes beyond the horror of every-day life and takes the reader (and writer) into a world of magic, fantasy, science... Speculative fiction defines the best in humanity: imagination and the sharing of it with others.[139]

Such works can be mysteries, alternate histories and historical fiction. The scope and range of speculative fiction is large.

3.6.2 *Issues and concerns in Distances*

3.6.2.1 *Alienation*

The night Anasuya's mother, Lata, passes away, she decides to stay alone on the raft. In Sagara, women would do so to mourn the loss of a loved one, for meditation, and sometimes just to be solitary in order to create new songs. The sea is calm, similar to the one which precedes a storm. During night, a storm comes and carries her raft along to a far-off place. She is rescued by brown people, in a large boat. Anasuya remembers these people with extremely dry skin.

She is taken to the great City, which for her is 'the dry land.' The absence of water is quite disturbing for her. Lata is overcome by feelings of home-sickness and loss. On the journey, Anasuya constantly remembers her home, the sea, which served as her guiding light and a scared place. Yet, the memory of her place gives her feelings of guilt and loss.

According to a popular legend in Sagara, it is the Trickster wave which takes people away from their moorings and it is considered that the same took Anasuya away from her home. It is responsible for her moving outside the circle. Trickster is not always a wave, but can also come in the form of an underwater current or even wind. It plays tricks, deceives, and springs a surprise. Nevertheless, moving away from Sagara was not always discouraged. The Trickster wave had made a pact with the leviathans, which allowed one to venture out, satisfy their urge to explore newer places and then return. Yet this freedom was violated by the inhabitants and hence withdrawn. Leviathans are sea creatures who came and settled at the bottom of the sea.

So, as per the pact between the Leviathans and the Trickster, it was decided that those people of Sagara who desired to go into the outside world and explore newer spaces would be allowed to do so. As a matter of fact, such travelers were also given their due respect. But the pact was breached by some who brought back with themselves foreigners who wanted to "dive down into the ocean depths to find out who or what the leviathans were, or break in other ways the sacred rituals of the Sagaran people."[140] then stepping outside the circle began to be frowned upon. It is for this very reason that Lata, before she dies, says to Anasuya: "Remember what I have taught you, dearest of daughters! May you always be within the circle."[141] People in Sagara also believe that skin turns brown when one moves outside the circle and the sea washes out of them. Anasuya recalls a time before she came to the City, when she had seen a brown man amongst her green fellows.

Anasuya's green skin colour distinguishes her from the crowd at the City and often instills in her the feeling of being a foreigner. The green colour has been part of her identity ever since she can remember. However, in the opening pages we learn that she starts noticing brown flecks on her shoulder because the solisforms that gave her skin its green, exotic tint, depletes.

Anasuya is welcomed in the City and taken in to live in a pentad. She has a place to belong to and the companionship of four other people who admire her greatly. Yet she feels like a stranger, even after having lived in the City for four years. Even the act of going home from the Temple is a challenging task for Anasuya, as she couldn't bear the long trip over the walkways. Because of her green skin, she is deeply insecure and feels uncomfortable being watched by the others.

Irrespective of the excitement that Anasuya feels for her new life, work, and the various difficulties associated with it, and the originality in innovation, she began to experience a sense of void. She had stepped outside the circle by leaving the sea, and she felt alone and secluded, like "an arc, a segment, a thing broken in both space and time."[142] She yearns for the peace and the sense of belonging which her housemates possess. Anasuya is the closest to Palanik, a lean, pallid man. They travelled in the same ship to the City. He is a traveler, yet is very much at peace wherever he goes. He is no less than a guide for Anasuya, answering all her questions and resolving her doubts, especially about the mechanical working of things. Another of her room-mates is Marko, who works as a farmer, cook and stove-maker. He uses solar energy for his work. Then there is big Parul, a technician, who spends her day with machines and made the life of the City easy. She is described as round and curvaceous and enjoys eating. Marko tends to her by cooking a tasty meal using various spices and herbs. The fourth member is Lost Silaf. Silaf is a short and quiet woman, and takes care of the others when they are sick. She is also recovering from the loss of her lover's death and spends most of her time in the garden tending to herbs and flowers. For Anasuya, Silaf is no less than a mystery, yet she wished she could be as unself-conscious, as comfortable, as "unlost" as Silaf.

Palanik, Marko, Parul, and Silaf are Anasuya's housemates and they gave her everything: a home, companionship and even love. Yet, Anasuya worries that she cannot compensate for the same, and she has nothing to offer in return. Her knowledge, experience and *athmis* are of no use to them. Even though they are proud of Anasuya's achievements at the Temple, they can hardly understand the nature of her work. The sea, which is so significant for her, has little meaning for them.

There are also other people in the City who seem more alien than her, such as the Master, yet Anasuya cannot get over her own foreign status and her feeling of being away from home. At the City, what she misses most about Sagara is the difference in the atmosphere. She yearns for the sound of rain and water. It rains only about twice a year and on each occasion the brief rain seems to her a mockery of the plenteousness of the ocean. The City, as opposed to the natural habitat of Sagara, is very mechanical. The City always carries a certain odor of stone and metal, the invisible clutter of the machinery that smoothly underlies the workings of the city. The people of the City plant polyps in their bodies, and some even use them as full body armour.

Anasuya's feeling of being an outsider and her sense of unease in the City increases with the increase in the number of brown spots on her body. After she discovers the secret to faster than light travel, she works doubly hard on creating her artwork. It is during this time that Anasuya notices that "the soliforms were dying."[143] She was being troubled by black spots in the amnion as she worked on the *sthanas* and she realizes that she is the cause of these spots. Anasuya associates losing her mathematical vision with turning brown. Without her *athmis*, she expresses a wish to die. In the hope of a cure, Anasuya also approaches a healer, who, after examining her blood, assures her that the spiroforms are still thriving, but that it is difficult to say how long they will thrive. She is overcome by the feeling that she is doomed. By the time Anasuya finishes her masterpiece, she has turned completely brown and hence feels no need to paint the brown patches to green.

When Anasuya sees her reflection in the mirror, she has turned into that image of a woman with a brown face and dark eyes which would appear to her, during her work on the *sthanas*. Having lost her *athmis*, Anasuya feels the urge to return home and tell her people about the discovery of hyperspace; she had about fourteen years of time to do so, since the Tiranis would take that much time to reach home.

3.6.2.2 *Athmis*

As mentioned in the text, Anasuya is invited to be a part of the Temple of Mathematical Arts because of her *athmis*. This makes her not only unique but also desirable. The *athmis* is referred to as "The sudden crescendo of mathematical harmonies in her mind, as she floated in the marsh forest: in the fractual landscape,... The myriad geometries surrounding her."[144]

In addition, Anasuya's *athmis*, which is beautiful and benevolent, is quite common among her people. There are other kinds of *athmis* too, but less gracious than the one Anasuya got. For instance, some could perceive the dreams of another, or see different worlds, which were beyond the purview of rationality and sanity.

From the time Anasuya attains the *athmis*, she gains knowledge not only of the sea and its harmonies but also of various fields such as:

> the use of herbs to prevent or enable pregnancy,... She came to know the men by their individual geometries, their particular graces of speech and movement,... She learned the language of bodies.[145]

Hasha is Anasuya's lover, and his *athmis* is extremely intense. He dreams of unknown worlds which neither he nor anyone else has any knowledge about. He describes them as unusual yet magnificent. Hasha possesses a restlessness that both worries and thrills Anasuya.

Hasha would often share his thoughts with Anasuya and talk about the visions he has:

> Great, gleaming structures moving through emptiness,...He wanted to roam the world and find the places he saw in his visions, even though the elders said those places didn't exist except in his mind.[146]

Hasha is counseled by his elders to stay within the circle, since leaving is not suitable for the children of the sea. Yet they are unable to prevent Hasha from dreaming about the other worlds; his thirst for discovery remains unquenched until he meets a brown man on the shores of Sagara. This man confirms Hasha's visions and gradually they both disappeared. Then Anasuya knew that Hasha would never return. The *athmis* enables Anasuya to appreciate artworks and the beauty of nature around her better than before. At some point she also raises the question how one could separate god from non-god, especially if one's *athmis* was active in them. It is the gift of *athmis* that makes her so popular in the City and because of which she is able to solve the mathematical poem and discover hyperspace.

However, we learn that towards the final stages of discovery Anasuya turns brown, and that she then loses her mathematical sight.

3.6.2.3 Sthanas *and hyperspace*

As mentioned earlier, a set of mathematicians from Tirana travel for eighteen years with a set of mathematical equations. They come to the Temple of

Mathematical Arts seeking a solution. Of their five-member team, Nirx, the mathematician, has discovered these equations or a mathematical poem. The renown of the Temple of Mathematical Art is far and wide. No other place is more capable and popular than this for the resolution of a mathematical poem. This poem is then offered to Anasuya, their most accomplished worker.

The *sthanas* is also described as a mathematical country that is yet to be explored. Investigating the *sthanas* gave Anasuya an enthusiasm and excitement. The experience of immersing herself in the amnion as she works on the *sthanas*, and solves the mathematical equations, is described by the narrator elaborately as a sixth sense that revealed before her the synchronizations, natural and artificial, that formed the subtext of the creation and she looked for peculiarities, slithered over manifolds, and drafted out the abstract, mountainous territory of bizarre mathematical functions.

For Anasuya, her work on the *sthanas* is like making art because while making a join or cut; one has to make choices that were, at their core, aesthetic in nature.

Such a discovery and understanding also leads Anasuya to perform better in the amnion and achieve faster results. While working on mathematical problems she realizes that the *sthanas* were indeed a seven-dimensional, differentiable manifold, homeomorphic sphere, but with an exotic differentiable structure. Nirx was enormously pleased with this discovery.

The silver lines also identify the woman Anasuya sees during the sessions and she chooses to name her 'Vara.' Vara provides to her visions of an artwork of astonishing beauty, which inspires Anasuya to create art. She also discerns that the art which inspires her is inseparable from the mathematics of the *sthanas*. The same motivation is required to work on both. Nirx is also highly appreciative of this union of mathematics and art that is present in the working culture at the Temple, not be found where she comes from. Anasuya works hard at creating her artwork, and in the process creates one which is appreciated by many, which contains the image of Vara. She calls this a 'breakthrough,' although her best piece of art was yet to be made.

Anasuya knows that she is close to her final artwork, but is also aware that it will be possible only after she has understood Nirx's mathematics. The confluence of art and mathematics will give her the requisite knowledge. Anasuya's expertise in making art helps her increasingly to build mastery in solving mathematical equations. Furthermore, her gift has never helped her more.

Keeping in mind the idea that the union of art and mathematics is the key, Anasuya entered the amnion and followed across a silver line, which, according to her, was a curve where four-d subspace transected and was submerged in seven-d *sthanas*. Suddenly, she is able to see clearly and form a connection between things. Anasuya recalls a dream in which she saw Lata, who extends a strand of hair to her, as if enabling her to cross the horizon; there is also similar image of Vara with strands of hair flowing;

she is also reminded of the large distance that separates her and Nirx from their respective homes; she recalls a conversation she overhears between the Tiranis during which they were discussing an idea that can reform the universe; in addition, she hears of Kar-Pthath, a devotee of the Nameless Goddess, he "had wanted to discover how our reality lay coiled within the body of the Goddess. And it came to her why the Tiranis would travel for eighteen years each way for this secret." Vara had also been hinting at the same throughout as she often repeated, "I have no time... Take an empty space and create something in it..."[147]

Kar-Pthath had passed away a few years before Anasuya came to the Temple. His work is similar to that of Nirx, while Nirx's poem is intricate and elaborate, Kar-Pthath's work is simple and vague. Anasuya is shocked to know all this while the Tiranis had hid from her the true nature of the *sthanas*. She declares to them in a loud voice that she has uncovered the secret, "This sthanas of Nirx's equations. It is the geometry of mata-reality. The four-d manifold is our space and time."[148]

The Tiranis refer to the same as "hyperspace, the greater beyond."[149] This would set free humanity from the domination of sub-light travel and will bring people together at last. This discovery would enable movement from one planet to another in the shortest time span. It is also referred to as "near-instantaneous travel."[150] Both the engineers from Tirana and experts at the Temple would use the understanding of hyperspace and assemble a ship. The gift of mathematics which the Temple provides would allow its citizens to "navigate the universe!... The age of the slow ships will be over..."[151]

3.6.2.4 Love

As described earlier, Anasuya is welcomed in a pentad by her four house-mates. She receives warmth, companionship and closeness from them, and is privileged to find a home as against living in the common room of the Temple like most newcomers.

It is clear that Anasuya is most fond of Palanik in the house, yet she also has immense affection for her other lovers. They all make life special for one another.

Whenever Anasuya is at home, all the housemates rejoice and indulge in a feast accompanied by love making, referred to in the novella as *joran*. Marko cooks the meal using selective spices and herbs to bring out its taste. Parul is specifically fond of eating and Marko takes special efforts to satiate her taste buds.

In a traditional pentad, the *joran* took place regularly, with all the necessary customs involved, and, if need be, the members of the pentad would travel together. Here a person was singled out as someone who stimulated others and initiated the action, called the *kendr*.

Hence, Anasuya's *joran* was unconventional in its own unique way, like the distinct personalities of each of her lovers.

3.6.3 *Issues and concerns in Of Love and Other Monsters*

3.6.3.1 *Meta-mind*

Arun's particular passion in the novella is the study of minds that sets him apart from other people. He likes to go into a group of housewives haggling over turnips or a crowd at a cricket match. He studies the embryological prospect of the meta-mind. Arun, the narrator, shares with the readers that there are different kinds of minds. The first kinds he describes are the 'solitons', such minds remain unaffected by a meta-mind and walk through it as if nothing were there. They take nothing nor do they give anything. He could sense them well, but could not pull them into forming a meta-mind. Of 'solitions,' because their minds moved through his jumbled meta-minds the way a man walks through a large, empty field on his way home taking nothing leaving nothing behind.

A second category of minds are referred as 'blanks' by Arun. He could not sense these minds as they were closed to him. They "did not register on his radar."[152] Arun felt afraid of such minds and treated them with suspicion. Such minds made him anxious. Another category of minds is that which Arun calls 'sensitive.' Janani has such a mind. It means that although she did not possess the unique talent to create a meta-mind, she, however, could sense if one was trying to draw her into one.

Arun learns and practices the art of meta-mind at the market, during the time he lives under the guardianship of Janani. He would observe the vendors, and the various shoppers who bargained for fruits and vegetables. At that time he tried to sense the intricate topography of each mind full of emotional fluxes.

Arun also liked to play a game where he would lie on the branch of a large tree, close his eyes and try to guess who were all passing below him through their mind-signature. In case the passerby was a stranger, Arun could guess nothing about the person, not even if it were a male or female by reading their mind-signature. But, at the same time if it were someone he knew, he could read the inner contours of the mind.

It is during the same time, when Arun lives with Janani that Rahul Moghe tries to reach Arun by making a connection with his mind. Janani, as mentioned earlier, is a 'sensitive' and is able to sense if a meta-mind is being formed. She also cautions Arun to stay away from Moghe as he is dangerous and means harm to humanity. Moghe is the only other person who shares Arun's talent. At the same time, Janani encourages Arun to study, learn computers and develop a reading habit. With time and Janani's advice, Arun progresses significantly and also begins to read voraciously in Hindi and English.

Arun's knowledge and expertise in different fields such as computers, reading, and his hobby of meta-mind leads him to the understanding that sensing other minds through writing –whether English or Hindi or computer code – is a key that opens the doors to other minds.

Arun gradually improves his English; with the computer diploma, he receives a job offer in Delhi. His work is to check software for defects. His routine is relaxed and he finds the job easy. It is during this time that Arun begins to explore his talent in a more methodical manner. He realizes that there are only few people who are 'solitons' throughout and maintain that state of mind. However, all people assume a 'solition' state for brief periods of time. Apart from humans, in Delhi, Arun also experiments with animals. He is able to sense their minds, but finds it difficult to understand the essence of their thoughts. On a certain day when he was coming back from work, Arun saw a splendid bull standing in the midst of a road. Across the roads were a few cows that seemed to pay no attention to the bull. Arun senses that the bull was making an endless summons of desire to the cows, and the cows politely declined the offer. After this incident, Arun becomes aware of the fact that animals not only have the ability to sense one another's minds, but can also make contact mentally.

Arun's experiments with humans are taken to a new level and understanding when he reaches America, referred to as the "land of milk and honey."[153] Irrespective of the idea of individualism in which Americans believed, that every individual is unique and hence different, Arun came in contact with large sets of people who shared the same belief systems and mental processes. He was thrilled to find that seemingly the most competitive people who frequented Wall Street could form a seamless and stable meta-mind. It was equally easy for Arun to form a meta-mind with the suburban, extremely prosperous Americans. With the teenagers also, who asserted their individuality through their branded clothing and anxious looks, Arun found it easy to build a meta-mind. However, with this group there could be felt a dark undercurrent which bothered Arun, as if the dam was overflowing with water and about to burst. A similar disturbing experience occurs when Rahul Moghe finds Arun in America and creates a meta-mind of supreme power which is composed of around twenty minds, twisted and tangled together, not arbitrarily but with the convolutedness, order, and beauty of an integrated circuit. Arun is drawn out of bed and drives ten miles from his place to find that which was exercising such a strong hold on his mind. This meta-mind is built on the seventh floor of a building and it is leading its subjects one by one to jump from the window.

Arun discerns that he must intervene in order to save the people from dying and slips into the meta-mind. Arun undoes the meta-mind, but is attracted in the direction of Moghe as he recognizes the familiar waves of his mind. Moghe then communicates with Arun through the feelers of his mind, building an intimacy. Moghe tells Arun that the meta-mind he saw is only a trailer of what they can build together. Both their capacities, when combined, can create a magnificent meta-mind that can make the present one seem like a child. Moghe wishes to tell Arun the truth about their species, and who Arun really is. Moghe mutters to him, "You belong to me... you and I are one of a kind... both alien, both lost, both pretending to belong..."[154]

From the time Arun meets Moghe, he becomes preoccupied with questions about who he is, what had happened to him, whether he was really an alien and if Janani was his 'murderer.' After he moves to America, he changes several jobs, often living in a depressed and anxious state. Arun eventually moves to India and takes up a position as a lecturer at a college in South Delhi. He continues to experiment with mind-weaving; however, it was not with the excitement which he experienced in his earlier days. It was also a reminder to him that he was not human, which affected him largely. Arun would use his skills of mind-weaving to resolve arguments and also to help him to get to know the students better.

Binodini, Arun's colleague at college, emerges as a good friend and an interesting mind to study because her mind is strong, beautiful and its fluxes and transformations are smooth and controlled.

Binodini teaches sociology at the same college and Arun feels attracted to the shape of her mind. She conducts research into groups that believe in the existence of supernatural beings and UFO sightings. Together, they talk of such phenomena and watch SF films.

3.6.3.2 Love

Arun feels attraction and love towards both men and women in *Of Love and Other Monsters*. We are told at the very beginning of the novella that Arun has no recollection of the time before the fire. He can only remember that Janani rescued him from the fire. She is his progenitor who gives him a name and identity. Arun learns to do everything afresh. He says, "It was like learning to live again… all was new, strange, and endlessly fascinating…"[155] Most of his knowledge about the world was either given by Janani or by observing his surroundings, including sex and desire. It is significant to note that Arun's longings are 'nebulous,' and that they are not defined clearly. He is also not simply physically attracted to a person, but the shape of their mind. Hence, the beauty or intricacy of the mind is more significant. While Arun is drawn to the tea-seller's daughter, he is equally attracted towards a barber, thin, shy, clean-shaven man, whose appearance would not attract many.

Amongst the few people to whom Arun feels attracted both mentally and physically is Dulari. A fourteen-year-old girl, Dulari is a sex worker whom Arun rescues with the help of a local women's group. She is later given work at a clothing shop. Arun comes across Dulari while wandering through the streets of Old Delhi; he finds her standing in a doorway which turns out to be a brothel. Her mind feels to him as if she had struck him with a blow between his eyes. Arun senses helplessness about her so much so that he instinctively moves towards her. Underneath her frail body, Arun is able to admire the depth of her mind.

Another character who occupies a significant place in Arun's journey is Manek, his colleague in Delhi. We are told that Manek's mind is clear and simple like a neatly arranged room and his thoughts and emotions are quite coherent. Manek confides in Arun that he loves a young woman, but he cannot marry her because of class and caste issues and the beloved's family has started looking for a suitable match for the girl. Manek is in a depressed state of mind and grows close to Arun. Manek seeks in Arun the comfort he found in his partner. On a certain day, Manek visits Arun at his rented room, almost in tears and Arun hugs him empathetically.

Manek is followed by Sheela, a quiet, plain-looking woman who lives in the flat above Arun's. She is the oldest of daughters in her household and is unmarried. Her other sisters have been married off. What distinguishes her from Arun's other lovers is that she never spoke a word and conveyed her emotions by touch or glance. Arun finds Sheela to be fascinating yet he feels the most intense love for Sanakaran, a postdoctoral researcher he meets in a café in Boston.

As mentioned earlier, Sankaran is a 'soliton,' who walks through a meta-mind Arun weaves without being affected. In Sankaran, Arun finds a kind of innocence and child-like quality that was also common to Dulari, but without the agony. Sankaran arouses in Arun a sweet desire to touch his mind as well as body. He longs for his Sanakaran's touch, even if it is for an instant.

Arun spends as much time he can with Sankaran, sometimes on the pretext of cooking or learning the astronomical chart. Arun is distraught when he learns that Sankaran's family is looking for a bride for him and that he will soon be married. Arun says, "But for an accident of gender and the cruelty of convention, I would have married him in a minute."[156] Sankaran is a devotee of Lord Shiva and keeps a small stone Shiv-lingam in his room. This stone reminds Arun of how he would pretend to be a woman for his old lover, Manek. Arun is also reminded of *Ardhanarishwaram*, one of the manifestations of Shiva, half-man, half-woman. Yet he cannot marry Sankaran or try to convince Sankaran to marry a man.

Furthermore, Arun also has a sexual encounter with Janani after Rahul Moghe tries to make contact with Arun for the first time. Janani is concerned that Moghe may cause some harm to Arun and exhorts him to stay away from Moghe. That particular night, Janani makes love to Arun. After this, she informs Arun that they must part; he must make a living for himself, and stay away from Moghe.

Another pair of lovers can be found in Rinu Devi and Janani. Rinu is described in the novella as a good-looking, middle-aged woman who works as a tailor in Rishikesh. Janani joins Rinu after she parts ways with Arun. They had previously been in love for more than a decade. From Rinu, Arun learns that Janani was part of a network of people who could sense aliens. Whenever they receive news about an unusual event - they reach that place. In the case that they find an alien, such as Arun, they arrange a burning and take away their powers. Janani goes for a similar activity to Bangkok, but she herself is burned in the fire. Arun discovers that it is Rinu who had betrayed her lover. Janani is more dedicated to the network than she is to Rinu, which disappoints Rinu. That is why she betrays Janani by giving this information to Moghe. Janani is then killed by Moghe. Rinu always finds a second place in Janani's life. Jealousy pervades over her love.

3.6.3.3 Boundaries

We learn in the novella that Arun is an alien and that the only other person with his unique talent of meta-weaving is Rahul Moghe. We also learn that Arun has no recollection of his past and that the only information he receives is from Moghe and Janani. It is as if his life begins after the fire from which Janani rescues him. While he recuperates from the burns, Arun can sense things very faintly from his past, like symbols, numbers, words, shapes. Janani not only gives him a name, but also teaches him how to live. She tutors him on everything from how to brush his teeth, use the toilet, wash utensils, and chop herbs. Janani runs a small shop where she dispenses herbs for different ailments from stomach ache to unfulfilled love and this is how she makes a living. Arun feels that he has no identity; he has nowhere to go and takes refuge in Janani. The Hindi syllables feel unfamiliar to him, and he spends hours in front of the mirror, trying to recognize his own face. Everything seems strange, new and exceedingly fascinating. Gradually, however, he finds himself thinking less about his old life and gets engaged in daily activities.

However much Arun tries to fit it and think of himself as human, he is often reminded of things from what may be his past. After Arun registers for computer classes on Janani's insistence, he discerns that he had the aptitude for programming. Working with numbers, instructions, logic and symbols always invoke in him a feeling that these have to do with things he learned in his old life. Another thing that makes Arun stand out from others around him is that he does not understand the social conventions of being a man or a woman. He does not behave according to stereotypes. Observing others, the realization returns to him that he is different.

Arun can be seen as the prototype of a sensitive male who can treat a woman with respect without looking at her as an object of desire. He is not compelled to observe the stereotype that women at clubs are there for flirting. Women can confide easily in him and feel safe in his company. Such a man may appear as an 'alien' or rare, but there is a hint from the narrator that this would be conducive to a safer and livable world for women. Arun watches cooking shows as well as cricket and wrestling, again breaking gender stereotypes. He is not overshadowed with the idea of emphasizing his maleness. In fact, Arun affirms that his skill of sensing minds has empowered him to look at human beings as a life form that goes past 'man–woman categories.'

Arun is extremely unhappy when, due to the conventions of society and the sameness of gender, he cannot marry Sankaran. He feels bound and suffocated in these boundaries that humans have created for themselves, which prevent them from expressing themselves. This injustice also reminds him of 'Ardhanarishwaram': half-man, half-woman, manifestation of Lord Shiva. His point is that if God can be both a man and woman, then why not him. In fact, Arun rectifies his concept of 34 genders. His conception considers each gender to be a colour in a spectrum, yet there is no clear demarcation between the colours as one bleeds into another. When Arun feels worried about being an alien or human, Binodindi assures him that the two terms are just labels. One need not get carried away by the meanings they carry.

Arun learns the truth about himself from Moghe that he does not belong to earth, but in fact they owe loyalty to a different star, 'Sapt-Rishi.' Arun comes to know that they both are aliens to earth and all along they have been pretending to belong. Yet they have not received the kind of acceptance expected by them.

Moghe maintains that such divides or stifling boundaries do not exist in their world. He tells Arun the truth about his people. According to the ancient tradition, their species was in the early stages of evolution when they went among the stars and colonized a number of worlds, the earth being one of them. But shortly afterward, their own world sank into an age of darkness and unconsciousness. Moghe adds that, in place of melding and fusing with one another to achieve solidarity and fellowship, they put up barriers. This began their downfall.

People from Moghe's star also built ships to reach the colonizers. Unfortunately, for ages there was no contact between them and the colonized world. It was mandatory that the colonizers return in order for their history to be complete. It is for this reason that Moghe and his fellow men set out and landed on the Earth to search for their kinds. On Earth, Moghe faces a lot many difficulties, which includes escaping from a burning arranged by humans. His spaceship gets destroyed and he is to wander endlessly from one continent to another in search of the colonizers.

The colonizers not only took over the native species, which includes both humans and animals, but also fused with the mind-shapes of the natives. This shows that they turned native to such an extent that they forgot who they were. It is the task of Rahul Moghe to free the original colonizers from their ongoing state. This is possible only with the help of Arun. Together, they can build a meta-mind to send a message across into space for help. They would have to form a mind-weave between a minimum of hundred thousand human minds. Moghe emphasizes:

> that this great melding of minds will free the original colonizers from their current state. They will realize who they really are. They will leave with us when the ship comes. Even if they cannot take corporeal form, we can find some way to take them with us. To go home...[157]

Since Arun was burnt by Janani, he could no longer change form like Moghe; his power to do so has been taken away by the network. However, Moghe brings to him a liberation that he had not experienced with anyone else. Arun resents the boundaries humans have built on the basis of which they discriminate. These boundaries prevent humans from communicating on a personal level and instead get stuck in the formal binary divides of man–woman, body–mind. What the humans lack is the ability to communicate from mind to mind, which may be dormant. According to Arun, this ability may be present in those humans who were colonized.

Arun and Moghe suggest that it may be possible for humans to revive their ability to communicate with one another freely through their minds, to rise above the prejudices and biases that we harbor towards one another. There is a kind of cruelty that humans exhibit for one another that is pointless. This can also be seen in the behavior of Janani and her network toward the aliens. They would sense the alien, arrange a burning and take away their powers. These aliens would be left lifeless, often found either in mental hospitals, or begging and wandering the streets. This is a very inhuman and harsh treatment for a set of people that are harmless. They only came to Earth to recover their own species to take back to their planet. In fact, while searching for Moghe, Arun realizes that humans were responsible for many calamities and disasters. Arun follows the trail of disasters and unexplained violent events only to discover that they were the results of human actions and not those of any aliens. Hence, one can rightly say that 'humans' and 'aliens' are just labels; it is actions which determine your true nature.

Notes

1   Hasan, Md. Mahmudul. "Commemorating Rokeya Sakhawat Hossain and Contextualizing her Work in South Asian Muslim Feminism". 2013, p. 45
2   Hasan, Md. Mahmudul. "Commemorating Rokeya Sakhawat Hossain and Contextualizing her Work in South Asian Muslim Feminism". 2013, p.45
3   Hossain, Yasmin. "The Begum's Dream: Rokeya Sakhawat Hossain and the Broadening of Muslim Women's Aspirations in Bengal". 1992
4   Hasan, Md. Mahmudul. "Commemorating Rokeya Sakhawat Hossain and Contextualizing her Work in South Asian Muslim Feminism". 2013, p. 45
5   Singh, Amardeep. "Where Women Rule and Mirrors are Weapons". *Lehigh University*. May 14, 2006. Web. July 15, 2013. http://www.lehigh.edu/~amsp/2006/05/where-women-rule-and-mirrors-are.html.
6   Hossain, S. Rokeya. "Sultana's Dream". *Penguin*. January 14, 2005. Web. June 25, 2013 http://digital.library.upenn.edu/women/sultana/dream/dream.html.
7   Hasan, Md. Mahmudul. "Commemorating Rokeya Sakhawat Hossain and Contextualizing her Work in South Asian Muslim Feminism". 2013, p. 42
8   Ibid., p. 42
9   Ibid., pp. 42–43
10 Ray, Bharathi. *Early Feminists of Colonial India: Sarala Devi Chaudhurani and Rokeya Sakhawat Hossain*, 2002, p. IX
11 Hasan, Md. Mahmudul. "Commemorating Rokeya Sakhawat Hossain and Contextualizing her Work in South Asian Muslim Feminism". 2013, p. 47
12 Ibid., p. 47
13 Hasan, Md. Mahmudul. "Commemorating Rokeya Sakhawat Hossain and Contextualizing her Work in South Asian Muslim Feminism". 2013, p. 48
14 Hasan, Md. Mahmudul. "Commemorating Rokeya Sakhawat Hossain and Contextualizing her Work in South Asian Muslim Feminism". 2013, p. 49
15 Ghoshal, Somak. August 24, 2013. Web. August 25, 2013. http://www.livemint.com/Leisure/DKDlAqUKyUTCHlJgB5enoI/Writers-At-Work--Manjula-Padmanabhan.html.
16 Inflibnet. Shodhganga. "Chapter VI. Charting a Vision for the Future: Manjula Padmanabhan's Escape and Arun Joshi's The City and The River". p. 14

17   Ibid., p. 14

18   This information has been collected from Vandana Singh's website http://users. rcn.com/singhvan/.

19   Singh, Vandana. "About the Author". Web. May 25, 2014. http://users.rcn. com/singhvan/AboutAuthor.html

20   Singh, Vandana. Antariksha Yatra. "Alternate Visions: Some Musings on Diversity in SF". May 27, 2014. Web. May 31, 2014. http://vandanasingh.wordpress. com/2014/05/27/alternate-visions-some-musings-on-diversity-in-sf/.

21   Ibid.

22   Singh, Vandana. Antariksha Yatra. "Alternate Visions: Some Musings on Diversity in SF". May 27, 2014. Web. May 31, 2014. http://vandanasingh.word-press.com/2014/05/27/alternate-visions-some-musings-on-diversity-in-sf/.

23   Ibid.

24   Ibid.

25   Ibid.

26   Singh, Vandana. Antariksha Yatra. "Alternate Visions: Some Musings on Diversity in SF". May 27, 2014. Web. May 31, 2014. http://vandanasingh.word-press.com/2014/05/27/alternate-visions-some-musings-on-diversity-in-sf/.

27   Ibid.

28   Ibid.

29   Ibid.

30   Singh, Vandana. Antariksha Yatra. "Alternate Visions: Some Musings on Diversity in SF". May 27, 2014. Web. May 31, 2014. http://vandanasingh.word-press.com/2014/05/27/alternate-visions-some-musings-on-diversity-in-sf/.

31   Singh, Vandana. "Younguncle Comes to Town". Web. May15, 2014. http:// users.rcn.com/singhvan/YuncleUS.html

32   Goodwin, H. Geoffrey. "An Interview with Vandana Singh". August 2006. Web. September 2013. http://www.bookslut.com/features/2006_08_009677. php.

33   Goodwin, H. Geoffrey. "An Interview with Vandana Singh". August 2006. Web. September 2013. http://www.bookslut.com/features/2006_08_009677. php.

34   Singh, Vandana. "If You See Something, Say Something: The Scientist as Activist". *Climate Change: Learning, Communicating, Acting.* February 4, 2014. Web. June 5, 2014. http://climatechange4perspectives.wordpress. com/2014/02/04/if-you-see-something-say-something-the-scientist-as-activist/.

35   Chabria, S. Priya. "The Autobiography of a Goddess-Translating The Autobiography of a Goddess: Concept". September 2013. Web. May 2014. http://www.kaurab.com/themudproposal/priya-chabria/Aandaal-Project.pdf

36   Ibid.

37   Sarma, Dibyajyoti. "Priya Sarukkai-Chabria: Writer forever". *I write, riot.* September 23, 2006. Web. May 2013. http://writeriot.blogspot.in/2006/09/ priya-sarukkai-chabria-writer-forever.html.

38   Ibid.

39   Sarma, Dibyajyoti. "Priya Sarukkai-Chabria: Writer forever". *I write, riot.* September 23, 2006. Web. May 2013. http://writeriot.blogspot.in/2006/09/ priya-sarukkai-chabria-writer-forever.html.

40   Ibid.

41   "Sultana's Dream" (1905) was originally published in *The Indian Ladies' Magazine*, Madras, in English. This edition is transcribed from *Sultana's dream and Padmarag: two feminist utopias* by Rokeya Sakhawat Hossain; translated with an introduction by Barnita Bagchi. New Delhi (India): Penguin, 2005.

42   *Zenana* is a part of the house meant specifically for upper class women; it is a way of segregating them.

43   The *zenana* is called *mardana* after the men are placed there.

44 Singh, Amardeep. "Where Women Rule and Mirrors are Weapons". *Lehigh University*. May 14, 2006. Web. July 15, 2013. http://www.lehigh. edu/~amsp/2006/05/where-women-rule-and-mirrors-are.html.

45 Hasanat, Fayeza. "Sultana's Utopian Awakening: An Eco-critical Reading of Rokeya Sakhawat Hossain's *Sultana's Dream*". *Asiatic*. Vol.7.2, 2013, p. 118

46 Maulana Abul Kalam Azad was a significant figure in the Indian Independence movement and an Indian scholar. He also became the first Minister of Education after Independence.

47 Sutra, Videshi. "Bengali Feminist Sci-Fi: "Sultana's Dream" by Roquia Hussain". February 6, 2014. Web. March 8, 2014. http://videshisutra.com/2013/02/06/bengali-feminist-sci-fi-sultanas-dream-by-rokheya-shekhawat-hossein/#_ftn2.

48 Ibid.

49 Valiyamttam, Rositta J. "Rositta Joseph: Manjula Padmanabhan's Escape". *Muse India*. Issue 60, March–April 2014. Web. April 2014. http://www. museindia.com/featurecontent.asp?issid=46&id=3753

50 Padmanabhan, Manjula. *Escape*. 2008, p. 406

51 Valiyamttam, Rositta J. "Rositta Joseph: Manjula Padmanabhan's Escape". *Muse India*. Issue 60, March–April 2014. Web. April 2014. http://www. museindia.com/featurecontent.asp?issid=46&id=3753.

52 Valiyamttam, Rositta J. "Rositta Joseph: Manjula Padmanabhan's Escape". *Muse India*. Issue 60, March–April 2014. Web. April 2014. http://www. museindia.com/featurecontent.asp?issid=46&id=3753.

53 Matthan, Ayesha. "Legend of the clone". *The Hindu*. April 1, 2008. Web. January 10, 2013. http://www.thehindu.com/todays-paper/tp-features/tp-metroplus/legend-of-the-clone/article1411808.ece

54 Ibid.

55 Ibid.

56 Singh, Vandana. *Of Love and Other Monsters*. 2007, p. 19

57 'City' is used here as a name of a place, hence capital 'C' is used.

58 Singh, Vandana. *Distances*. 2008, p. 2

59 Mathegraphia is the art of being skilled in mathematical operations as has been mentioned in the text.

60 Hossain, Yasmin. "The Begum's Dream: Rokeya Sakhawat Hossain and the Broadening of Muslim Women's Aspirations in Bengal". *South Asia Research*. 12.1, 1992, p. 2

61 Ibid., p.3

62 Ibid., p.3

63 Hossain, S. Rokeya. "Sultana's Dream". *Penguin*. January 14, 2005. Web. June 25, 2013 http://digital.library.upenn.edu/women/sultana/dream/dream.html.

64 Hossain, S. Rokeya. "Sultana's Dream". *Penguin*. January 14, 2005. Web. June 25, 2013 http://digital.library.upenn.edu/women/sultana/dream/dream.html.

65 Hossain, Yasmin. "The Begum's Dream: Rokeya Sakhawat Hossain and the Broadening of Muslim Women's Aspirations in Bengal". *South Asia Research*. 12.1, 1992, p. 7

66 Ibid., p.8

67 Hossain, Yasmin. "The Begum's Dream: Rokeya Sakhawat Hossain and the Broadening of Muslim Women's Aspirations in Bengal". *South Asia Research*. 12.1, 1992, p. 9

68 Subramaniam, Aishwarya. "Rev. of Sultana's Dream by Rokeya Sakhawat Hossain". *Strange Horizons*. September 30, 2013. Web. January 10, 2014. www.strangehorizons.com/reviews/2013/09/sultanas_dream_comments. shtml.

69 Lakhi, Mukti. "An Alternative Feminist Modernity: Feminist Utopia and the Quest for Home in Sultana's Dream". *Post Graduate English Journal*. Issue 14. 2006, p. 14

70   Lakhi, Mukti. "An Alternative Feminist Modernity: Feminist Utopia and the Quest for Home in Sultana's Dream". *Post Graduate English Journal*. Issue 14. 2006, p. 15
71   Defamiliarization is the process of making the familiar seem unfamiliar.
72   Hossain, S. Rokeya. "Sultana's Dream." *Penguin*. January 14, 2005. Web. June 25, 2013 http://digital.library.upenn.edu/women/sultana/dream/dream.html.
73   Ibid.
74   Lakhi, Mukti. "An Alternative Feminist Modernity: Feminist Utopia and the Quest for Home in Sultana's Dream". *Post Graduate English Journal*. Issue 14. 2006, p. 17
75   Lakhi, Mukti. "An Alternative Feminist Modernity: Feminist Utopia and the Quest for Home in Sultana's Dream". *Post Graduate English Journal*. Issue 14. 2006,
76   Ibid.
77   Ibid.
78   Hossain, S. Rokeya. "Sultana's Dream". *Penguin*. January 14, 2005. Web. June 25, 2013 http://digital.library.upenn.edu/women/sultana/dream/dream.html.
79   Ibid.
80   Ibid.
81   Lakhi, Mukti. "An Alternative Feminist Modernity: Feminist Utopia and the Quest for Home in Sultana's Dream". *Post Graduate English Journal*. Issue 14. 2006, p. 19
82   Ibid., p. 20
83   Lakhi, Mukti. "An Alternative Feminist Modernity: Feminist Utopia and the Quest for Home in Sultana's Dream". *Post Graduate English Journal*. Issue 14. 2006, p. 20
84   Hossain, S. Rokeya. "Sultana's Dream". *Penguin*. January 14, 2005. Web. June 25, 2013 http://digital.library.upenn.edu/women/sultana/dream/dream.html.
85   Lakhi, Mukti. "An Alternative Feminist Modernity: Feminist Utopia and the Quest for Home in Sultana's Dream". *Post Graduate English Journal*. Issue 14. 2006, p. 13
86   Hossain, S. Rokeya. "Sultana's Dream". *Penguin*. January 14, 2005. Web. June 25, 2013 http://digital.library.upenn.edu/women/sultana/dream/dream.html.
87   Hossain, S. Rokeya. "Sultana's Dream". *Penguin*. January 14, 2005. Web. June 25, 2013 http://digital.library.upenn.edu/women/sultana/dream/dream.html.
88   Ibid.
89   Hossain, S. Rokeya. "Sultana's Dream". *Penguin*. January 14, 2005. Web. June 25, 2013 http://digital.library.upenn.edu/women/sultana/dream/dream.html.
90   Ibid.
91   Ibid.
92   Ibid.
93   Hossain, S. Rokeya. "Sultana's Dream". *Penguin*. January 14, 2005. Web. June 25, 2013 http://digital.library.upenn.edu/women/sultana/dream/dream.html.
94   Padmanabhan, Manjula. *Escape*. 2008, p. 125
95   Ibid., p. 75
96   Padmanabhan, Manjula. *Escape*. 2008, p. 18
97   Valiyamttam, Rositta J. "Rositta Joseph: Manjula Padmanabhan's Escape". *Muse India*. Issue 60, March–April 2014. Web. April 2014. http://www.museindia.com/featurecontent.asp?issid=46&id=3753.
98   Ibid.
99   Poddar, Namrata. "Female foeticide and infanticide is the cancer that slowly kills us". Web. 2014 http://www.oneyoungworld.com/sites/www.oneyoungworld.com/themes/custom/oneyoungworld/pdf/Essay4.pdf.
100   Padmanabhan, Manjula. *Escape*. 2008, p. 75

101 Rositta, Joseph Valiyamattam. "Personal and national destinies in independent India a study of select Indian English novels". *Shodh Ganga*. September 19, 2013. Web. May 15, 2014. https://shodhganga.inflibnet.ac.in/bitstream/10603/8645/13/13_chapter%206.pdf. p. 15
102 Ibid., p. 15
103 Ibid., p. 16
104 Ibid., p. 16
105 Padmanabhan, Manjula. *Escape*. 2008, p. 146
106 Ibid., p. 146
107 Ibid., p. 127
108 Ibid., p. 269
109 Ibid., p. 269
110 Padmanabhan, Manjula. *Escape*. 2008, p. 270
111 Ibid., p. 64
112 Ibid., p. 66
113 Ibid., p. 146
114 Padmanabhan, Manjula. *Escape*. 2008, p. 237
115 Padmanabhan, Manjula. *Escape*. 2008, pp. 97–98
116 Ibid., p. 99
117 Chabria, Priya S. *Generation 14*. 2008, p. 16
118 Ibid., p. 17
119 Hereafter, Clone 14/54/G will be referred to as Clone
120 Chabria, Priya S. *Generation 14*. 2008, p. 33
121 Originals are the few human beings surviving in the Global Community. They are given special care and attention so that their race continues to produce offspring, which are vital for the social betterment of the Global Community. They are cloned to assure their existence even after their demise.
122 Chabria, Priya S. *Generation 14*. 2008, p. 35
123 Chabria, Priya S. *Generation 14*. 2008, p. 15
124 Ibid., p. 15
125 Ibid., p. 11
126 Chabria, Priya S. *Generation 14*. 2008, p. 68
127 Ibid., p. 103
128 Ibid., p. 106
129 Ibid., p. 107
130 Ibid., p. 133
131 Ibid., p. 280
132 Ibid., p. 30
133 Ibid., p. 282
134 Ibid., p. 177
135 http://hinduism.about.com/od/gurussaints/p/adishankara.html
136 Chabria, Priya S. *Generation 14*. 2008, p. 150
137 Ibid., p. 149
138 Ibid., p. 87
139 Lilly, N. E. "What is Speculative Fiction." *Green Tentacles*. March 2002. Web. April 2013. http://www.greententacles.com/articles/5/26/.
140 Singh, Vandana. *Distances*. 2008, p. 119
141 Ibid., p. 120
142 Ibid., p. 48
143 Ibid., p. 111
144 Ibid., p. 19
145 Ibid., p. 22
146 Ibid., pp. 22–23
147 Ibid., p. 83
148 Ibid., p. 85

149 Ibid., p. 82
150 Ibid., p. 88
151 Ibid., p. 92
152 Singh, Vandana. *Of Love and Other Monsters*. 2007, p. 12
153 Ibid., p. 19
154 Ibid., p. 35
155 Ibid., pp. 3–4
156 Ibid., p. 25
157 Ibid., p. 10

4 Radical elements and the use of conjunctions

4.1 Introduction

According to a popular definition, "a conjunction (abbreviated CONJ or CNJ) is an uninflected linguistic form that joins together sentences, clauses, phrases, or words … some common *conjunctions* are 'and,' 'but,' and 'although.'"[1] At the level of grammar it is used to connect two sentences; however, at the semantic level it enables the writer to express a dissimilarity or opposition.

> A compound sentence is a conjunction if its component sentences are joined by 'and.' It is a disjunction if they are joined by 'or.' The component sentences are, respectively, conjuncts, which are conjoined, and disjuncts, which are disjoined. 'Conjunction' and 'disjunction' can also mean the logical operations of forming such expressions. 'And' and 'or' here have only their joining force, without signifying, e.g. temporal order (as in 'He came and went'). 'Or' is usually inclusive ('either and 'perhaps both'), but can be exclusive ('either but not both'). Sometimes alternation replaces 'disjunction,' with alternant and alternate for 'disjunct' and 'disjoin.' Occasionally 'disjunction' and 'alternation' are distinguished, 'disjunction' being kept for the exclusive sense. Conjunctions in the ordinary sense ('and', 'or' etc.) are in logic called connectives…[2]

The focus of this chapter is to highlight and emphasize the conjunctions within the chosen texts.

When speaking of conjunctions, those ideas are underlined which contribute to bringing out the intent of the writer. These are the auxiliary ideas and elements which help to the maintain continuity in the text, contribute towards proving the authenticity of facts and also render a pleasing reading. It is interesting to note that the various 'connectives' serve different purposes. They not only maintain the literary quality of the text and link the imaginary world of SF with the living world, but also ensure a gratifying experience.

Conjunctions are noted at the level of words, phrases, sentences and this chapter includes examples of each. Conjunctions are also pointed out at the level of ideas, the various subthemes, incidents, characters or facts.

4.2 Different forms used as conjunctions

4.2.1 Word

In the opening lines of "Sultana's Dream," "But" is a connective word as it helps to take the narrative forward. The narrator speaks of falling asleep. In such a case perhaps the narrative would come to an end. The use of 'But' indicates that Sultana may not have dozed off; she describes her state as "wide awake," and what she experiences and learns is perhaps real. This arrangement places the story between the realm of the imaginary and real world, not leaving it as a work of mere fantasy. Another significant connector appears shortly afterwards in the story when Sultana, feeling awake, takes a walk with Sister Sara. The word "and" is significant here. The quoted lines indicate that it is Sultana's acceptance of an invitation for a walk, which she later finds is Ladyland, which allows the various issues in the story to unfurl. Just as they start to walk, Sultana finds that it is broad daylight and that the city is crowded. Sultana is extremely shy of being outdoors without her veil. Interestingly, she notices that there are no men on the streets. It is from this juncture in the story that Sultana learns just how much Ladyland differs from colonial Calcutta and how she can be as empowered as the women in Ladyland.

Sultana is reluctant to be outdoors, and she is told that such are the attributes of men in Ladyland. Hence she should not behave in such a manner. A few more exchanges between Sultana and Sister Sara reveal how women have managed to imprison the men within their homes.

Men referred to their scientific discoveries as romantic imagination. The women receive an opportunity to reply to their comments, not by words but by deed. The military officers take charge to fight the enemy, but the enemy's army advances closer to conquer their nation-state. The country is in a state of panic, especially the men. Most men are on the battlefield, which also includes sixteen-year-old boys. Many of them are either killed, wounded or tired of fighting. It is at this point that the women get together to devise a way to end the war and save their people and country. This plan necessitated that the men enter the *zenana*, renamed as *mardana* to denote the place segregated for men.

They attack the enemy with concentrated sunlight, this combination of heat and light aimed together became unbearable for the enemy and in a state of panic they all ran away. Because of fear and horror, they left their weapons behind and as they ran they were scorched in the same heat and light. After this incident, no one dared to attack Ladyland and the rule of the Queen was established. We are also told that ever since the men were put in the *mardana*, there have been no incidents of crime or sin; hence there is no police, or magistrate, in Ladyland.

The incident mentioned above is cited by Sister Sara to Sultana for a special purpose, since she would like Sultana to tell her fellow women that a place exists where women have the opportunity, respect and freedom to live independent lives. The need for women's education is evident, and the author shares its potentials and possibilities with the reader. It is underlined that if one uses their 'brain power' such an idyllic state can also be achieved in colonial Bengal. The author, through recounting this incident, also emphasizes that it is possible to do away with crime and criminals, without any bloodshed.

The topic of women's education in colonial Bengal was a controversial one, more so during the so-called Bengal Renaissance. Women were mostly kept away from public debates regarding the relevance of their education, and whether or not education should be given to them. Debates were also centred on the point that which subjects should the women be allowed to study, if at all. Most women, those had access to education around this time, were teenage brides who were taught by their large-hearted and good-natured husbands. Such an education, in many cases, took place secretively, without the knowledge of elders. In their daily lives women continued to show no signs of their education and to carry on with their conventional role. Rokeya also received her education in a similar manner, first through her elder brother and sister and eventually from her husband who taught her the English language.

Women's education received approval in colonial Bengal since it was promoted as one of the prerequisites of being a good wife. The belief propagated was that an educated woman would prove to be a better partner and a capable mother. Yet, in "Sultana's Dream" through the scientific inventions and progress that the women make, it is clear that the primary purpose of education must be to encourage learning of all kinds. Women are depicted as more worthy of receiving education, as compared to the men who use it to make weapons of war. Women use the gift of education to use nature's abundance for the well-being of their state, converting the entire country into a garden. Women emerge as the real champions in the story as they are successful in saving the country from enemies, making use of their innovations and knowledge of science.

"Now years back from that day, she drew her shift over the bare brown spot on her arm, and remembered. And thought: the sea dies in me."[3] Before these lines and the use of the word 'And' which connects and, in fact, brings back the story to the present, Anasuya digresses to talk about her past, her lover Hasha and how she reached the City. The author quickly shifts the scene by the use of the above sentences from talking about Anasuya's home and this time there to talk about a time when she is almost brown and also losing her mathematical sight. The phrase "the sea dies in me" embodies that thought.

In addition, an example of a word as a conjunction can be seen in the following paragraph: "She learned the language of bodies,… But most of all she learned the young man whose name was Hasha."[4] The word 'But' here acts as a conjunction which provides the transition from talking about what Anasuya learns as part of her training once she acquires her *athmis* to talking about Hasha, her lover. The *athmis* in Hasha is particularly prominent. In the absence of this word, the narrative would seem disconnected and lose its literary quality. Hasha's *athmis* enables a better understanding of Anasuya's *athmis*. Both their gifts are in contrast to one another. While Anasuya's *athmis* is ennobling, benevolent and peaceful, Hasha's *athmis* leaves him restless with visions of far-off worlds which he wants to visit and explore, which his elders forbid him from doing.

The three Uncles are debating whether they should continue with the herbs and potions which have slowed her growth and keep her forever hidden in this state, or tell Meiji about this and how she is the last surviving female. They continue to debate on this until Youngest uses the conjunction 'But' to focus on a more pertinent issue. His point is that even if they explain to Meiji the truth of her situation of being the sole member of an already extinct species and allow her to decide whether she would like to stay with her uncles and lead a life of an almost confinement or travel to a safer place, Meiji will be unable to understand the implications of what they convey. Her thinking has not developed fully to suit her age and circumstances, and she has no knowledge of women. The conjunction allows the reader to enter a very sensitive area that goes beyond the purview of making a choice. That Meiji does not even have the basic information to make a choice. And she is also not used to making a choice; she may not like to decide on her own. Meiji declines the right to decide and shows little inclination to accept her liberty. It makes little difference to her if she stays or leaves as she has no knowledge of life outside her home when she lives in the basement of the estate of the three brothers.

4.2.2 Phrase

A set of phrases which kick-start Manjula Padmanabhan's *Escape* and also provide a general idea of the novel are: "There are those who told us, the larger mission is impossible. It can't be done. To them we said, Be Bold."[5] Although it is mentioned that these lines are taken from the manual of Generals, who have exterminated the species of women, they can also be read as a declaration by the author on behalf of all the readers that although the task of saving the girl child from foeticide may seem impossible, it can be achieved. The message conveyed to the readers is that being bold and courageous is sufficient to solve any problem. The important step, of course, is to first acknowledge the issues.

Furthermore, a phrase that is also taken from the manual by the Generals is self-explanatory and brings out a major theme of the novel: "They were agents of mortality. By eliminating them, we eliminated mortality."[6] The reference is here to the species of women which has been eliminated completely from the country in which the story is set. Many references indicate that the referred place is India. This idea surfaces throughout the novel in different ways, either through the story of Meiji or through such captions from the manual of Generals.

Additionally, the phrase "The next time I saw Sankaran, I didn't see him" plays an important role as a conjunction. This particular line signifies that after his marriage, the shape of Sankaran's mind is no longer the same. Arun says upon meeting him, "I didn't even feel the quiet, clean wave of his mind wash over and refresh my soul."[7] This change appears in Sankaran after he marries to please his family. The marriage had clouded his mind with contradictions, which prevented him from being his original self. Again, social conventions are to blame. But this incident also takes Arun's attention away from Sankaran, and he can concentrate on finding Moghe and Janani.

In addition, the utterance, "I don't remember ever being free"[8] is an interesting point of study in the novel *Generation 14*, since it throws light on the theme of the treatment of women. This phrase comes from the 'visitation' named *The Watcher*. The events are conveyed through a female parrot. The given phrase epitomizes the female parrot's plight during 1857 and also that of other women of that time, in a Nawabi household. Although the parrot is free to eat and sleep, it is in a state of imprisonment. Similar is the case of women in *zenana*, who are free to eat, sleep and undertake other daily activities but are imprisoned in the *zenana*. The parrot's tongue is peeled to make its voice sweeter, its wings are clipped and its claws are capped, so that it may not hurt the Khan-Sahib's Begum. The parrot also feels trapped in a 'false sexuality', as the Begum refuses to accept the parrot as a female. This experience disturbs the parrot. While the parrot is in control of the Begum, the Begum is in turn at the behest of her husband Khan-Sahib. This is the kind of enslavement that the phrase discloses.

Chabria uses the phrase "The War against the Earth" to describe the state of decadence depicted in *Generation 14*. It is a world populated with clones, and the last few surviving human beings. The many life forms, of both flora and fauna, have been destroyed and extinct. Even the weather patterns have been disturbed. The ancestors did not take careful measures to ensure a regeneration of decaying forms. Negligence on their part led to many wars and a mechanization in the society. We are told that the official name for "The War against the Earth" is "The First Age of the Global Community." The first age merely focused on developing thirteen generations of clones. The 'War' is not just a violent war but a gradual destruction of humans, animals and vegetal.

4.2.3 Expressions/Idiomatic expressions

The expression, and the explanation of it given by Lata, prove to be a useful conjunction in *Distances* as it gives us more information about Anasuya and her Yra as,

> Yra's athmis gave her the ability to breathe under water and understand the language of the fish. That's why you can stay under water longer than most people![9]

The given lines provide us a history of Anasuya and another mother, Yra, who gave birth to Anasuya. Yra could swim under water and also decode their language. Hence, it is clear that Anasuya inherited this ability from her mother to stay under water for longer periods and the readers know that Anasuya solves the mathematical equations after she is immersed in water in the amnion. This information helps us to understand Anasuya and her ease with water and her fish-like activities. Her words "human beings, how they could be, simultaneously friend and betrayer. Murderer, mother, lover kind"[10] are significant reflections on the actions of humans.

Also, an expression that appears towards the start of the novel, *Generation 14*, continues throughout until it has manifested the point the author is trying to make. It's a chant, "'Buddham, Saranam Gacchami, Sangam Saranam Gachhami...'"[11] When Clone researches about this, she finds that the chant belongs to the period between 1st BCE and 8th CE to be commonly found in the caves of Ajanta. Further on in the novel, we learn that these words are chanted by acolytes in a monastery by young boys, who have been sent there to receive education. We are told that Bodhisattvas live amongst us on Earth, but we don't realize their presence. Yet, they are all around us, in some form or the other. Through other examples also, the author underlines the importance of goodness and kindness which Buddha preached. This is another subtheme of the novel.

4.2.4 Sentence(s)

A conversation between Nirx and her assistant Vishk proves to be both a conjunction and a clue which helps the story to progress in the right direction. Anasuya can understand their language; through the conversation she gets to know the nature of discovery which the Tiranis are expecting. Keeping this in mind, she uncovers a mysterious element in the solution-space, which the Tiranis had been keeping a secret. Taking a clue from the fact that the *sthanas* represents something unique and secret, Anasuya is able to direct her energies in the right direction and in no time she unravels that it has to do with faster-than-light-travel, which she also calls meta-reality. Hence, this particular set of sentences can be seen as a conjunction.

Another set of sentences which emphasizes one of the main themes of the novella is an exchange of dialogue between Arun and Rahul Moghe. Moghe says, "If your so-called friends could see you as you are, they would hate and revile you. I am the only friend you have, my love. We owe allegiance to a different star..."[12] These lines come in the middle of an incarceration which Arun goes through. During this process, Rahul Moghe, who is also an alien like Arun and possesses the same ability to form a meta mind, reveals the truth about Arun's origin. Moghe tells Arun that he was burnt by Janani and that his real powers were taken away from him. That is a major reason why Arun is unable to identify with many things on Earth. What disturbs him most is the divides which humans have established between man and woman and mind and body. The story also emphasizes that divides such as human-alien and mind-body are simply labels and that one must not become obsessed with the meanings they carry.

4.2.5 Paragraph

In these writings, there are many examples when a paragraph acts as a conjunction. It not only ensures the connectivity, but also helps the author to leave a hint about the real nature of the *sthanas*. It is towards the end of the novella that we learn that the strangeness Anasuya perceived in the "solution-space" was due to the fact that it represented a physical system, which Nirx had not disclosed.

In Manjula Padmanabhan's *Escape* there are many paragraphs that act as a conjunction and provide a lead about the kind of environmental degradation that is going to be described in the following pages. Through such paragraphs, one can note that most of the ecosystem and animal life has been destroyed. This will be dealt at length as the novel progresses, allowing the reader to take a cue of what even their world's situation could be if each individual does not assume responsibility to take corrective action. It could mean paying attention to the environment and also saving the girl child. In the novel a connection is continually drawn between women and nature.

Another paragraph regarding the killing of a pregnant female hare acts as a conjunction to the subject of female foeticide. Youngest kills a hare and finds that she was pregnant. This incident visualizes the atrocity, which shows the foetus that is about to die, while the mother dies before her children. This is also Meiji's first experience of seeing a mother and her children. She has never seen a woman and this instance in the novel introduces her to this concept, even if it is through an animal. Though the memory will travel with her, it takes her a while until she understands and learns about women.

A paragraph on cigarette papers in *Escape* provides information about the prevailing state of degradation and backwardness. Instead of moving forward, the civilization has in fact receded to the ancient ways of being. There is no money or currency available for transactions since these means have been discontinued by the Generals. Instead a barter system is in place. We are told that there are no mines, no refineries or any surviving heavy industry. All of the signs of progress have been scrapped. In a dronery, Youngest sees the kind of objects that we use in contemporary times, as relics of the past. They have been made redundant. He also saw a hat-stand that served the purpose of hanging fused light bulbs. Along with this there were the air conditioners and a car sliced into two halves, kept but serving no real purpose.

As the novel, *Escape*, progresses, the leap of Meiji is sharply indicated as she grows from a girl into a woman. The paragraph regarding this transition clearly indicates that Meiji is now more mature and that she can better articulate her situation. She is also able to address her anxieties and difficulties, which she couldn't do earlier. Before that she was ignorant of many things had little or no questions for her Uncle. As she travels, her mind and body also develops. She says, "But I've changed." The paragraph is significant because it marks her entry into womanhood directly from her childhood behaviour.

Furthermore, a paragraph which helps the reader to better understand one of the major themes in *Of Love and Other Monsters* is in the words of the narrator, Arun:

> I thought about the notion that Janani was as much my murderer as my progenitor. She had burned me, Moghe had said. I understood now that I am stuck with this body, this gender, because of that. Unlike him, I could no longer change form; nor could I tell friend from foe.[13]

Here, we are able to understand why Arun could love both men and women and could see women as something beyond objects of desire. It is because Arun and his likes could change into any form; man, woman or even of an animal. These were merely forms for them and held no real meaning. Arun professes that there are not just two genders, but many, and each is like the colours in a rainbow, where one flows into another. With such a view, love for each one is possible, without any mental blocks of divides on any basis. He calls them stifling boundaries, which man himself has created.

In addition, a paragraph at the beginning of *Generation 14* helps to understand the protagonist and the process of mutation she is undergoing. Unusually for a clone, she feels impelled to think, and to act according to her will.

The novel provides many examples to show the reader that the protagonist, Clone 14/54/G, is no ordinary clone. She is on the verge of mutating and possesses most of the traits of her Original. This is an interesting area for the author to explore as she feels that we are moving towards an era of cloning. She also contemplates the kind of relation we are going to have with clones. The paragraph perhaps indicates that clones may become as capable as humans of perceiving their conditions and commenting on it. In fact, the Clone is quite human as the Original tends to express herself through the Clone.

4.2.6 Metaphor

A popularly held belief in Sagara is that if one leaves the homeland or is made to do so, it is the work of the Trickster wave. It fools you into "stepping outside the circle."[14] During early times, a pact was made between the Trickster wave and Leviathans that lived at the bottom of the ocean. According to the pact, those who wished to travel and explore were free to do so and accepted happily when they returned. This carried on for some time but the trust was breached when inhabitants of Sagara brought along foreigners who attempted to disrupt the life of people or tried to interrupt or break their sacred rituals. This can also be read as applicable to people on Earth, who end up exploiting and manhandling its resources, and exhausting the non-renewable resources. When such things happen, nature is displeased and reacts in its own way, showing its discontent through calamities. Nature offers warnings, which, if ignored, leads to irreversible disasters. Anasuya is also carried away from Sagara on a raft, while she is asleep. She associates her turning brown with losing her *athmis* and a result of "stepping outside the circle." Anasuya also believes that the Trickster wave led Hasha away from Sagara.

A strange metaphor is used to refer to women in Manjula Padmanabhan's *Escape*. The metaphor is that of a drone, which is half human, half clone. These drones are also mostly deaf and dumb, only capable of performing set functions. In fact, the protagonist, Meiji, also thinks that she is like a clone because, like them, she is also not growing. Meiji is not sufficiently, either physically or emotionally, for her age. She is sixteen, yet she looks like a child. Connected to this idea is another metaphor that surfaces in the story, that of sculpting. The three uncles, who are in charge of Meiji's destiny, are compared to a sculptor. They not only control her growth but also shape her destiny.

Furthermore, Meiji's Uncle, Eldest, uses the metaphor of a plant to describe the growth and evolution of Meiji from a girl to a young woman, once she moves out of the Estate and begins her journey. Another reason for him to use the metaphor can possibly be to make it easy for Meiji to understand the process. Eldest tells her, "'You will climb out of this safe underground seed case in which you have been germinating for so long.'" [15] A similar metaphor is used by the Generals in their manual and it definitely refers to the women, whose lives they have extinguished, "Destroy the plant and its roots will rise up to haunt you. Destroy roots and the plant will cease to exist." [16] By the time Meiji acquires an understanding of what puberty is, and what it signifies, she begins to despise her Uncles for bringing her into a world that is hostile to her. Referring to herself as a plant, she accuses them of "planting seeds of flesh and blood." [17] The metaphor of fruit is also used in the novel to refer to women. Additionally, Meiji is also compared to a 'juicy plum' by the narrator as the salesman ogles her when he sees her dressed in a pair of fitted jeans and a t-shirt. Another metaphor which the Uncles use to talk about Meiji is that of a boat.

Middle is referring to Meiji and her process of reaching puberty, which she will because the Uncles plan to stop giving her hormone suppressants once she embarks on her journey. The metaphor, a 'boat,' also signifies a release from the control of her Uncles and a freedom to grow and live naturally. The Uncles fear what lies in store for Meiji once she reaches the stage at which she is in control of her own circumstances. Although the Uncles wish that kind of freedom for her, she fears the outside world which may harm her. This can be compared to the contemporary situation in many parts of India, where parents wish to allow their daughters more freedom, yet restrict them and sometimes even stop their education and basic rights, fearing their exposure to evil forces in society.

4.2.7 Simile

Meiji compares her uncle, Youngest, to a General when he speaks bitterly to her. The reaction comes when Youngest reprimands Meiji for repeatedly calling him Uncle after several warnings of not doing so. He wants her to address him as 'Brother', and this is necessary for her own safety. Owing to the challenging circumstances, Youngest is tougher on her and Meiji responds by calling him as ruthless and barbaric as a General. This exchange in the novel is significant as it marks the beginning of Meiji turning into a woman. She begins to convey a maturity that she had not shown before. Youngest can sense in her a bitterness and an overflow of emotions when she attacks Youngest with her words.

Additionally, the simile of a wolf appears in *Escape*, when Eldest uses it to describe his own self. He asserts that after the Change, circumstances were such that he became as ruthless and ferocious as a wolf. He had to hunt down many competitors to establish himself, and also to protect Meiji from outsiders. This simile appears towards the beginning and gives the reader an idea of the perturbed and hostile circumstances which will increasingly pervade the story as the action progresses. This is one of the first hints to the reader of the decadent state of the nation and one also learns gradually the reason for it is the extinction of women. Meiji is also referred as a *project* in the novel and this also refers to her objectification.

In *Generation 14*, the city of Kashi is compared to a fish at the time of floods, and the piece of land that is still visible. *Matsya* foregrounds that that the shape of Kashi is like a fish that saves it from floods. Hence, it is the shape of Kashi that leads the Matsya to make this comparison. His superstition is also that he need not fear, despite the flood. The fish seeks the higher truth through meditation, and believes, like the others, that the flood is a good sign. Matsya expects that its illumination is at hand and all illusions will be and it could become part of the Brahman, the Eternal Reality however nothing like this happens on the contrary ultimately, it is caught in a fish hook and is extremely disappointed.

Another simile appears in the visitation of the Dumb Madwoman of Dauli, in *Generation 14*. In a state of grief and anger, she likens herself to lightening. She says that the death of her son and many others in the battle of Kalinga has opened her eyes like the effect of lightening. She questions Ashoka whether he needed such a large-scale bloodshed for his mind to follow the path of *dhamma*. Despite knowing the story of Ashoka's repentance, she still holds him responsible for the loss of many people's lives. This story is linked to the idea of endless wars fought in history, referred to in the main plot. The narrator emphasizes that all wars cause only death and bloodshed.

4.2.8 Analogy

Meiji makes a strange comparison between her Uncles and her generators. She thinks that her Uncles have created her, just as drones are created within laboratories with the help of machinery. That is why she says, "you *are* my… generators!"[18] She means to say parents, but she has never heard the word being used, nor does she understand its meaning. The mechanized state of their nation-state has also affected her vocabulary. Until this time, she had been thinking that the drones were real people. The Uncles, in some ways, can be seen as Meiji's generators, as they control her life. As mentioned, she has never met people except for her Uncles. They not only control her physical and mental development but also her daily activities, ranging from what she will study, to what games she will play. At a later stage in the novel, Meiji again uses the word, generator, but this time she is more aware of the meaning. Yet she uses it knowingly to taunt Youngest and calls him her generator, although he prefers her to use the word 'father' as he is both her Uncle and biological parent. Other analogies are those of mind as a net, or knitting wool, aliens as the mitochondrion. In *Of Love and Other Monsters*, the narrator, Arun, whose skill is to bring many minds together and form a connection between them, talks of it: "After some practice I was able to draw the minds into a kind of net, to weave the separate threads of jangling thought-processes into-not a tapestry… but a jumble of knitting wool, such as a kitten might do."[19] Hence, the mind is visualized as a kind of net.

Arun also compares the aliens who came and settled in human minds to the mitochondrion, a membrane-bound organelle, an interesting analogy that he learns from Rahul Moghe. This analogy brings out the situation of Arun's species, that they have become one with the humans that they may not even like to return to their original habitation if given a choice. Despite this, the likes of Janani hunt them down for no fault of their own.

4.2.9 Subtheme as a conjunction

The General often gives interviews to propagate and popularize his ideas to the outside world; he manifests that he and his likes condemn individuality. The General and his clones are identical. He declares, "We're identical… there's always another to take his place."[20] This declaration brings out one of the subthemes of the novel, which is the destruction of individuality and the spread of commonality: no individual is unique and hence can be replaced by another. General and his army of soldiers have destroyed the species of women and the ecosystem, and turned the whole country into a desert. Two-thirds of the entire population have been extinguished. Through the process of cloning, Generals have not only cloned themselves and the Boy Soldiers, but also animals and humans to form drones. As a result, there is a monotony and dullness in the lives of people where, except for the living human beings, most of the things are identical. The vestiges of the past have been devastated. However, the citizens are responsible for their own downfall and existing conditions as they accepted money from the outside world to store their toxic waste. Gradually, the land turned into a radioactive wasteland and the General and his brother cunningly took over the administration of the nation-state. This also shows that one must choose their leaders through discretion and one reaps the consequences of their actions accordingly. These ideas surface throughout the novel from time to time. This theme of condemning individuality is also referred to as the theme of replaceability as recorded in the novel:

'Our theme today is replaceability'... Everyone and everything is replaceable. No-one is uniquely precious. Not even the Generals... We are everywhere at once. We think the same thoughts. If one of us passes away, another takes his place without feeling loss or bereavement. We have banished the pain of loss. The pain of... *death*.[21]

The use of subthemes as a technique helps the writer to change the direction of the main story and keeps them (sub-themes) closer to the theme. This technique is being used by the writer to serve various purposes, such as to provide additional information, bringing new settings, introducing new characters, creating interest among the readers, and so on. But in SFs the technique is applied specifically to create absolute the effect of conjunction. Among the subthemes in the works are: exploitation of girls in places like brothels, treatment of living beings other than humans etc.

Arun, the protagonist in *Of Love and Other Monsters*, rescues a four-teen-year-old girl Dulari from a brothel through the use of money and an NGO that works for women. He is able to save her from being marketed and sold as a commodity day in and out. After he saves Dulari, Arun also secures her a job in a clothing shop that employs young and malnourished women. Dulari's life improves, but this is not a normal life for a fourteen year old. She cannot afford to go to school and she leads a dull, monot-onous life. Arun feels sorry for her, yet he cannot do much, fearing what people will think of him. Hence, the particular subtheme addresses not only the situation of many children who are forced into different kinds of labour, but also considers the mental blocks in our society which prevent people from coming out to help such victims.

Another subtheme that appears in *Of Love and Other Monsters* is that of the treatment meted out to living beings other than humans. We learn in the story that aliens like Arun and Moghe are burnt alive to turn them into humans and to take away their special powers. They are seen as aliens. In fact, we discover that Arun and Moghe never cause any harm to the humans, and that they are the ones that are in danger throughout. Moghe lands on Earth only to find his people, those who had reached Earth but were not able to return. In fact, their ancestors had become one with the animals and had forgotten their lives on another planet. They lived in the most benign manner. Similarly, the author, Vandana Singh, is concerned with the way animals and other organisms are treated in the society. She has emphasized that we must be compassionate towards species other than human beings, cats and dogs.

4.2.10 *Character as a conjunction*

The figure of the Queen becomes an important character that allows Rokeya to bring certain ideas in front of the readers which would not reach them otherwise. Hence, she also serves the purpose of a connective. The Queen is able to put her ideas to practice and in very little time two universities for women were established.

These discoveries are a proof of the capability of women and the need for society to acknowledge their potential. In Rokeya's contemporary society, there was a need to encourage women to come out of the confinement of their homes and explore their aptitude. Such ideas necessitate that women must be given a chance to bring progress and prosperity to the society. Unlike Sultana, who has hardly any understanding of science, women in Ladyland have a sound scientific sense. If Sultana had studied science, she would have known the things Sister Sara was talking of. It is perhaps this difference that Rokeya wanted to point at and, in the absence of such information, the idea would not have reached the reader.

In Manjula Padmanabhan's *Escape*, Windseeker can be seen as an important character who aids Youngest and Meiji in their journey across the Waste. As Meiji and Youngest approach the first boundary post of the Waste, they encounter a stranger in the desert, named Windseeker. He not only shares the meal with them, but also warns them of Boy Warriors approaching. Since Youngest gets to know about this impending danger, he is able to avert it with Windseeker's help. Windseeker accompanies them on their journey to the South and saves them from the feral dogs, which attack humans in the dark, old men and young children are particularly vulnerable, but the dogs may also attack an adult man, if they find a heavy sleeper who does not stir awake in time to defend himself. For instance, Windseeker awakes when he senses the dogs and does his best to drive them away, all the taking care of Meiji and Youngest, and acting as their guardian. He leaves Meiji and Youngest to carry on with the rest of their journey and leaves them at the Station House, where they are able to rest and replenish their food stock. Yet, even at this point, the Windseeker provides useful advice so that Meiji can be protected from the eager and evil eyes of onlookers. Although Youngest refers to Meiji as 'him' throughout, the Windseeker suspects that Meiji is a girl. After such valuable advice and guidance, the Windseeker leaves to never surface again in the novel, yet plays a crucial role in the plot and its development.

Two more characters surface in *Escape*, and they appear from time to time, only at the behest of Meiji. She alone can interact with these characters, as they are figments of her imagination. They are actually her reflection in the mirror which she talks to and she calls them Mister Frog and Mister Piggie. They mostly appear when she wants to talk about things that baffle her the most, yet she cannot talk to Youngest about them. At the very beginning of the novel, a suitor appears to see Meiji; even after warnings, he leaps at Meiji just to get a glimpse of the girl. Seeing this, drones attack the man and break his neck, killing him instantly. Meiji is frightened and chooses to discuss the matter with her imaginary friends.

Through these characters, Meiji can point attention to the traumatic experience that many Indian girls go through, of meeting a suitor or being married off at an early stage. The experience can be extremely disturbing and leave the girl at this stage full of worries. This can also be seen as a subtheme of the novel.

The character of Rinu Devi in *Of Love and Other Monsters* also functions as a conjunction, as she helps to carry forward the plot. When Arun decides to come to India from the USA, to meet Janani and attend Sankaran's wedding, he has no clue what he is to discover. Since he arrives early to attend Sankaran's wedding, Arun takes off for Rishikesh to meet Janani and seeks answers to questions such as why she burnt him. He doesn't find Janani, but meets Rinu Devi. Rinu and Janani had been living together and they were lovers. From Rinu, Arun learns that Janani was part of a network of people who could sense aliens. They then organized a burning and took away their powers, just as they had done in the case of Arun. The kinds of Arun are then mostly sent to mental hospitals, or can be found begging on the streets. Janani pulled Arun from the fire well in time to save him. Yet his powers died in the fire. Learning this, Arun recalls reading in Janani's last letter to him, which said that he was burnt in order to make him human. Eventually, Janani dies in one such burning.

Similarly, Binodini surfaces as an important character. She appears only to make Arun realize that he should not run from Rahul Moghe but find him instead. Only he could answer the questions which had been bothering Arun, about his origins and his life. Additionally, the characters of Couplet and Fireheart appear as a conjunction in *Generation 14*. The Clone is captured with the hope that she may convey her Original's ideas, which she was to uncover before her death. Hence, the Clone is given a drug which would compel her to say the truth. The Clone conveys, in prose, that the enemy lies in us, and that we are responsible for our own acts. She gives examples of wars that have been fought in history, the war of Kurukshetra, or the attack in New York. Since the Clone appears to be blaming the Global Community for the state of the world, she is at risk. It is both Couplet and Fireheart who come to her rescue at several points in the novel. They protect her by saying that the Clone does not seem to be voicing her Original, and she is hallucinating. Hence, the Clone is not to be blamed.

4.2.11 Author's personal observations

The words of Youngest in *Escape* appear to be the author's personal observation. The context being that the brothers expose Meiji, the young girl, to suitors often and this leaves the girl traumatized as the men often try to attack her, even for a small glimpse of her. Youngest is appalled at such an experience and he requests the brothers not to engage in such an activity. He says, "If you will never act upon something you know, then it's the same as not knowing it…"[22] The suggestion here is that if one is aware that a certain act will lead to major repercussions, and even then if one doesn't take heed, then it is as good as not being aware of it. This can be seen as a statement of anger by Youngest towards his brothers to stop showing Meiji in front of suitors which intimidates her. These can also be seen as the author's personal views. The author perhaps expects the readers to gauge the future through the novel, that if one does nothing about the problem in front of them, then he/she might as well have no knowledge of it.

A significant observation and intervention by the author is also found in *Escape*. The purpose is to highlight Meiji's subtle transition towards becoming a woman. Being subtle, attention needs to be given to note that theme. The given lines are an aftermath of an argument between Meiji and Youngest. From this point onwards, many changes in Meiji are noticed, which were not a part of her as a child.

Further, although the lines are uttered by Arun, they come across as the author's idea of how an ideal society should be. According to her, the minds of people must be in harmony with one another, rather than dividing people along the lines of man-woman, or man-aliens and so on.

4.2.12 Author's peculiar observations

The following lines are to be seen as the author's peculiar observations in Vandana Singh's *Distances*:

> the orders and patterns of the world are meant to be discovered, experienced, and celebrated. Only some knowledge can be utilized for our needs, and that too with great circumspection...[23]

Here, the author creates space for further investigation with her personal suggestion that there is no end to any investigation. Whatever we visualize from a distance are not always in a complete form. A close look would certainly reveal the issues and concerns associated with that. Therefore, 'what they are for' terms as a meaningless question.

Another peculiar observation by the author is found in *Of Love and Other Monsters* by Vandana Singh. The narrator claims that his ability to read minds enables him to see human beings as entities beyond man-woman categories and he finds that there are not just two, but at least thirty-four gender categories. He labels them the 34 climactic zones of the human mind.

It is clear that there cannot be as many as 34 genders, yet what the author wants to emphasize is that there should be no bias when accepting people who belong to a different gender or colour. She is making a plea to dismiss discrimination on the basis of gender, colour, caste or creed. Being a human who possesses the quality of love is sufficient for associating with one another. The protagonist of the story, Arun, feels attracted to Sankaran. He cannot express his love to Sankaran or marry him, because they belong to the same sex. The 'social mores' discourage Arun. This experience seems to disturb the author.

Further, another observation that demands attention is: "How does a man who is not a man or a woman, not a human or an alien-how does such a being confess his love to another man."[24] This is a reflection made by Arun when he is unable to confess his love to Sankaran. This comes across as a peculiar observation by the author who highlights the agony of a man, also an alien, who is crushed by society's conventions. Had he been on his own planet, he could have easily married Sankaran, yet being an Indian, he feels he will be unable to convince Sankaran. The quoted lines arouse the reader to reflect on the shackles that humans have created for themselves that impair their own freedom to love and be happy. Such things need to be done away with.

4.2.13 Story

When Nirx shows interest in knowing about the history of the City and how the Temple of Mathematical Arts came into being, she is taken by Turel and others to the Temple of Two Lovers to hear their story. According to the story, in the old times, Ekatip and Shunyatip were lovers. They could change forms, becoming both men and women, and spend most of their time in love. However, they significantly discovered the Number, which they kept as secret and hid it in a cube of bone. The Nameless Goddess attempts to steal the cube from the two by changing different forms, first by assuming the role of sand and working up a storm. The Nameless Goddess then becomes a beautiful women and the three engage in a passionate orgy. During this time, an outsider joins them, unnoticed by the group. It is none other than "the lesser god Anhutip himself, who was known as a mischief maker." He is known for changing appearances and playing tricks. Anhutip becomes successful in stealing the magic cube and replaces it with a stone. Just as Ekatip and Shunyatip realize that it is a stone and not the magic cube, Shunyatip, who had kept the cube in his mouth the whole time, spits it out. Anhutip takes charge of the moment and picks up the stone, and it turns into the cube, which he had earlier turned into a stone. Now the lovers no longer had the proficiency over Number. Anhutip took the magic cube and extracted more information from it than the Two Lovers after that he ingested it and kept it in his body until he had understood all forms and relations; after that he breathed out the world as it is now, in all its assorted magnificence, including sand, rock, empty sky, and water along with all the creatures of the world.

The story is significant in the sense that it provides an understanding of how the people of the City became such experts at mathematics so that people from nearby planets were drawn to them for help. Additionally, the whole story revolves around the premise of mathematics and hence one can say that the story of the Two Lovers serves as a conjunction.

Notes

1 *Merriam Webster Thesaurus.* May 15, 2014. https://www.merriam-webster.com/dictionary/conjunction.
2 Proudfoot, Michael and A.R. Lacey. *The Routledge Dictionary of Philospohy.* Routledge. 1976, p. 10
3 Singh, Vandana. *Distances.* 2008, p. 123
4 Ibid., p. 22
5 Padmanabhan, Manjula. *Escape.* 2008, p. 1

6 Ibid., p. 23
7 Singh, Vandana. *Of Love and Other Monsters.* 2007, p. 53–54
8 Chabria, Priya S. *Generation 14.* 2008, p. 145
9 Singh, Vandana. *Distances.* 2008, p. 47
10 Singh, Vandana. *Of Love and Other Monsters.* 2007, p. 23
11 Chabria, Priya S. *Generation 14.* 2008, p. 36
12 Singh, Vandana. *Of Love and Other Monsters.* 2007, p. 35
13 Ibid., p. 41
14 Singh, Vandana. *Distances.* 2008, p. 119
15 Padmanabhan, Manjula. *Escape.* 2008, p. 89
16 Ibid., p. 82
17 Ibid., p. 405
18 Ibid., p. 108
19 Singh, Vandana. *Of Love and Other Monsters.* 2007, p. 5
20 Padmanabhan, Manjula. *Escape.* 2008, p. 147
21 Ibid., p. 218
22 Padmanabhan, Manjula. *Escape.* 2008, p. 4
23 Singh, Vandana. *Distances.* 2008., p. 96
24 Singh, Vandana. *Of Love and Other Monsters.* 2007, p. 52

5 Contradictions through disjunctions

5.1 Introduction

Social forces always find expression in culture, even when they work unseen, and the problem is stated falsely if culture and society are torn apart from one another and are regarded as fully independent spheres which, as such, react upon one another. The social process is contained in the very structure of cultural life itself so that it is never for one moment free from its influence.[1]

Karl Mannheim's main thesis in *Man and Society in an Age of Reconstruction* is that one of the major reasons for our difficulty in grasping literature and its cultural significance is the disjunction between the social structure and the culture. Here, the social structure stands for the system of social relationships between persons, who are entrenched in a system of norms and rules. The concept of culture stands for the symbolic expressions in the field of ideas and art of the involvement of individuals in those interactions. Therefore, the disjunction arises both in real life and in literature because of the complexities involved in finding appropriate symbolic expression to grasp the meaning of experiences in contemporary society.

Any work of literature is constructed by making use of language; therefore, the implication of a sentence – that is, the proposition that it articulates – is conventionally structured as a set of possible worlds. This refers explicitly to those worlds in which the sentence is true. Therefore, the proposition articulated by a sentence conventionally stands for its truth circumstances. As per the writer of the text, the alternate world is real. The circumstances created in the SF world are such that we tend to believe in the writer. Thus, the proposition articulated by a sentence arrests the instructive content of that sentence, i.e., the information that is delivered by a speaker in voicing the sentence. Despite all of these efforts there is always a gap between the intended meaning and the received meaning; however, the concept of disjunction can be deliberately employed by a writer to foreground the discrepancy. In such cases, the intended meaning lies in the disjunction.

This particular treatment of disjunction as generating sets of alternatives is the main focus of this chapter which will analyze "disjunctive antecedents, unembedded disjunctions, and disjunctions under the scope of modals."[2]

One dictionary definition describes disjunction thus:

> A compound sentence is a conjunction if its component sentences are joined by 'and.' It is a disjunction if they are joined by 'or.' The component sentences are, respectively, conjuncts, which are conjoined, and disjuncts, which are disjoined. 'Conjunction' and 'disjunction' can also mean the logical operations of forming such expressions. 'And' and 'or' here have only their joining force, without signifying, e.g. temporal order (as in 'He came and went'). 'Or' is usually inclusive ('either and 'perhaps both'), but can be exclusive ('either but not both'). Sometimes alternation replaces 'disjunction,' with alternant and alternate for 'disjunct' and 'disjoin.' Occasionally 'disjunction' and 'alternation' are distinguished, 'disjunction' being kept for the exclusive sense. Conjunctions in the ordinary sense ('and', 'or' etc.) are in logic called connectives...[3]

The focus of this chapter is to highlight and emphasize the disjunctions within the chosen texts.

5.2 Conjunction as a disjunction

In Vandana Singh's novella, *Distances*, the following lines are examples of conjunctions becoming disjunctions. Anasuya can see the *sthanas* and its various dimensions, as she works on it in the amnion, yet she is unable to comprehend what it stands for. The purpose of the writer here is to connect the two pieces of information and to see if it helps Anasuya to understand the *sthanas*, but the narrative loses its connectivity for a short period as attention is drawn to the metaphor of hunting, Anasuya's mother, Lata and Sagara.

5.3 Different forms used as disjunctions

5.3.1 Word as a disjunction

There are many paragraphs which indicate that Anasuya, even as she emerges from the amnion, from her work on the *sthanas*, continues to think of the image of the woman she sees, whom she later names Vara. She is completely absorbed and occupied with her effort to find an answer to what the 'mysterious woman' may be referring to. The message definitely seems important not only to the project, but perhaps also to something personal, as indicated, and might even pertain to Anasuya's future. Her train of thoughts follow her even in the shower. Yet, it is the word 'But' which puts a stop to her meditation; she is made to postpone the thinking. Hence, the word 'But' is used here as a disconjunction, disturbing both the flow of thoughts and the story.

Another example of word playing as 'disjunction' can be seen in *Escape* when Youngest asks Meiji if she has any questions about either the journey, or its implications. Additionally, Meiji must also know the truth about herself and the circumstances of her birth. Meiji is reluctant to participate in any conversation as she is not used to asking many questions or taking her own decisions. This has been part of her education, which the Uncles gave her. Youngest's attempts to get Meiji to ask any questions at all is declined. Youngest's efforts are in vain because Meiji is not interested in the conversation; hence the story must take a different course. As a child, Meiji is unable to realize the seriousness of the situation. Since they have already embarked upon their journey, Youngest has little time to explain to her what things, people and hurdles they might encounter. He also has to explain to Meiji that she will gradually turn into a full-grown woman. Instead of understanding the consequences of such a journey, Meiji starts to think of a name that she may adopt in order to mask her identity. Meiji can be seen as symptomatic of those women who have been denied the agency of freedom of choice and conditioned into accepting it.

5.3.2 Paragraph as a disjunction

Once Youngest and Meiji cross the Waste, they feel much safer, although the danger does persists to some extent. They take refuge in the home of Budget, a fellow estate owner, and a person who has done business with them at some point and has agreed to be host them. Here, Youngest and Meiji venture out to buy essential things and to replenish their supplies. After buying clothes for Meiji, they approach a recreation spot, which is called the Point. It is actually a sea, where one has to wear a radiation suit for safety. While Meiji goes to the seashore, like many others, to gather the waste that the sea brings to the shore, Youngest prefers to sit and watch. As Youngest gazes towards the onlookers, he becomes nostalgic about his past, remembering a time when he would go for picnics with his family to the seaside and the land was not contaminated with radioactivity.

There are a number of paragraphs in the novel that convey the decadence of the present situation, and Youngest is inclined to compare it to the happy, glorious past he spent with his family. What are now washed up against the shores of the sea, are remains of what used to be the parts of cars, homes, and buildings in the time before the Change. The scene of visitors at the sea is the same, yet no one is picnicking like they used to, when people would bring food from home. The air is also not as fresh as it used to be. This kind of nostalgia for the past can also be regarded as that of the author, who depicts an image in front of the reader, comparing and contrasting a pleasant vision versus a devastating one. It is for the reader to assess and decide the one they would like for themselves. The paragraph can be seen as a disjunction because Youngest loses track of Meiji, while he daydreams. All along he had been so protective and mindful of Meiji's safety. Yet he lets her roam on her own and for some time and has no knowledge of her whereabouts. References to memories of the past are quite pertinent in showing the contrast to the reader, yet they divert attention from Meiji's story.

5.3.3 Simile

Pedha Mudhiaya, in the 'visitation' named 'The Sentence', compares his situation to the walls of a circular prison. "Like the walls of this circular prison. I think I'm spinning in this dark airless cell. By now they should have told me who is going to do the job tomorrow."[4] From the beginning of this 'visitation,' Mudhiaya is concerned with the question of who will behead him for the theft he has committed. This question haunts him more than the punishment itself. This question revolves in his mind like the prison walls which circle around him. Although the story is a disjunction, the simile used here helps to convey Mudhiaya's inner turmoil.

5.3.4 Story

The narrative of *Distances* is interspersed with a few stories, which are similar to folk tales. One such is the story of the Cave of Delusion. This story involves a man named Dara, who seeks shelter in a narrow opening in a cliff and gradually enters a cave. He tries to search for water but finds none and falls asleep. When he wakes, through a ray of sunlight he finds that water has reached the cave. He drinks water to quench his thirst and tries to pass water, but is unable to do so. He continually feels thirst, drinks water, but finds it difficult to urinate. He repeats this several times until Dara sees his reflection in the water in the faint light. Dara's image speaks to him and conveys that he is in a state of delusion, which includes the water that is also deceiving him. He needs to move out of this cave and return to the sea, where he belongs; otherwise he will have to remain where he is, all alone. In a state of fear, Dara runs into the cave's walls and wakes up from his dream. He finds that he is not alone, and his body is weak and fragile. Perhaps the author has attempted to use the story as a conjunction, but it comes out as more of a disjunction. It does not serve the purpose of conveying any specific point that is pertinent to the main narrative; its only purpose is that it expects to fulfill is a moral lesson to the society.

The story of Pedha Mudhiaya, a palace guard, is also a disjunction in the narrative of *Generation 14*. Most 'visitations' that appear in the midst of the plot tend to carry a purpose of conveying a theme or subtheme or taking the action of the story further. In this particular story, the Mudhiaya steals a ruby ring from a courtesan in order to please her handmaid, Vanithamma. The theft is discovered and although Mudhiaya pleads guilty, the courtesan insists that he be killed. Throughout the 'visitation,' Mudhiaya regrets ever having met Vanithamma and committing the theft. The story serves as a moral lesson not to steal or to pursue someone endlessly, even if it lands you in trouble. Other than that, it makes no contribution to the main plot.

5.3.5 Disjunction becomes conjunction

Just as Sister Sara advises Sultana to not be afraid of men in Ladyland, the attention of the narrative is taken to the aesthetic beauty of the place.

Sultana appreciates the greenery in Ladyland; for example, a patch of grass appears to her like a "velvet cushion."[5] There are moss and flowers everywhere along the sidewalks. The place gives the likeness of being in a garden, even amidst the busiest of streets. The inclusion of this idea appears as a disjunction, distracting the reader and does not appear to relate to any of the story's main ideas. This can be seen as a device used by the author to arouse the interest of the reader by delaying information about where the men might be and why Sultana should not be wary of men as she walks on the streets in Ladyland. Just as the reader might feel curious to move forward, Sultana is also impatient.

Towards the end of the story, however, we learn that through the use of the disjunction, the author was building up to introduce the larger point about the importance of preserving nature and optimizing on its benefits. That is why even Sister Sara's house is built in the midst of an appealing garden. She keeps it cool by using plants. Another example where a disjunction becomes a conjunction when we learn that Sultana is convinced that it is unsafe for women to venture out of *zenana* as they are weaker and need the protection of men. Hence, their confinement is justified. In order to clarify to her that women are not weak, Sister Sara uses a number of examples, which may or may not be connected to the plot and hold relevance only until the point is conveyed. They classify as connectives leading to a greater understanding and carrying forward the course of events.

Sister Sara uses the example of wild animals. She says that it is unsafe for women to be outdoors if there are men on the streets or if there is a wild animal in the market. She compares men with wild animals. Another example she uses is of lunatics. Sister Sara poses the following question: if a lunatic flees from an asylum and causes havoc in the city, troubling mankind and animals, what would be the best thing to do? Sultana responds that in such a situation, the lunatic should be caught and sent back to the asylum. Sister Sara then poses another question: if so is it also wise to keep the sensible people in an asylum and free the insane? Sister Sara makes this point to emphasize that in Sultana's country, this is practiced.

The author is attempting to make clear that women's position of subservience is also a result of their own negligence. The men cannot be held entirely to blame. Just because a lion is more powerful than a man, there is no reason for a man to let the lion control it. Rokeya wants the women of her times to know that they are equally capable of inverting the situation, and that women can also put the men in *purdah*. She uses such ideas to shock the Bengali Muslim women out of their apathy and to take charge of their situation. Rokeya, for example, is against the idea of women accepting jewels in compensation for their enslavement, visualizing bracelets as handcuffs. Rokeya emphasizes that a woman's true jewels must be books and she stresses the cause of women's education. It is only then that women would be able to realize their rights, abilities and potentials. They needed to wake up from the conditioning that women are weak and that they are best suited to stay indoors, do household work and take care of babies. In the story, Rokeya reiterates the importance of recognising that the power of brain is greater than physical strength.

As the story moves forward, another disjunction appears which seemingly puts a break in the progression of events. While talking to Sultana about the need to catch and put the men in *purdah*, the conversation shifts to household work, such as stitching, embroidery and needlework. When the reader pays attention, however, it becomes clear why the author often interrupts and inserts these seemingly extraneous pieces of information. Yet what Rokeya wants to emphasize here is the power of women, their multi-tasking abilities. Sister Sara affirms that women can manage all the tasks on their own, and that they should not leave even the embroidery work for men, as they lack patience. Sister Sara can both embroider and complete office work. In fact, she is able to finish her work in two hours, pinpointing the inefficiency of men, who spend seven hours in the office every day. She claims they are only productive for one hour and that they waste six hours in smoking. If women like Sultana are given the opportunity for education, even they can prove to be more fruitful and inventive than men.

Even after Janani goes to live in Rishikesh and sends Arun to a neighbouring town, she continues to write and also sends Arun's properties to him before he was burnt. At this point the packages which Janani sends make no sense to Arun. Arun cannot correlate with them. Hence, their relevance seems pointless and the mention of these remains from the fire, seems as a disjunction in the story. No real purpose is served by these things. Yet later on, when Arun learns from Moghe that he is an alien and was burnt by Janani, then these remains from the fire begin to make sense to him. He is able to relate to the photographs and the pieces of ceramic artifacts that she sends. We learn here that all things finally fall into place, as compared with the first time that Janani sends Arun's things.

Additionally, when the Clone requests the regular rations meant for a clone, she is instead given a few options: American breakfast, continental food, Japanese food or the food given to 21st century Indian widows. "Sir, would you care instead for the austere meal of twentieth Indian widows? A small plate of watery lentils and dirty rice with a spoonful of snake-gourd curry appeared."[6] The abrupt appearance of this reference to the meal served to widows in the 21st century appears as a disjunction, serving no real purpose, other than just a mention to the readers. Yet, as the narrative moves to the 'visitation' of the parrot, the situation is comparable. Both this reference of the meal and the captive status of the female parrot and other women in *zenana* highlight the limited improvement in women's status between the 19th century and the 21st century. Such ideas are a major theme in the novel, being carefully spread throughout its pages. The Clone is, however, more confident and assertive and there are instances where she is in control of her circumstances. All of these changes in the Clone are inspired by her Original.

Notes

1 Bell, Daniel. "The Disjunction of Culture and Social Structure: Some Notes on the Meaning of Social Reality." *Daedalus*. 94.1 (1965): 208–222. p. 208.
2 Alonso-Ovalle, L. *Disjunction in Alternative Semantics*. Ph.D. thesis, University of Massachusetts, Amherst. 2006. p. n. a.
3 Proudfoot, Michael and A.R. Lacey. *The Routledge Dictionary of Philosphoy*. Routledge. 1976, p. 10
4 Chabria, Priya S. *Generation 14*. 2008, p. 172
5 Hossain, S. Rokeya. "Sultana's Dream." *Penguin*, 14 January, 2005. Web. 25 June, 2013 http://digital.library.upenn.edu/women/sultana/dream/dream.html.
6 Chabria, Priya S. *Generation14*. 2008, p. 122

Conclusion

The present research focused on the ability of the chosen SF texts to sensitize the readers and inspire in them a radical perspective and an acknowledgement of the need for change. Depending upon what the author has chosen to focus on, among the issues covered in such recent literature are the need to become aware of environmental and ecological or an acknowledgement of matters relating to issues affecting girls and women. Even though in most of the chosen texts the setting is India, the writers have tried to portray issues that are pertinent the world over and that require immediate attention. What helps reinforce the ideas of the authors is the mode of SF, its imaginary setting, which allows them to explore issues and concerns more freely than any other genre.

'Radical potential' as a concept has been defined in the introductory chapter. Accordingly, a text which possesses radical potential discusses serious political or social views which may appear as either outrageous or extraordinary to many readers. The presence of radical potential in a text is the key factor which instills in the reader the ideas for change and the ways in which they can bring about the extreme change, which is necessary to change or model the existing conditions. SF is the genre best suited to convey the radical potential, as it permits the author to touch upon areas considered as taboo by many mainstream writers. These observations were arrived upon after the study. The author uses an alternate setting to discuss sensitive political, social or ecological issues and gives voice to those who are marginalized, such as women, people of colour, transgender or bisexuals. The fragile issues of race and gender are also communicated effectively through the genre of SF. Hence, upon careful study and analysis, it has been established that SF is best at bringing out the issues which need serious and immediate attention. The radical potential in SF not only serves to introduce such ideas but also to arouse in the readers a consciousness to act accordingly. All such observations have been noted during the course of investigation under the purview of the research.

In order to clearly bring out the intensity of radical potential in Indian SF, four representative texts were carefully chosen. The fact that they are all female authors reflects the common issues they address. They give a primacy to social issues dealing with women, along with issues related to the environment or technological developments. Various subthemes were also discovered and studied to uncover the radical potential they hold. Hence, more radical ideas were found than expected. The subthemes not only maintained the continuity of the plot, but also emphasized the main ideas.

The aim of the present study was to draw attention to Indian SF, a largely ignored and unknown area of literature. Through the research, attempts were made to present a specialized study of Indian SF to inspire researchers and make it available to a large set of people. This was more so necessary because there is hardly any detailed study of any aspect of SF. All the blogs and books available on Indian SF mentioned in the introductory chapter were studied carefully to assess the level of research carried out on the subject to date. It was found that most studies deal with similar topics such as the evolution of SF in India and the West, and the major themes dealt in SFs. Hence, there is a dearth of specific studies which focus on any single and relevant aspect, rather than offering a general study of Indian SF. That is why the present study has concentrated on the radical potential, covering the social, gender, environmental and technology issues.

The concept and importance of studying the radical potential in works of SF as discussed in the introduction stands as the testimony to such a hypothesis, which was not casually dealt upon; rather, the intensity is felt in the texts under discussion. SF is truly radical in its ability to present both the society in which the work is set and the world of the reader from a radical perspective. Additionally, the use of an imaginative/alternative society that represents the future scenario places the author in a very comfortable position to pose difficult and important questions which might perturb the author and affect the society. Only SF can confront the readers with a fantastical situation where there is no escape, offering to the readers a space to envision their future and what they can do to avoid such a scenario.

SF authors have the convenience of choosing to write in any of its subgenres. The subgenres enable a specialization such that the author would only discuss the aspects which disturb them the most. For instance, the short story and novel respectively, "Sultana's Dream" and *Escape*, mainly discuss social and gender issues. There are, of course, other subthemes, but the focus remains on these two aspects. The outcome of both the works also favours a reform in their direction. The focus of the writer remains fixated on the goal, which is to convey a set of ideas to the reader through a future situation; the events of the text revolve around that. There is little space for digressions. Indeed, even if there are any digressions, they ultimately lead back to the central ideas.

The justification provided in the introduction to carry out a study of the radical potential in Indian SF was kept in mind throughout the research. A detailed investigation was made to ensure whether or not there are any works available in India that deal with the aspect of Indian SF. Once this was confirmed, the research was taken further. As speculated, it was also decided that SF is essentially a genre that presents to the readers a future situation and makes them aware of the widespread and unrestrained conditions of the society. This idea is also linked to the hypothesis of the proposed research: that Indian SF has immense potential as a radical literature. The points highlighted in the hypothesis were to explore the intensity of radical potential in the works and note the way in which the chosen texts possess the ability to initiate a movement towards increased responsibility, especially amongst the younger generation, so as to analyze future changes from a critical perspective. During the study, particular focus was given to the collection of evidence which also led to the conclusion that such radical potential is clearly present in the chosen works. It was also deduced that a large percentage of readers would be able to understand the intent of the author in presenting SF as a mode of social criticism. In fact, based on the available reviews of the chosen texts of Indian SF, one can also assert that SF has the ability to foresee political and social reforms and also comment upon them.

As mentioned in the hypothesis, SF has the potential to inspire future scientific developments and discoveries. Although no new scientific discoveries had been made after reading the chosen texts, yet this still remains a possibility. Rokeya Sakhawat Hossain, in "Sultana's Dream," talks of the use of solar heat for cooking and using the same to drive away the enemy by directing sunlight in their direction. There is no evidence that this incident in the story led to developments in the use of solar heat, but there still seems a chance of it being true. Similarly, Manjula Padmanabhan's *Escape* talks of some unique inventions used by Youngest and Meiji on their journey. Among many innovations in the novel, for example, they travel in a chariot that leaves no shadow and a ring which carries a dart to kill the enemy or helps to hunt a prey. SF includes such ideas and leaves it to the reader's imagination how they can use them to their advantage. What authenticates them in each instance is the presence of a reasonable scientific explanation. Apart from such scientific discoveries, Priya Sarukkai Chabria also introduces a near-possible future discovery: the creation of human clones. The author provides a picture of a world populated with clones. It further suggests that the role of humans can decrease along with their number. Additionally, since clones will inhabit the same world, it is imperative that the humans consider what kind of relations they plan to have with such clones. According to the author, a world with clones will not be conducive to the growth and development of the society; SF writing posits that, as shown, if treated as machines then the clones will rise in revolt against the few surviving humans.

Moving on to the methodology, it was decided to acquire the knowledge of the theories of cultural materialism, feminism and ecofeminism, for an effective analysis of the chosen texts. Each theory was helpful in its own individual way, allowing focus on, and also interpretation of, relevant themes and ideas. The theory of cultural materialism helped to give priority to the issue of tussle between subordinate and dominant classes. The theory emphasizes on the marginalized, which was relevant to the present study. Cultural materialism also enabled the interpretation of those issues in SF which a mainstream reading would neglect. It helped in an in-depth analysis of the most sensitive issues, by pinpointing the oppressed voices in the society. Although SF as a mode tries its best to give primacy to the silenced voices, yet it is the use of the theory of cultural materialism that helped to put ideas in a better perspective. In addition, the theory helped to connect issues identified in the text with similar issues that are relevant in the daily world, such as the lack of moral values or the current obsession with money. Additionally, the theory enabled an engagement with issues of class, gender, sexuality and race.

Feminist theory helped to put into perspective the issue of gender discrimination found in all the chosen texts. After a careful reading of the theory, it was possible to identify, explore and comment upon issues of discrimination, subjugation and patriarchy in the texts. It also became possible to articulate and observe the differences in treatment of women based on their social status, class, race, ethnicity and age. Also, since feminist theories have investigated the dissimilarities between women in different time periods and places, it was helpful to locate similar points in the texts. How the issues of race, nation, class, age correspond with the issue of gender was also probed in the research. The theory assisted in noting how important it is to give a voice to women and to appreciate their contribution to the society. For instance, Rokeya Sakhawat Hossain made enormous contributions to the cause of female education and emancipation. She dedicated her life to it and even opened the first school for Muslim girls in 1911 in Calcutta. Additionally, the feminist theory was helpful in investigating the reason for women's marginal status in the chosen texts. In "Sultana's Dream," the narrator Sister Sara comments that the women are also partly to blame for their marginalized status. They must not submissively endure their situation of confinement at home; rather, they should assert their rights. Rokeya had suggested that women must not accept jewels in return of education because jewels are weapons that bind women even further. Her true jewels should be books. Feminist theory and its four types, gender difference, gender inequality, gender oppression, and structural oppression, helped to find the underlying voices of women and their effort to usher change through their writings.

The theory of ecofeminism enabled to identify the link between women, environment and ecology. The theory helped to explore common issues of gender, class, race and environment in the chosen works. It was also possible to include marginalized groups in the discussion. Since the authors have taken special care to include issues of environment, its degradation accompanied by a fall in the status and treatment of women, the theory of ecofeminsim was extremely valuable in this regard. The correlation between woman and nation was also traced.

Further, a study of the author's personal information, including their family background and education, was helpful in understanding the themes and issues chosen by them to write on. Although no attempt was made to draw a parallel between the author and any character, it is clear that issues which are of deep concern to the author helps shape their writings. The research showed that Rokeya Sakhawat Hossain belonged to a period when the practice of child marriage and purdah was quite prominent. Accordingly, these issues are highlighted throughout her writings. Rokeya's father prevented his daughters from receiving any formal education, unlike his sons. Rokeya secretly received her education from her eldest brother and sister and, later, from her husband. Hence, the issue of female education is very close to Rokeya's heart and pervasive throughout her works. She continually emphasized that a society cannot progress if around one-half of its population is illiterate. Through Rokeya's literary, political and educational activism, it was learned that she strove for the elevation of women's position in the society, especially of Muslim women, who were denied a chance for education and freedom, more so than their Hindu sisters. Hence, the adequate knowledge of Rokeya's background was especially helpful in contextualizing the issues she raises. Also, it was beneficial to know that Vandana Singh has a background in physics, in fact she has a PhD in theoretical particle physics and she teaches physics in a college. The scientific matter present in her works results from her comprehensive knowledge of science. Moreover, since her teenage years she has been a participant in environment groups. This explains her continuous engagement with nature and efforts to conserve its resources. This concern was also noted in her novellas. Chabria, for example, spent a period of eight years to research history 'from 2500 B.C. to the 24th century.' She made use of this information to form the various 'visitations' which she situates in different time periods in *Generation 14*. These details about her background allowed an appreciation and understanding the storehouse of knowledge that the author possesses.

When considering the themes covered in Indian SF, it would be worthwhile noting whether the themes observed in Chapter 2 are also to be found in the chosen texts. The theme of social and environment issues was found in all the chosen texts, albeit to varying degrees. The authors have concentrated upon various kinds of pollution, air, water, or soil, which are a menace to the ecology. In addition, danger to wildlife and many non-renewable sources of energy were also important issues. The simultaneous abuse of nature and women was another recurrent theme. These works of SFs show how environmental and ecological degradation can impact on society and also lead to natural disasters.

A popular theme of Indian SF, the theme of cloning, was found in both Manjula Padmanabhan's *Escape* and Priya Sarukkai Chabria's *Generation 14*. Both the stories feature human or sub-human clones. In fact, human cloning is the main element of the novel, yet Chabria uses it to discuss the meaning of identity, both internal identity and that of the nation. The clone symbolizes a world that is bound to result in communal violence. Chabria poses the question to the reader whether we will learn from our mistakes we have made in the past and rethink our identity and motivation. Although many writers of Indian SF feel that the theme of cloning is inspired from mythological epics such as the *Mahabharata*, the chosen authors do not show any such indication of such a belief.

Similarly, it has been shown that the imaginary world portrayed in SF literature and films is inspired from imaginary worlds described in Indian epics. Dr. Srinarahari has given the example of the *Ramayana* and the *Mahabharata*. It is claimed that the "Pushpak Vimana" created by Vishwakarma inspired the idea of air travel. It can be speculated that the air-car used by Sultana and Sister Sara to travel to the Queen might have taken inspiration from it. Also, Vandana Singh might have the *mathsya lok* in mind, when she envisioned Anasuya, a fish-like creature who came from Sagara. There can be many such conjectures in literature. The authors provide no such clues or information about drawing on the epics for inspiration for their characters or settings. Yet one can also say that most Indian authors would have read or listened to the Indian epics. For instance, Vandana Singh mentions in the biography section on her website that she had grown up listening to her grandparents, her uncles and aunts recounting tales from the *Mahabharata* and the *Ramayana*. A similar pattern could be seen in the case with Chabria, who would eat her meals as a child while her grandmother churned out stories from the *Ramayana*. So, the theme of mythology is not present in a direct way but an indirect presence can certainly be detected.

Moving further, the theme of gender bias was also found to be prominent in most of the works of Indian SF selected for analysis in this novel. By placing the story in an unreal, unfamiliar setting, the authors are able to offer an oblique critique of the patriarchal set-up of Indian society. The problems of the present world, more so of India, are re-examined in order to provide the reader with a new perspective of a situation which they had been taking for granted. For instance, Manjula Padmanabhan talks about a current worry that India is facing and she places the story in a future setting to look at it from a new angle, a rather far-sighted one. The concern here is over the declining sex ratio of girls in comparison to boys. A corresponding situation was found in "Sultana's Dream." The author, Rokeya, places the story in an alternative future society, but the issues she raises are contemporary and relevant to her society.

Further, the theme of space travel appears in Vandana Singh's novellas, *Distances* and *Of Love and Other Monsters*. Both include visitors from another planet, which set the events in motion. All the other issues and ideas ensue from the theme of space travel. On the basis of the description of themes commonly found in Indian SF, it was also deduced that the trope of time travel accompanies space travel. In *Distances*, the secret to faster-than-light travel is discovered, which makes the process of travelling across space less time consuming.

One of the most significant themes in SF is the presence of technology, which may or may not lead to scientific discoveries. This theme was found and noted prominently in the chosen texts. With the exception of Rokeya, who received no formal education, yet who applies logic in her explanations, the other three authors appeared to have a sound scientific knowledge and that was apparent in their elaboration of SF devices. As mentioned earlier in the book, the authors had their own ways of depicting technology in SFs. They chose to depict it in different ways, as an existing technology, or at times a realistic portrayal of a far-fetched technology, or just as a simple plot device that appears scientific, but has no foundations in science.

In addition, LGBT themes were also found in the chosen texts. Works like *Of Love and Other Monsters* do not merely include the presence of a bisexual character, who is later found to be an alien; rather, the author also articulates through his consciousness the main issues of the novella. For instance, the alien, named Arun, is appalled by the distinctions humans make between themselves which prevents them from expressing their love to one another. The binary divides are between man and -woman, mind and body, human and alien, and so on. The novella emphasizes for the reader that all of these words are just labels. Transgender characters are also present in *Escape*. It can be concluded that the LGBT readership identifies with the aliens in such works of SF.

Linked to the LGBT theme is the theme of love, a theme which was found to be pervasive in the selected texts. The texts with LGBT characters stress the importance of loving one another and discard all mental divides. The idea emphasized through love is that of equality and companionship. In these writings, prevalent social norms are shown to be sidelined in favour of affection and compassion for one another. *Escape* shows love between uncles and their niece, love for animals, love between cousins, who become lovers in testing times.

Finally, the theme of spirituality present in Indian SF was also to be found in the selected works. The theme played the functional role of drawing the attention of readers towards the question of religion, faith, the meaning of life, destiny and what it means to be human. SF through this theme demonstrates its innate and unique ability to ask many intense and probing questions which other genres often cannot. In *Generation 14*, an acolyte deduces that goodness is all around us, only to achieve that one has to be positive and alert to perceive it. Additionally, the *matsya* in *Generation 14* speaks of *maya*, a gigantic illusion that envelops the human mind and also proves to the reader that one must get rid of it. *Matsya* also exposes the pilgrims who visit Kashi to purify themselves of their sins just by taking a dip in the water. He clarifies that knowledge or illumination cannot be sought like that.

After a discussion of the relevant themes, it is important to include the responses for the chosen texts, in terms of reviews, criticisms, inspiration for other texts, adaptations, etc. based on the research and reviews, it was found that Rokeya's Sakhawat Hossain's "Sultana's Dream," originally published in 1905, continues to be a celebrated and significant work of feminist SF in India to the present day. In fact, the work is venerated and is widely held to be the earliest work of SF from India. It was composed at a time when India was dealing with the twin situations of being oppressed by colonialism and patriarchy. The element of role reversal in the story where men instead of women are segregated in the *zenana*, called the *mardana*, has inspired a number of writers. Most recently, a writer was motivated to include in her writing the idea of *mardana*. She is Kameron Hurley, the fantasy writer. She used the idea in her book, *The Mirror Empire* (2014). Hurley has often underlined the influence of "Sultana's Dream" on her book in general and on feminist SF and Fantasy in general.

It is to be noted that ideas which were central to Rokeya in 1905 are still relevant in contemporary times. She was a visionary and her work, as is written in many reviews, still seems as if it was written yesterday, with respect to the concerns she raises. According to Mahvesh Murad,[1] what Rokeya identified as problems in 1905 can also be seen in today's times:

> why should women be taught to stay safe, when men are not taught to not threaten or abuse or rape or be a danger to women? The idea of restricting women in the zenana (or even in forced purdah) *by* men for their own protection *from* men is completely absurd- just as much back then as it is now, and Hossain isn't afraid to point out that 'it is not safe so long as there are men about the streets, nor is it so when a wild animal enters a marketplace.[2]

Amongst many, one aspect that is largely appreciated by critics, including Murad, is Hossain's impartial judgement for both me and women. Hossain does not blindly attack the men; she also condemns the women for their shortcomings. Hossain enables Muslim women to see beyond the myths spread by the narrow-minded patriarchal systems of her time. Through "Sultana's Dream," Hossain sets an example for other women to realize that the tenets of a male-dominated society can be questioned if women welcomed the idea that their life is not restricted to daily household work, and that it is possible to dispute the status quo. Rokeya is given the prestige of being one of the first few feminist reformers from India, who wrote continually about women's emancipation in Bengali, rather than English, to capture a wider audience.

Most of the reviews of "Sultana's Dream" available online applaud the endeavour and initiative taken by Hossain to advance the cause of female empowerment and education. Her efforts are described as bold, taking account of the time period in which she was writing. Reviewers appreciate the extraordinary presence of wit, style and grace in her writing. Her approach to technology is also referred as interesting in comparison to other SF writers of her time, such as Verne. Rokeya suggested ways and means to reduce women's labour so that they would be free to undertake creative ventures, which would change the world for better. The issues raised by Rokeya are acknowledged by both readers and reviewers, even if some show a degree of disapproval for the utopian land she describes.

Other critics have found the tale impressive in the first reading, especially the role reversal, which involves women managing the state. What is also held in high regard is the audacity and courage with which Rokeya wrote in 1905 and the social work undertaken by her. She chose her own profession at a time where education for women was not allowed. According to one of the book reviews:

Despite being an extremely short story, it still succeeds in making a strong point. Injustice is terrible and religion, in this case Islam, is no excuse! Women have the right to walk the streets with no fears. They have the right for the best education opportunities because they are as much capable of inventing as men are. They can rule countries and defend themselves and their lands. They can even drive flying cars![3]

Yet such reviews are limited and most of them do write at end that one must not forget that Rokeya wrote the story shortly after she learned English. Also, it is to be kept in mind that English was her fifth language.

The popularity of the story can be noted by its republication in 2005 by Penguin, with an introduction by Barnita Bagchi. "Sultana's Dream" was first published in 1905 in the *Indian Ladies' Magazine* in Madras in English. One of the reviewers, Jerry Jose, says:

The things that looked like science fiction in her 'wonderland', when observed now, were actually prophecies and solutions for 21st century- Solar Energy, Hydrogen weather balloons, Commercial Aviation and even competitive academics. And there is a special charm in her writing, a narrative cuteness that keeps men from being offended, be it then, be it now.[4]

Like most reviewers, Oeveraas also acclaimed the work to be, above all, topical and thought-provoking, which maintains the freshness of the text even after 100 years of its publication.

Manjula Padmanabhan's *Escape* has received reviews in newspapers, blogs, magazines and websites. One of its earliest reviews was done by Sumana Mukherjee in 2008 in *The Hindu*. She acknowledged in Padmanabhan's writing a humanism that accepts all kinds of defects, despite the dystopic mode in which *Escape* is written. Even though, she appreciates the tale, she critiques Padmanabhan's handling of certain events in the story. Mukherjee felt that the author lost track of the narrative, more specifically in the section devoted to Swan's nest, a unit where subhuman clones are manufactured. She adds, "Yet so compelling is her larger narrative, so complete her imagined meta-reality, that you go with the flow, like the boat that will carry them to the City at the edge of their world."[5]

Jai Arjun, who regularly writes in his blog *Jabberwock*, insists that the novel *Escape* operates on various levels. It can be read as an adventure story, a well-written work of speculative fiction, and a thoughtful study of characters. He compliments Padmanabhan on her skill at balancing the internal conflicts of Meiji and Youngest with the rest of the story as it describes the external landscape and other characters or special creatures they encounter. According to Jai Arjun, SF works such as those of Padmanabhan have changed the perception of Indian SF, transforming to from something regarded primarily as children's literature to being regarded as mainstream, serious fiction. A similar contribution has been said to have been made by Vandana Singh and Priya Sarukkai Chabria. They have extended the boundaries of SF to broaden the prospect of what can be investigated in the genre. *Escape* is an open-ended novel and many reviewers and critics have speculated on the possibility of a sequel coming on the scene.

Hence, based on the reader's response on the selected texts, mentioned above, one can say that they have impacted the readers in a positive manner. Even the critical points of shortcomings on the part of the author go to signify that the works have been read and analyzed by the readers. The reviews do not just stress that the texts were a leisure read; they impelled the readers to assess the situation text in the text and the real world. Not only could they find a similarity in the issues pertinent to the real world but also find an underlying message and motivation to bring a worthwhile change in the society. Hence what the author has presented to the reader was not just a narrative but encoded within it were serious political and social problems of the society. Yet the narratives were able to engage the readers and not make it seem like a manual of social, environmental and technological issues. This was also part of the radical potential embedded within the chosen texts, to serve more than one purpose, to delight and also alert the readers. The authors do not compel the readers, but merely advance the issues before the readers and often the solutions and then it is up to the reader how they choose to act upon it. Many readers, in the form of critics, bloggers and so on, have written about the issues raised and hence passed on the ideas to another set of readers. This is another way to speak of the radical potential inherent in the chosen works.

As noted in Chapter 4 and 5, the various conjunctions and disjunctions identified in the text also justified the presence of radical potential in the texts. These ideas helped to bring out the writers' purpose. The conjunctions are the supplementary ideas and elements which not only helped take the narrative forward, but also contribute towards proving the authenticity of facts and also ensured an enjoyable reading. The various conjunctions in the texts serve a variety of different purposes. Firstly, they were useful in preserving the literary value of the text; secondly, they maintained the tie between the imaginary world of SF and the real world; and finally, they ensure a delightful experience. Even the disjunctions at various points have led to a conjunction, and hence they have contributed to further development of the issues and themes.

There is scope for further exploration of the radical potential inherent in Indian SF. For the present study, only selected texts were chosen, because an exhaustive study would be very time-consuming. Yet there are many texts available which can be studied for the nature of the radical potential they contain. This would not only bring the works of Indian SF to the fore and make it a popular genre; it would also open up new areas of investigations for SF. The present study is a contribution to the generation of further scholarly interest.

Notes

1 Mahvesh Murad lives in Karachi, Pakistan and writes regular reviews for books and takes interviews of writers on her radio show. She holds specific interest in dystopian fiction.

2 Murad, Mahvesh. "Under the Radar: *Sultana's Dream*". *Science fiction. Fantasy. The universe. And related subjects.* TOR.COM. October 17, 2014. Web. November 15, 2014. https://www.tor.com/2014/10/17/under-the-radar-sultanas-dream/.

3 Reem. "*Sultana's Dream* by Rokeya Sakhawat Hossain, Durga Bai (Illustrations)". *Goodreads.* September 15, 2014. Web. October 21, 2014. https://www.goodreads.com/book/show/948061.Sultana_s_Dream.

4 Jose, Jerry. "Sultana's Dream by Rokeya Sakhawat Hossain, Durga Bai (Illustrations)". *Goodreads.* June 29, 2017. Web. October 21, 2017. https://www.goodreads.com/book/show/948061.Sultana_s_Dream.

5 Mukherjee, Sumana. "A humanist plea". *The Hindu.* December 7, 2008. Web. October 21, 2017. http://www.thehindu.com/todays-paper/tp-features/tp-literaryreview/a-humanist-plea/article1438258.ece

Bibliography

Primary Sources

Singh, Vandana. *Distances*. New Delhi: Penguin, 2008a.
———. *Of Love and Other Monsters*. Washington: Aqueductpress, 2007.
Hossain, Rokeya S. "Sultana's Dream." 1905 http://digital.library.upenn.edu/women/sultana/dream/dream.html
——— *Sultana's Dream and Padmarag*. New Delhi: Penguin, 2005.
Padmanabhan, Manjula. *Escape*. New Delhi: Zubaan, 2008.
Chabria, Priya S. *Generation 14*. New Delhi: Zubaan, 2008.

Secondary Sources

Adams, Robert. *Science Fiction*. London: Routledge, 2000.
Aldiss, Brian *Billion Year Spree: the History of Science Fiction*. London: Wiedenfeld and Nicolson. Updated in 1986 as *Trillion Year Spree*. London: Gollancz. 1973/1986.
Algere, Sara M. "The Case of Vandana Singh: Reading Indian Science Fiction, with a Warning about Wrongs." *Academia*. 2018. Web. September 25, 2013 https://ddd.uab.cat/pub/presentacions/2018/182669/CONFERENCE_PRESENTATION_Sara_Martin_on_Vandana_Singh.pdf.
Asimov, Isaac. *My own view; 'Asimov on Science Fiction'*. Great Britain: Panther Books, 1981.
Banerjee, Suparno. "Other tomorrows: postcoloniality, science fiction and India" *LSU Doctoral Dissertations*, 2010. 3181. Web. July 26, 2013 https://digitalcommons.lsu.edu/gradschool_dissertations/3181.
Banker, Ashok K. "Ashok Banker talks about his sci-fi book". *Woodpie blog*, September 19, 2013. Web. May 15, 2014. http://blog.woodpie.com/ashok-banker-talks-sci-fi-book/
——— *Gods of War*. New Delhi: Penguin, 2009.
Bell, Daniel. "The Disjunction of Culture and Social Structure: Some Notes on the Meaning of Social Reality". *Daedalus*. vol. 94 no. 1 (1965) pp. 208–222.
Best Science Fiction Books. *BestScienceBooks.com*. September 19, 2015. Web. November 15, 2015. https://bestsciencefictionbooks.com/space-western-science-fiction.php.
Britannica. "Utopia." *Encyclopaedia Britannica*, July 22, 2014. Web. August 2014. http://www.britannica.com/EBchecked/topic/620755/utopia.

Broderick, Damien. *Reading by Starlight: Postmodern Science Fiction*. London and New York: Routledge, 1995.

Chabria, Priya S. "The Autobiography of a Goddess-Translating The Autobiography of a Goddess: Concept." September 2013. Web. May 2014. http://www.kaurab.com/themudproposal/priya-chabria/Aandaal-Project.pdf

Chakraborty, Arnav. "Two stories lead India's modern science-fiction charge into the sci-fi magazine Strange Horizons." May 20, 2018. https://scroll.in/article/879596/two-stories-lead-indias-modern-science-fiction-charge-into-the-sci-fi-magazine-strange-horizons.

Chandler, Otis. "*GoodReads*." *GoodReads*, October 19, 2013. Web. April 15, 2014.https://www.goodreads.com/book/show/2493.The_Time_Machine.

———. "GoodReads." *GoodReads*, February. 2015. Web. April 15, 2014 https://www.goodreads.com/topic/show/1757873-what-is-space-opera.

Chattopadhyay, Bodhisattva. "Speculative Utopianism in Kalpavigyan: Mythologogerm and Women's Science Fiction." July 2017 https://www.res-reachgate.net/publication/324828709_speculative_utopianism_in_kalpavigyan_Mythologerm_and_Women's_Science_FictionMarch2020. March 2020

Childs, Peter and Roger Fowler. *The Routledge Dictionary of Literary Terms*. London: Routledge, 2006.

Clute, John and David Langford. "SFE Content". *SFE: The Encyclopaedia of Science Fiction*, February 28, 2013. Web. June 13, 2014. http://www.sf-encyclopedia.com/archives/hard_sf/124546.

Clute, John and Peter Nicholls. Eds. *The Encyclopedia of Science Fiction*. London: Orbit, 1993.

Clute, John. "SFE Content." *SFE: The Encyclopaedia of Science Fiction*. 2011. Web. January 17, 2013 http://www.sf-encyclopedia.com/entry/bengal.

Connery, Brian A. and Kirk Combe. Eds. *Theorizing Satire: Essays in Literary Criticism*. New York: New Directions Pub. Corp., 1994.

Dugal, Simrat Kaur and Charu Maithani. Indian Foundation for the Arts, 2013. Web. 2013. http://www.indiaifa.org/simrat-kaur-dugal-charu-maithani.html.

Edwards, Elise. *Race, Aliens and the US Government in African American Science Fiction*. Berlin: Deutsche Nationalbibliothek, 2011. 6–21

Garimella, Sujata. "The Mahabharata: A science Fiction". *India Opines*, October 2013. Web. December 2015. http://indiaopines.com/mahabharata-science-fiction/.

Google Books. n.d. Web. July 2013. https://books.google.co.in/books?id=vShY-fiP_6sAC&printsec=frontcover&dq=LGBT+themes+in+speculative+fiction.

Ghoshal, Somak. August 24, 2013. Web. August 25, 2013. http://www.livem-int.com/Leisure/DKDlAqUKyUTCHlJgB5enoI/Writers-At-Work--Manjula-Padmanabhan.html.

Gilarek, Anna. "Marginalization of "the Other": Gender Discrimination in Dystopian Visions by Feminist Science Fiction Authors, December 4, 2012. Web. January 2013. http://www.degruyter.com/view/j/texmat.2012.2.issue-2/v10231-012-0066-3/v10231-012-0066-3.xml.

Goodwin, H. Geoffrey. "An Interview with Vandana Singh." August 2006. Web. September 2013. http://www.bookslut.com/features/2006_08_009677.php.

Goswami, Dinesh C. *The Hair Timer: An Anthology of Science Fiction Stories*. Delhi: NBT, 2014.

Hamm, Ryan. "Sci-fi Spirituality." *Christianity Today*, August 14, 2012. Web. January 2014. http://www.christianitytoday.com/biblestudies/articles/theology/sci-fi-spirituality.html.

Hasan, Md. Mahmudul. "Commemorating Rokeya Sakhawat Hossain and Contextualizing her Work in South Asian Muslim Feminism." *Asiatic*, vol. 7, no. 2, 39–59. (December 2013).

Hasanat, Fayeza. "Sultana's Utopian Awakening: An Ecocritical Reading of Rokeya Sakhawat Hossain's Sultana's Dream." *Asiatic*, vol. 7, no. 2, (December 2013).

Hausman, Ricardo, Laura D. Tyson et al. "The Global Gender Gap Index 2013." 2013 Web. February 2014 http://www3.weforum.org/docs/WEF_GenderGap_Report_2013.pdf.

Hoagland, Ericka, and Reema Sarwal. Eds. *Science Fiction, Imperialism and the Third World: Essays on Postcolonial Literature and Film*. North Carolina: McFarland & Company Inc., 2010.

Hollinger, Veronica. "Contemporary Trends in Science Fiction Criticism, 1980–1999." *Science Fiction Studies*, vol. 26, no.2 (July 1999), pp. 232–262.

Huntington, John. *Rationalising Genius: Ideological Strategies in the Classic American Science Fiction Short Story*. New Brunswick, NJ, and London: Rutgers University Press, 1989.

Inflibnet. Shodhganga. "Chapter VI. Charting a Vision for the Future (Manjula Padmanabhan's *Escape* and Arun Joshi's *The City and The River*)." n.d. Web. July 2013 http://shodhganga.inflibnet.ac.in:8080/jspui/bitstream/10603/8645/13/13_chapter%206.pdf p. 14

James, Edward. *Science Fiction in the 20th Century*. Oxford: Oxford University Press, 1994.

James, Edward and Farah Mendlesohn, eds., *The Cambridge Companion to Science Fiction*. Cambridge: Cambridge University Press, 2003.

Jones, Gwyneth. *Deconstructing the Starships: Science, Fiction and Reality*. Liverpool: Liverpool University Press, 1999.

Korsnack, Kylie. "Transcending Boundaries: An Interview with Vandana Singh." *Los Angeles Review of Books*, LARB, November 25, 2017, https://lareviewofbooks.org/article/transcending-boundaries-an-interview-with-vandana-singh/. November 25, 2017

Khan, Sami A. "The Others in India's Other Futures." *Science Fiction Studies*, vol. 43, no. 3 (November 2016), pp. 479–495.

Kumar, Shanti. "Mixing Mythology, Science and Fiction: The Sci-fi genre in Indian Film and Television." University of Texas, December 1, 2006. Web. January 10, 2013. http://flowtv.org/2006/12/mixing-mythology-science-and-fiction-the-sci-fi-genre-in-indian-film-and-television/#.

Kumar, Radha. *The History of Doing*. New Delhi: Zubaan, 1993.

Koshy, Jacob P. "Indian science fiction authors fret niche, hope for more readers." *Livemint*, November 22, 2008. Web. February 2013. http://www.livemint.com/Home-Page/5D0QJCOCaWeMTd40UyTIgK/Indian-science-fiction-authors-fret-niche-hope-for-more-rea.html.

Lakhi, Mukti. "An Alternative Feminist Modernity: Fantastic Utopia and the Quest for Home in *Sultana's Dream*." *Post Graduate English Journal*, No. 14 (September 2006), 1–28.

Lal, Mohan. Ed. *The Encyclopedia of Indian Literature*. New Delhi: Sahitya Akademi, 1992.

Lilly, N. E. "What is Speculative Fiction." *Green Tentacles*, March 2002. Web. April 2013. http://www.greententacles.com/articles/5/26/.

Little, Judith A. *Feminist Philosophy and Science Fiction*. New York: Prometheus, 2007.

Mathur, Suchitra. "Caught between the Goddess and the Cyborg: Third World Women and the Politics of Science in Three Works of Indian Science Fiction." *The Journal of Commonwealth Literature*, vol. 39 (September 2004), pp. 119–138,

Matthan, Ayesha. "Legend of the Clone." *The Hindu*, April 1, 2008. Web. January 10, 2013. http://www.thehindu.com/todays-paper/tp-features/tp-metroplus/legend-of-the-clone/article1411808.ece.

Melzer, Patricia. *Alien Constructions*. Austin: University of Texas Press, 2006.

Merriam Webster. "Conjunction." *Merriam Webster Thesaurus*. May 15, 2014. https://www.merriam-webster.com/dictionary/conjunction.

Mishra Arvind, Manoj K. Patrairiya et al. Eds. *Science Fiction in India: Past, Present and Future*. Jaipur: Ayush Books, 2011.

Mishra, Arvind. "Science Fiction in India. January 13, 2012. Web. August 2013. http://indiascifiarvind.blogspot.in/2012/01/mythological-ideas-for-sf-story-themes.html.

Mohan, Vishwa. "J&K Floods a Grim Reminder of Increasing Climate Change Impact in India: Centre for Science and Environment." *The Times of India*, September 10, 2014. Web. November 2014. http://timesofindia.indiatimes.com/city/delhi/JK-floods-a-grim-reminder-of-increasing-climate-change-impact-in-India-Centre-for-Science-and-Environment/articleshow/42194924.cms.

World Heritage Encyclopaedia, "Biopunk." World Heritage Encyclopaedia, ed. By World Library Edition, Project Gutenberg Self-Publishing Press, October 10, 2014. Web. October 2014. http://www.self.gutenberg.org/articles/eng/Biopunk.

Naik, Preetigandha. "The Science-Fictionalisation of Science Fiction and Image Advertising in Harvest by Manjula Padmanabhan." *Fafnair - Nordic Journal of Science Fiction and Fantasy Research*. 7 (January 2020), pp. 11.

Narain, Sunita. "The Origins." *Down to Earth*, January 4, 2012. Web. January 2013. http://www.downtoearth.org.in/content/science-meets-fiction?page=0,2.

Narlikar, Jayant. *Geography and You*, February 6, 2014. Web. February 7, 2014. http://www.geographyandyou.com/science/sceience-national/20-storeis/science-and-tech/national/597-writers-need-to-take-up-sci-fi-genre-jayant-narlikar.html.

Nathonson, Jeremy A. *Britannica*, Encyclopaedia Britannica Inc. February 1, 2010 Web. July 30, 2019, https://www.britannica.com/technology/solid-waste-management.

Palodkar, Rupali. "Ecofeminism in India: Disappearing Daughters in Padmanabhan's *Escape*." *The Quest*, vol. 25, no. 1 (June 2011), 55–61.

Poddar, Namrata. "Female Foeticide and Infanticide is the Cancer that Slowly Kills us." n.d. Web. 2014. http://www.oneyoungworld.com/sites/www.oneyoungworld.com/themes/custom/oneyoungworld/pdf/Essay4.pdf.

Ray, Bharathi. *Early Feminists of Colonial India: Sarala Devi Chaudhurani and Rokeya Sakhawat Hossain*. Delhi: Oxford University Press, 2002. p. ix.

Sarma, Dibyajyoti. "Priya Sarukkai-Chabria: Writer forever." *I write, riot*. September 23, 2006. Web. May 2013. http://writeriot.blogspot.in/2006/09/priya-sarukkai-chabria-writer-forever.html.

Sarval, A. and Geetha B. Eds. *Exploring Science Fiction Text and Pedagogy*. New Delhi: SSB Publications, 2011.

Scholes, Robert. *Structural Fabulation: An Essay on Fiction of the Future*. Bloomington: Indiana University Press, 1975.

Shah, Salik. "Notes on Indian Science Fiction: The Parallel Worlds of Jayant Narlikar and Vandana Singh." *MithilaReview.com*, Mithila Review, May, 2016. Web. April 2018 http://mithilareview.com/shah_05_16/.

Singh, Amardeep. "Where Women Rule and Mirrors are Weapons." *Lehigh University*, May 14, 2006. Web. July 15, 2013. http://www.lehigh.edu/~amsp/2006/05/where-women-rule-and-mirrors-are.html.

Singh, Vandana. "Alternate Visions: Some Musings on Diversity in SF." *Antariksha Yatra*. May 27, 2014a. Web. May 31, 2014. http://vandanasingh.wordpress.com/2014/05/27/alternate-visions-some-musings-on-diversity-in-sf/.

———. 2012. Web. January 12, 2013. http://users.rcn.com/singhvan/.

———. October 2014b. Web. November 2014. www.vandana-writes.com.

———. "Indian SF: Science Fiction and Fantasy Stories." March 1, 2014c. Web. April 8, 2014. http://indiansf.in/about/.

———. "If You See Something, Say Something: The Scientist as Activist." *Climate Change: Learning, Communicating, Acting.* February 4, 2014d. Web. June 5, 2014. http://climatechange4perspectives.wordpress.com/2014/02/04/if-you-see-something-say-something-the-scientist-as-activist/.

———. *Infinités.* Paris: Denoël, 2008b.

Srinarahari, M. H. *International Report from India.* "Popularizing Science Writing and celebrating Science Fiction: A Report of the 14th Science Fiction Conference in India." Kochi, 2014a.

——— "Koi Mil Gaya, India's First Science Fiction." September 4, 2014b. Web. September 10, 2014. http://www.concatenation.org/articles/koirevised3.html.

——— "Indian Science Fiction: History and Contemporary Trends." *Academia*, n.d. Web. December 20, 2018 https://www.academia.edu/10442469/Indian_Science_Fiction_History_and_Contemporary_Trends. A Concise Review of Indian Science Fiction."

——— "A Concise Review of Indian Science Fiction." *Academia*, 2019. Web. 2020 https://www.academia.edu/38885288/A_concise_review_of_isf.

Sterling, Bruce. "Encyclopaedia Britannica." August 8, 2014. Web. September 10, 2014. http://www.britannica.com/EBchecked/topic/528857/science-fiction/235730/Space-travel.

Subramaniam, Aishwarya. "Rev. of Sultana's Dream by Rokeya Sakhawat Hossain." *Strange Horizons*, September 30, 2013. Web. January 10, 2014. www.strangehorizons.com/reviews/2013/09/sultanas_dream_comments.shtml.

Suvin, Darko. *Positions and Presuppositions in Science Fiction.* Canada: Macmillan P, 1986.

Sutra, Videshi. "Bengali Feminist Sci-Fi: "Sultana's Dream" by Roquia Hussain." February 6, 2014. Web. March 8, 2014. http://videshisutra.com/2013/02/06/bengali-feminist-sci-fi-sultanas-dream-by-rokheya-shekhawat-hossein/#_ftn2.

Thomas, Isabel. "Science Daily. Should scientists pursue cloning?" *Science Daily*, Raintree, 2013. Web. 2013. https://www.sciencedaily.com/terms/human_cloning.htm.

Vandermeer, Jeff. *The Southern Reach*, October 7, 2007. Web. May 15, 2014. http://www.jeffvandermeer.com/2008/10/07/in-search-of-indian-science-fiction-a-conversation-with-anil-menon/.

Valiyamttam, Rositta J. "Rositta Joseph: Manjula Padmanabhan's *Escape*." *Muse India*. Issue 60, March-April 2014. Web. April 2014. http://www.museindia.com/featurecontent.asp?issid=46&id=3753.

Walton, Jo. August 23, 2012. Web. June 16, 2014. http://www.tor.com/blogs/2012/08/some-thoughts-on-anthropological-science-fiction-as-a-sub-genre.

Yasmin, Hossain. "The Begum's Dream: Rokeya Sakhawat Hossain and the Broadening of Muslim Women's Aspirations in Bengal." *South Asia Research*, vol. 12, no.1 (1992).

Yim, Grace. "Human Cloning: Science Fiction or Reality?" *The Science Quarterly*, August 2004. Web. January 2013. http://www.scq.ubc.ca/human-cloning-science-fiction-or-reality/.

Zaidi, Zeashan. "The War of Reflections." July 8, 2014. Web. August 11, 2014. http://zeashanzaidi.blogspot.in/2014/07/the-war-of-reflections-part-6-last-part.html#more.

Index

For Product Safety Concerns and Information please contact our EU
representative GPSR@taylorandfrancis.com
Taylor & Francis Verlag GmbH, Kaufingerstraße 24, 80331 München, Germany

www.ingramcontent.com/pod-product-compliance
Lightning Source LLC
Chambersburg PA
CBHW071116100726
47908CB00008B/2391